GRASS OF
THE EARTH

GRASS OF THE EARTH

Immigrant Life in the Dakota Country

Aagot Raaen

With a New Introduction by

Barbara Handy-Marchello

MINNESOTA HISTORICAL SOCIETY PRESS

St. Paul

Cover: Harvey Dunn, *After School*, South Dakota Art Museum
Collection, Brookings, South Dakota

Portrait of Aagot Raaen from Aagot Raaen Photograph Collection,
North Dakota Institute for Regional Studies, North Dakota State
University, Fargo; all other photographs are from the Hatton-Eielson
Museum and Historical Association, Hatton, North Dakota

Borealis Books are high-quality paperback reprints of books chosen
by the Minnesota Historical Society Press for their importance as
enduring historical sources and their value as enjoyable accounts of
life in the Upper Midwest.

♾ The paper used in this publication meets the minimum
requirements of the American National Standard for Information
Sciences–Permanence for Printed Library Materials, ANSI
Z39.48-1984.

MINNESOTA HISTORICAL SOCIETY PRESS, St. Paul 55102

International Standard Book Number 0-87351-295-2
Manufactured in the United States of America

10 9 8 7 6 5 4 3 2

Library of Congress Cataloging-in-Publication Data

Raaen, Aagot.
    Grass of the earth : immigrant life in the Dakota country /
Aagot Raaen ; with a new introduction by Barbara Handy-
Marchello.
        p. cm.
    Originally published: Northfield, Minn. : Norwegian-American
Historical Association, 1950.
    ISBN 0-87351-295-2 (pbk. : alk. paper)
    1. Raaen family. 2. Raaen, Aagot. 3. Norwegian Americans–
North Dakota–Biography. 4. North Dakota–Biography.
5. Frontier and pioneer life–North Dakota. I. Title.
    F645.S2R3 1994
    978.4′043982–dc20
                                                        93-44859
                                                          CIP

TO

Beata Mark, who knows the truth of this story

and

Isabelle Berg, whose patient understanding
has been of infinite help.

Aagot Raaen, about 1952

Introduction to the Reprint Edition

The story of family settlement on the prairies and plains has often been portrayed as an experience that ensured family cohesiveness, built strong character in healthy children, and provided every family with a piece of the American dream—land of their own.[1] A close reading of historical records indicates that few homesteaders enjoyed such blessings while turning grasslands into farmland. For European immigrants there was an additional burden of cultural separation. Language, foodways, religious practice, and sometimes family were lost to immigrants seeking land and wealth under the Homestead Act. Ole E. Rølvaag explored the experience of Norwegian immigrant farmers in *Giants in the Earth*, his powerful novel of settlement in Dakota Territory. Beret and Per Hansa suffered hardship, isolation, illness, and fear on their homestead. Their relationship was torn, their faith tested, their future uncertain. Land in itself and the implicit wealth to be accumulated from working the land did not soothe the pain of leaving family and community in Norway, nor quiet the fear of the immense task before them.[2]

Rølvaag's novel has its historical reflection in Aagot Raaen's family biography, *Grass of the Earth*. Raaen's parents, immigrants from Norway, claimed a homestead in northern Dakota Territory in 1874. There are some notable differences in the characters, however, which serve further to dispel the myths of settlement. Raaen focuses on the way the family's poverty, unending hard work, and distress affected the children's health, access to education, adult relationships, and values. Raaen also presents her father as the antithesis of the ambitious, confident, and gregarious Per Hansa who believed so strongly in the power of the land. Thomas Raaen was not interested in farming or land. He was a lonely man with few friends on the prairie to share his intellectual interests. Neither is Raaen's mother, Ragnhild, Beret's counterpart. Incredibly patient, hardworking, and forgiving, Ragnhild never demanded more of Thomas than he readily offered.

Aagot Raaen, born December 3, 1873, carefully recorded her family's history, although she did not publish all of the material. Raaen's other books, an extensive genealogy of her father's family and a sequel to *Grass of the Earth* entitled *Measure of My Days*, along with unpublished manuscripts, census information, and other historical records, provide the evidence that supports and enhances Raaen's family biography.[3]

When Thomas Raaen ("Far" in the book) emigrated from Hol, Hallingdal, Norway, in 1869, he was already a mature man of forty-two. As a young man in Norway, Raaen had trained at the Linnes School of Agriculture but eventually decided on a career in the Norwegian army. After eighteen years of service as an officer, he lost his military position and pension when he began to drink to excess. With no future in Norway, he immigrated to Worth County, Iowa, where he lived with his sister, Birgit Mark, and her family. He earned his living there as a furniture maker, but drinking made him unwelcome in his sister's home. Birgit Mark "cleverly manipulated" him into a marriage to Ragnhild Rødningen, which was celebrated on February 28, 1873.[4]

Ragnhild Rødningen ("Mor") was born to a peasant family in Etnedalen, Valdres, Norway, and worked on farms from an early age. Her parents and some of her siblings emigrated in

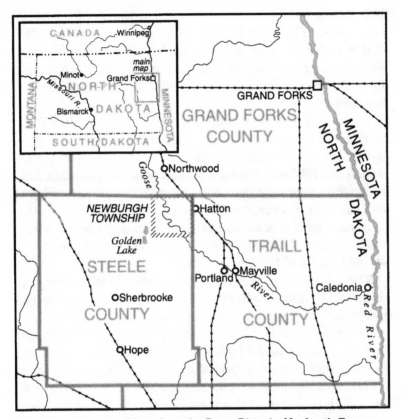

The Raaen homestead lay along the Goose River in Newburgh Township. The farm was well situated for access to wood, water, market towns, and—when it arrived—the railroad.

1861, but Ragnhild continued to work in Norway for several more years. The work was hard and the pay very low. She told her children that she was paid $2.50 plus clothes and shoes for a year's work and had a single day off in two years. In 1870 at the age of thirty-one, Rødningen emigrated to join her family in Iowa.[5]

In the spring of 1874, a little more than a year after their marriage, Thomas and Ragnhild set out in a covered wagon to take up a homestead in Dakota Territory. While Ragnhild waited in Hillsboro, Thomas walked west to Township 148, Range 54 (eventually named Newburgh Township for Ragnhild's brother, Halvor Berg) where he claimed 120 acres in the southeast quarter of section five and forty acres in the southwest quarter of section four. The land lay across the steep, wooded banks of the Goose River.[6]

The following spring, Thomas and Ragnhild with their children moved into a sixteen-by-fourteen-foot, one-room log house with one window and one door. This would be their home until they built a larger log house in 1883. Here, daughters Aagot and Ragnhild (born in 1875 and known to the family as "Laddi") would be joined by Kjersti (1877) and Tosten (1879). Another baby, Birgit, died two weeks after birth. Her brief life is described in this book, but her birth date and place in the birth order are not known. Most likely, Birgit was born between Kjersti and Tosten. Ragnhild gave birth to Tosten when she was forty. After his birth she was unable to conceive again.[7]

Ragnhild had another daughter, Julia, who was born in 1871, approximately two years before she married Thomas Raaen. Julia was raised with the Raaen children, although it is unlikely that Julia was Thomas's daughter. It is impossible to know under what circumstances Ragnhild conceived her first child, but there are at least three possible explanations. First, pregnancy often preceded marriage among the peasants of Norway, in which case she could have been Thomas's child. Engagements were rarely broken, so pregnancy and

The Raaen family in about 1881; left to right, Aagot, Ragnhild holding Tosten, Kjersti standing in front of Julia, and Thomas holding Laddi. Aagot later wrote that, "one thing treasured as a memento by the children is a tin type of the family where she [Ragnhild] and the children are attired in clothes of her own making" ("Thomas Raaen and Ragnhild Rødningen," 10).

even childbirth before marriage was fairly common and not considered socially significant. Second, on Norwegian farms it was common practice to house hired men and women in the same quarters, which frequently led to out-of-wedlock births, and Ragnhild may have been pregnant when she left Norway. Finally, Ragnhild apparently traveled alone from Norway to Iowa, and as an unescorted woman, she was vulnerable to rape. In a brief biography of her mother, Aagot Raaen wrote that Ragnhild endured "many privation[s] and much suffering which she accepted because she felt they were a just [re]tribution for the mistakes she had made." If this is a reference to Julia's birth, it is the only one Raaen made. Julia is not a part of the family in this book and does not appear in any of Raaen's papers. By the age of fourteen, Julia was living and working in the home of some of her mother's relatives in Newburgh Township.[8]

Raaen wrote *Grass of the Earth* from the rather odd perspective of her youngest sister, Kjersti. This device allows Raaen to gain some critical distance in dealing with her own life and also permits the innocence of little Kjersti to soften some of the hard edges of the family's experience. Her childish wonder and simple language suggest that Raaen intended the book for young readers. Although Tosten is everyone's favorite (Raaen doted on him until his untimely death in a 1928 auto accident) and might have been a logical choice for the narrative voice, the female perspective is important because it is Ragnhild and her daughters who are responsible for most of the work and income that provide for the family's needs and make the payments on the farm mortgage. The book ends with Kjersti's death. Her life span forms the framework within which the family established a farm and fought to save it from predatory lenders and Far's improvidence.

In the first few chapters, Raaen sticks to a fairly predictable, but marvelously detailed, description of pioneer life. Mor and Far work at the necessary tasks of survival in the house, barn, and fields. The children do their assigned chores, play with homemade toys, and learn about the natural world around them. Although there is sadness, the children learn that loss is a part of life, and in spite of it, their "home breathed harmony and happiness."[9]

With Chapter 11, Raaen begins to uncover the dark side of pioneer life. Thomas often retreated to "the Shadows," drinking bouts during which he used up the precious cash from the sale of the crops or livestock. He would be absent from the family, sometimes for weeks, leaving Ragnhild to manage the farm, the livestock, and the small children on her own. During the time Thomas was in "the Shadows," he became the prey of thoughtless neighbors and unscrupulous businessmen. While in this condition, he signed a mortgage and brought it home for Ragnhild's signature. The homestead could be mortgaged because Thomas had used Ragnhild's small inheritance to commute the homestead claim and gain title to it. Reluctantly she signed. She felt unable to protest, because Thomas was "the head of the house, his authority was felt to the extent that the rest adjusted their lives to the conduct he expected of them." A mortgage, however, was "the burden" that Ragnhild could hardly bear. From that point on, she would never know a moment of rest from work or worry. The mortgage, combined with Thomas's drinking, ensured that the family would be continuously involved in a "pitiless struggle for existence," never able to enjoy a comfortable margin against poverty in spite of their efforts.[10]

Raaen stops short in her description of "the Shadows" in *Grass of the Earth*. Elsewhere, among her papers, is a brief piece on her parents in which she reveals that, when drunk, Thomas was extremely violent. His abusive behavior began, she stated, when Ragnhild told him about hiding some of the liquor so that his drinking bouts would not last so long. When under the influence of alcohol, he would accuse Ragnhild of hiding the liquor and attack her. Ragnhild suffered permanent scarring and headaches and lost some of her teeth from Thomas's blows. As the attacks escalated, Ragnhild had to leave the house and, at least once during a winter storm, make her way to a neighbor's house with baby Tosten in her arms and the four little girls at her side.[11]

Ragnhild considered divorce and spoke occasionally to her children about it. Divorce was rare among Norwegian pioneers, but not unthinkable. Raaen tells of her mother going with a neighbor to see a lawyer about a divorce (p. 126), but the lawyer refused to file papers for a woman with no money. Ragnhild's own poverty and her sense that her troubles were punishment for some transgression apparently kept her from seeking a divorce from Thomas.

Family violence was not unknown among pioneers. Many memoirs suggest that physical attacks were fairly common in pioneer families. Often a father's hurtful behavior was attributed to the frustrations and disappointments of farming under isolated conditions in a land of little rain. Most writers, unwilling to mar their fathers' reputations and perhaps not clear about their own ambivalent feelings regarding their experiences, offer little more than a suggestion that abuse was a part of their childhood. Mari Sandoz's biography of her Swiss immigrant father, Jules Sandoz, offers one of the few historical depictions of domestic violence among homesteaders. It is clear that Sandoz wrote to honor her father's accomplishments in promoting the settlement of the western Nebraska sandhills. She would have us understand that his violent behavior was related to his disappointments in love, his frustrations with neighbors, lawsuits, and the government, and his position as patriarch of the household. Without diminishing the fear, the pain, and the danger of his attacks, Sandoz accepted Jules's ill treatment as a part of his powerful and complex personality.[12]

Had Raaen seen a way to include Thomas's rages in her book, she probably would have been able, like Sandoz, to paint a truer portrait of him. She attributed his alcoholism to his mother's indulgence and his violence to drinking. But when he was not drinking,

Thomas was a man of remarkably fine moral character. He was scrupulously honest, and was particularly careful to see that his children did not associate with those in the community notorious for gossip, immorality, or profanity. . . . He was a profound philosopher, a man who carried no grudges, a man who despite the misfortune and misery occasioned by his weakness for alcohol found opportunity to do many kind acts.

The Goose River Church (later called Hol), which Thomas Raaen had helped to organize, applied *kjerketukt* (exclusion from church membership) to Thomas because of his drinking. Aagot Raaen believed throughout her life that the church had been unfair in this action and had created greater problems for Thomas and the family. He did not refrain from drink but became a "silent, moody man, seldom conversing even with members of his family." Thus the Thomas we meet in the book is distant, an outsider even in his own home. The family carried on its activities in his absence or while he slept or read. He made demands on the members of the family but rarely interacted with them outside of work.[13]

Thomas's "weakness" meant that Ragnhild was entirely responsible for the support of her family until the children were old enough to contribute income from their own labor. The work she did was typical of most North Dakota farm women. For some of these women, the income they earned contributed to their family's comfort, but in years of poor crops or on farms with large mortgages, their labor and earnings were as essential to survival as were Ragnhild's. Women demonstrated a wide variety of abilities in the work of house, barn, and fields. They toiled long hours with prodigious strength. Women who lacked certain skills or tools exchanged what they had with neighbors to get what they needed. The Newburgh community regularly traded labor and goods without distinctions between men's and women's work. Kjersti "dug a well" for Mor by working in a neighbor's house. Housework (women's work) was swapped for well-digging (men's work). The labor of children was an important part of the barter process. Children were "lent" to do housework in a home where the woman had recently given birth. This exchange not only meant that Newburgh women would receive a necessary rest after childbirth but also ensured that the lending family would receive like aid when needed.[14]

The work they did cost women their health, sometimes their lives, and occasionally their sanity. Ragnhild's health problems included a prolapsed uterus, a mangled arm from a threshing accident, fallen arches, and high blood pressure. She also lost many of her remaining teeth. When she made the thirty-mile trip to Grand Forks to see the doctor, she found there was little he could do for her. The doctor, like the lawyer that Ragnhild and her friend consulted, may have seen a poor country woman who could not afford treatment and would never get the rest she needed for her health. At one point, poor health, overwork, and worry caused Ragnhild to "lose her bearings," but with help from her children and one of her brothers, she managed to recover. Other pioneer women, perhaps with fewer resources, were not so lucky. In the North Dakota population as a whole between 1886 and 1928, women were actually less likely to be hospitalized for mental disturbances than were men, but European immigrants were hospitalized far more often than were Yankee Americans. The cultural chaos of immigration apparently took a greater toll than the social isolation of the homestead, which has so often been considered dangerous for women's mental health.[15]

The Raaen homestead was located in a community of Hallingdal immigrants who organized Newburgh Township in the northeast corner of Steele County. The settlers claimed good land with access to wood and water. The agricultural census of 1885 indicates that, on average, Newburgh farmers were better off than the rest of the farmers in Steele County. The average total value of Newburgh farms was a little higher than the county average, and the value of farm production was half again as high as for the rest of the county. The main crop was wheat, but farm income was supplemented by the sale of animal products. Nearly one-third of the county's 392

The second log house on the Raaen homestead; the photo is undated and the people not identified

head of sheep were kept in Newburgh. Most farms had a few dairy cows and some poultry. The farm women of Newburgh Township made 2.3 times more butter than women in the rest of the county and half of all the hard cheese.[16]

The Newburgh farms ranged from prosperous to poor. Nearly two-thirds of the farms fell below the average value of $3,062. Some thriving farmers had claimed or purchased a good deal more than the 160-acre homestead. Others had sold off portions of their land to pay debts. The Raaens were among the poorest. Thomas had never claimed nor bought more than his homestead right, which was valued at two thousand dollars in 1885. The total production for that year was estimated at $750 while the township average was $2,115. The Raaen family kept draft stock, seven head of beef cattle, four milk cows, three pigs, three sheep, and twelve hens. The children milked the cows, and Ragnhild produced 250 pounds of butter in 1885, a little more than the average Newburgh farm woman. Their small flock laid twenty-five dozen eggs, about half the average. Ragnhild traded surplus butter at H. M. Heen's General Merchandise store and other stores in Hatton to reduce the debt incurred for supplies the family could not produce on its own.[17]

Distinctions based on wealth ordered social relations in Newburgh Township. Although the Raaens owned their farm, the children were aware that the family occupied a lower socioeconomic position than many of their neighbors. Their poverty was readily identifiable in the clothing the children wore to school. Aagot was known as the "calico girl" or "gray girl" because of her simple wardrobe (p. 161). Kjersti was teased because her hair was tied with string instead of ribbon. Aagot and Kjersti had to work both in their own home and for wages in other people's homes, which limited their access to education. Because of her promise to help Mor, Aagot would not complete her teacher-training course until she was nearly thirty. The mortgage on the farm enforced the poverty. While neighbors began to prosper, the Raaen family remained dependent on the children's income to meet the mortgage payments.

In Newburgh Township, class and ethnicity were closely linked. Working in other people's homes introduced Kjersti and Aagot to the social life of wealthy town women who hired country girls to do their housework. If lucky enough to find work in a Yankee home, the girls could earn more money, learn English, and perhaps receive some fine cast-off clothing. Urban Yankee women led a life that Ragnhild could not have dreamed of and probably would have thought sinful in its apparent idleness. Although Aagot painfully felt her poverty, particularly when compared to her employers' comfort, she was ambivalent about her situation. She wanted fine clothes, travel, and, above all, education, but she regarded her childhood of hard work and deprivation as excellent training for life.[18]

Work formed the boundaries of Aagot's life as she tried to

*Kjersti Raaen,
no date*

spare her mother and sister from overwork as well as pay for her education. By contrast the world of Yankee Americans seemed easy. Although many Yankees homesteaded and suffered as much as the Raaen family, the only Yankees the Raaens actually knew lived prosperously in the towns and cities of North Dakota. They were mythologized as nonworkers with beautiful clothes who lived on "bread as white as snow and on cake, pie, pudding, and jelly" (p. 90). Aagot, Kjersti, and Tosten conflated Yankee dominance with wisdom and wealth. Yankees were supposed to "know everything" (p. 90), and the key to that knowledge for the Raaen children was the English language.

The Raaen children had their introduction to the English language when the Mobeck school opened in 1887. Nine-year-old Kjersti and seven-year-old Tosten were eager to attend, but Aagot, by then thirteen years old, doing housework about the neighborhood, and responsible for much of the household and field work on the homestead, could spend little time in school. Aagot read her brother's and sister's texts when she could not attend and slowly became accustomed to the new language. When she took a housekeeping position with a Yankee family in the town of Hope, she had an opportunity to speak English exclusively for one year. Letters between Aagot and Tosten show their effort to learn English. Initially they wrote in Norwegian with just a few paragraphs in English. Little by little the pattern reversed until, by 1900, the letters were written almost entirely in English with only a few Norwegian phrases or words.

The immigrants' children not only gained a second language, they began to adopt American customs. Aagot bought Mor a hat, and Kjersti bought her a coat. Her daughters were proud that Mor no longer had the appearance of a Norwegian peasant with her shawl and kerchief. Many of the neighborhood children would have their names Anglicized in school. Tosten briefly became Tom Rouen, but he eventually settled on Tom Roan (the same spelling the Yankee census taker used for the family surname). Aagot, however, refused to change her name and never recognized Tosten's Anglicized spelling of the family surname.[19]

Raaen gives us little information on the effect of Americanization of the children on their immigrant parents. Ragnhild Raaen never learned to speak or read English. When she and her friends testified at the trial of Olaug Aasen for the murder of Peter Lomen, all of the women required interpreters. Norwegian was the language of their homes, their neighborhood, and the town of Hatton where they traded. The Lutheran churches of Newburgh used Norwegian exclusively until well into the twentieth century and then changed gradually to English as the young people began to lose their command of Norwegian. The transition was painful for the older members, and the church recognized that the shift to English was the final step in the loss of Norwegian traditions.[20]

The Raaen children, with the exception of Laddi, were confirmed in the Goose River Church, but Thomas never attended church after his exclusion. Ragnhild rarely attended services after Laddi became an invalid and, most surprisingly, did not belong to the Ladies' Aid Society. The Ladies' Aid was extremely important to the financial well-being of pioneer churches and provided social activities and relaxation for women. Ragnhild felt she could not contribute (members paid dues, supplied food for their meal, and donated time and materials to make items to sell for the support of the church and charities) to the Ladies' Aid on an equal basis with the other members. She could "give only of that over which she had an authority and that was service and sharing her simple home." Removed by poverty, her husband's drinking problem, and probably his violent behavior from this association with neighboring women, Ragnhild nevertheless helped those even more needy than herself. She frequently furnished room and board to those in want, cared for infants when their mothers were ill, and prepared food for neighbors unable to provide their own.[21]

The Goose River Church community experienced a revival during the 1890s. Among the itinerant ministers was a young woman named Lena Myrold. Her presence created division in the congregation and contributed to the splitting of the church. Her message was simple, but her presence was controversial because women were not assigned any role in church that allowed them to speak publicly. Only men could hold a seat on the church council. Only men were ministers, Sunday school teachers, and *klokkere* (sextons). Thomas, Ragnhild, and their children attended Lena Myrold's revivals and were moved by them. Aagot in particular noticed the power of Myrold's sermons. She wrote to Tosten when Myrold returned to Goose River in 1902, "It is something so strange about that Line [*sic*]; it seems that she can do more than any one else." The presence of a woman preacher among Dakota settlers heightened the paradox of the role of women in the settlement. Daily life and community survival depended to a great extent on women's labor and skills, but most forms of public power were closed to them by law or by custom. Even the quiet spiritual message of a Norwegian-speaking woman, if delivered publicly, generated discord in an otherwise homogeneous community.[22]

The women of Newburgh challenged male dominance only when it threatened their economic well-being. Ragnhild and her neighbors marched into Hatton one January day in 1890 to close the saloons where Thomas and the other men drank away the income from the sale of the year's crops. The events of that day took place at an odd moment in North Dakota history. The state had entered the union two months earlier with a prohibition clause in the constitution. The saloons were allowed to remain open until July 1890. But Ragnhild and her friends could not wait until then. Their property and prosperity were at risk, and their labor was wasted when the income paid for liquor. The challenge, however, was directed only toward the community at large where the women could act in concert. In her own home, that very morning, Ragnhild obeyed when Thomas told her to leave the hatchet at home.[23]

Thomas died in 1903 after nearly thirty years on the Goose River prairies. He finally conquered alcoholism about ten years before his death. After his death, Ragnhild paid the debts and sold half the farm to pay off the mortgage. The sale left Ragnhild enough money to support herself and Laddi. But not all her troubles disappeared with the mortgage. In her last years, she could not forget "the burden" and the sacrifices she and her children had made to pay the debt. In 1920 after Laddi's death, Ragnhild moved to Hatton where she spent a couple of years before moving to the nursing home in Northwood. She died November 6, 1923, at the age of eighty-four.[24]

Tosten studied at Augsburg College, becoming the first college graduate from Newburgh Township. He was ordained in the Lutheran church and served churches in Duluth and Cloquet, Minnesota, (as T. T. Roan) until his death in 1928. He married and had three children.[25] Aagot's endless work paid off as she realized her dreams of education and travel. The restless energy and intellectual curiosity she inherited from her father drove her to pick up bits and pieces of education until she finally received a bachelor's degree from the University of Wisconsin in 1913. She later described her education as

Three months in rural schools, twelve months at Concordia [College, Moorhead, Minnesota], four years at the Mayville [North Dakota] Normal School, one year at the Minnesota University, six weeks summer school, and three semesters here [Unversity of Wisconsin]. Most of the credits I got at Fargo College were earned outside of school [and] so were many of my credits here.

After leaving Wisconsin, she spent a year in advanced study at the University of Berlin.[26]

Work and curiosity took Raaen to Europe and Norway, Asia, and South America. She taught school in different parts of the United States, returning from time to time to Newburgh schools. From 1917 to 1922 she was Steele County superintendent of schools. Late in life she was briefly married

The caption on the original undated photo says, "Tosten Raaen in his book corner in the old log house."

to Thomas Garman. She died January 7, 1957, in Fergus Falls, Minnesota.[27]

This pioneering story is a hard one, but it is unusual only in its frankness. The experiences of the settlers in this book were repeated on countless homesteads claimed by Norwegians, Swedes, Germans, and Yankees. Intensely aware that they were the last generation to experience the American pioneering tradition, many Dakotans wrote memoirs, but few were able to avoid the romanticism that Americans persistently associate with the frontier. Aagot Raaen found the courage to tell the story plainly, concealing very little. She knew that to honor her family, the life they lived must be "mercilessly laid bare." In doing so, she not only presented her family's considerable accomplishments in strong relief against a background of poverty, alcoholism, and overwhelming work, but she left a rare gift of an unvarnished history of the last pioneering era.[28]

BARBARA HANDY-MARCHELLO
University of North Dakota

Notes

I want to thank John Bye of the North Dakota Institute for Regional Studies for his help in finding further information and Eileen Mork of the Hatton-Eielson Museum for her friendly assistance in using museum materials. I also want to thank Sarah Rubinstein for editorial assistance and especially for taking an interest in republishing this book.

[1]Some of the material in this Introduction will appear in my doctoral dissertation on gender and settlement in North Dakota, which is currently in preparation for the Department of History at the University of Iowa.

[2]Ole E. Rølvaag, *Giants in the Earth* (New York: Harper & Brothers, 1927).

[3]Aagot Raaen, *Hamarsbøn-Raaen Genealogy* (Chicago: Eyvind Felland, 1959), and *Measure of My Days* (Fargo: North Dakota Institute for Regional Studies, 1953). Raaen's unpublished manuscripts, letters, and diaries are located in the Raaen Papers, Hatton-Eielson Museum, Hatton, N.Dak.

[4]Raaen, *Hamarsbøn-Raaen Genealogy*, 12–13; "Thomas Raaen and Ragnhild Rødningen," 2–3, Raaen Papers.

[5]"Mor," [1], Raaen Papers.

[6]*Illustrated Historical Atlas of Traill and Steele Counties, North Dakota* (Mayville, N.Dak.: J. J. Kelly and Company, 1892), 72; "Thomas Raaen and Ragnhild Rødningen," 3, Raaen Papers.

[7]*Hamarsbøn-Raaen Genealogy*, 25; "Mor," [1], Raaen Papers.

[8]"Ragnhild Raaen," [2], Raaen Papers. Julia appears in the 1880 federal census as a nine-year-old daughter in Thomas Raaen's household. In the 1885 territorial census she is listed as a helper in the home of J. H. Burgh (Berg). United States, Bureau of the Census, "Dakota 1880 Territorial Census," 287, "1885 Dakota Territory Census," 37, 28, microfilm copy in State Historical Society of North Dakota. On "night-courting" and premarital sexual behavior in Norway, see Jon Gjerde, *Peasants to*

Farmers: The Migration from Balestrand, Norway, to the Upper Middle West (Cambridge: Cambridge University Press, 1989), 89-92.

[9]The quote is from Aagot Raaen's "Introduction" to this book, page xxxi.

[10]"Thomas Raaen and Ragnhild Rødningen," 13-14, and "Mor," [2], Raaen Papers; *Hamarsbøn-Raaen Genealogy*, 13. Ragnhild's inheritance probably came from her father who claimed a homestead in Newburgh Township a couple of years before his death.

[11]"Thomas Raaen and Ragnhild Rødningen," 4-6.

[12]Mari Sandoz, *Old Jules* (New York: Hastings House, 1955). Among published accounts of homesteading in North Dakota, Pauline Neher Diede has written a family biography in which she hints that her father was sometimes violent in his behavior toward his wife and children; see *Homesteading on the Knife River Prairies* (Bismarck, N.Dak.: Germans from Russia Heritage Society, 1983).

[13]"Thomas Raaen and Ragnhild Rødningen," 7, Raaen Papers.

[14]Aagot cared for fifteen newborns in her years at home in Newburgh; "Ragnhild Raaen," [2], Raaen Papers. On rural women's lives, work, and relationships, see Deborah Fink, *Agrarian Women: Wives and Mothers in Rural Nebraska, 1880–1940* (Chapel Hill: University of North Carolina Press, 1992); Joan Jensen, *Loosening the Bonds: Mid-Atlantic Farm Women, 1750–1850* (New Haven: Yale University Press, 1986); L. DeAne Lagerquist, *In America Women Milk the Cows: Factors of Gender, Ethnicity, and Religion in the Americanization of Norwegian-American Women* (Brooklyn, N.Y.: Carlson Publishing, Inc., 1991); Glenda Riley, *The Female Frontier: A Comparative View of Women on the Prairie and the Plains* (Lawrence: University Press of Kansas, 1988). To compare Raaen's experience with that of other women in North Dakota, see Sophie Trupin, *Dakota Diaspora: Memoirs of a Jewish Homesteader* (Lincoln: University of Nebraska Press, 1984); Mary Dodge Woodward, *The Checkered Years: A Bonanza Farm Diary, 1884–88* (Caldwell, Idaho: Caxton Printers, Ltd., 1937; St. Paul: Minnesota Historical Society Press, Borealis Books, 1989); Carrie Young, *Nothing to Do but Stay: My Pioneer Mother* (Iowa City: University of Iowa Press, 1991).

[15]"Mor," [2], Raaen Papers; *Ninth Biennial Report of the North Dakota State Hospital for the Insane*, June 30, 1928, p. 35. This report summarizes patient population according to sex between June 30, 1886, and June 30, 1928. Data concerning immigrants and insanity is summarized from *Biennial Reports of the Trustees of the North Dakota Hospital for the Insane;* reports are available for the years 1892, 1908, 1910, 1914, 1918, 1920, 1926, and 1928.

[16]"1885 Dakota Territory Census," 9-15, 55-56. Some of this material has appeared previously in Barbara Handy-Marchello, "Land, Liquor

and the Women of Hatton, North Dakota," *North Dakota History* 59 (Fall 1992): 22–29.

[17]"1885 Dakota Territory Census," 56; Thomas Raaen's bill with H. M. Heen for 1895 is in the Raaen Papers.

[18]This sense of pride in her background is most evident in Raaen's second book, *Measure of My Days*.

[19]On Newburgh schools, see *Steele County, 1883–1983: A Centennial Commemoration* (Finley, N.Dak.: Steele County Historical Society and the Steele County Press, 1983), 241. The letters between Tosten and Aagot are in the Raaen Papers.

[20]*North Dakota v. Olaug Aasen* (May 15, 1890), County Clerk's Office, Traill County, N.Dak.; Ole Haugen, *Aurdal Through Seventy Years, 1874–1944* (Portland, N.Dak.: Aurdal Lutheran Church, 1944); *Golden Anniversary of Ebenezer Lutheran Church, 1898–1950* (Northwood, N.Dak.: Ebenezer Lutheran Church, 1950), 37.

[21]"Ragnhild Raaen," [1], Raaen Papers.

[22]*Golden Anniversary of Ebenezer Lutheran Church*, 27; Aagot Raaen to Tosten, April 1, 1902, Mayville, N.Dak.

[23]Handy-Marchello, "Land, Liquor and the Women of Hatton, North Dakota," 29.

[24]Raaen, *Measure of My Days*, 123–24; Raaen, *Hamarsbøn-Raaen Genealogy*, 12.

[25]Raaen, *Hamarsbøn-Raaen Genealogy*, 25.

[26]Raaen, *Measure of My Days*, 119, 129.

[27]Raaen, *Measure of My Days*, 182–249; Raaen Papers; Raaen, *Hamarsbøn-Raaen Genealogy*, 25. The Raaen family is buried in the Goose River Lutheran Cemetery. The markers read: Raaen, Rav. Tosten, Dec. 30, 1879–Oct. 10, 1928; Raaen, Kjersti, Mar. 8, 1877–Feb. 2, 1906; Raaen, Thomas, Mar. 4, 1827–Oct. 19, 1903; Raaen, Laddi, Apr. 16, 1875–Apr. 26, 1920; Raaen, Aagot, Dec. 3, 1873–Jan. 7, 1957; Raaen, Ragnhild, Mar. 11, 1839–Nov. 6, 1923; Red River Valley Genealogical Society, *Steele County Cemeteries* (N.p.: The Society, [1977]), 53.

[28]"Thomas Raaen and Ragnhild Rødningen," 16, Raaen Papers.

"Thou shalt know also that thy seed shall be great, and thine offspring as the grass of the earth."

Job v, 25

Foreword

The editor is glad to publish this unpretentious tale. It seems to be the prevalent scholarly fashion to frown on reminiscence as likely to be colored by a romantic haze or vitiated by nostalgic emotion. When buttressed with diaries and letters, as this story is, however, and when told by a realist, as this author is, reminiscence may serve a very useful purpose in the house of history, whose rooms too often are unheated and ill furnished. It supplies color for the bare frame, puts warmth and life within. Here is color, here warmth and life, here a moving, intimate, revealing American story.

The Raaen family in the Dakota country was not perhaps wholly typical of the Norwegian immigrants who turned the prairie sod and made garden of wilderness, but its experiences were typical enough. Miss Raaen's narrative is from the middle period of Norwegian settlement. It records the coming of the railroad, the saloon, the farm mortgage, and the sales agent rather than the earlier days of the unbroken prairie, the oxcart, the church, and the parochial school. The educated father did not remigrate to his native land, as many disillusioned intellectuals did a generation earlier — he found solace in drink instead! But despite his own frustrations — perhaps because of them — he instilled into his children a serene sense of basic values. An unconquerable integrity marks the character of the mother, that quiet, devoted, hard-working woman who on one occasion broke loose and played the role of a Carrie Nation in a wild invasion of the saloon. The children felt, as did their parents, a distaste for material-ism, however glittering its immediate rewards. They were not swept away by dreams of "practical" success — their ambitions took them into other fields where rewards were scarcely practical, rarely tangible. And the author reveals herself as a person of purpose and will whose drive for edu-cation and service was simply undefeatable.

Miss Raaen draws real people in describing her family. Far, Mor, Aagot, Kjersti, Tosten, and Ragnhild — these are not cardboard characters. They are not figures in a novel or imagined parts in a play. They are flesh and blood, kin to us, and we know them. Their story is a real story, even a dramatic story, not less real and dramatic because its pro-tagonists are plain people whose crises are the everyday tragedies of frontier life. The book is more than reminiscence — it is a book of history whose undertones vibrate in Amer-ican life, far beyond the Dakota settlement where the story runs its course.

THEODORE C. BLEGEN

Introduction

There came a period in my life when I had time to look back into the past. One by one, indelible pictures, stamped on my very being, crowded out everything else until I began to put them in writing. As I read family letters, diaries, and documents, I lived again dramatic scenes and events of the old neighborhood. The story naturally wove itself around my sister, Kjersti, from the time I remember her standing by the window counting snowbirds until she slipped into the unknown.

Have I pictured all? Oh, no! The most tragic scenes are omitted. There are heartaches that cannot be described, for there are worse things than loss of property, sickness, and death.

At first I dwelt in detail on descriptions of food and implements and on the way work was done, because these are pleasant memories; when Far and Mor were thus occupied, the home breathed harmony and happiness. On second thought I let the passages stand because they are pioneer history.

As I relived the past, I thought in the Norwegian language because that was the only one I knew before my fourteenth year. Translating as I wrote, I often could not find the English expression that would give the meaning I wanted.

To two friends I owe the presentation of this story. One is Hazel Webster Byrnes, librarian, Teachers College, Mayville, North Dakota — at present director of the state library commission, Bismarck — who read the manuscript and in her inspiring way insisted that it was worth publication; for more than a year she urged that the story be reworked and typed. The other is Isabelle Berg, teacher at Hayward Union High School, Hayward, California, who painstakingly read the manuscript, suggested changes and improvements, and typed it. Without the aid of these two, this story would have remained unpublished.

AAGOT RAAEN

HATTON, NORTH DAKOTA

Contents

Growing Up

Troubles and Solace

Education and Change

Childhood Days

CHAPTER I

The Blizzard

"Birds! many birds! Look! look! two, four, two, four!"

Aagot and Ragnhild fussed, "You can't count. Get away so we can see. Go sit on the *tinae*." They pushed four-year-old Kjersti away from the only window in the log cabin.

She looked longingly at the three chairs. Rarely was she lucky enough to be able to climb up on one of them, sit down, and let her feet dangle. She liked to feel the swing of her legs and hear the click of her heavy shoes against the rungs of the chair. Far and Mor and the older sisters seemed to have sole right to those chairs. But when no one was looking, Kjersti suddenly grew up. She stood on a chair, and, above the heads of the other children, she saw the wonderful world outdoors. Suddenly she was pushed rudely down and again told to sit on the *tinae*. Her sisters didn't have to sit on the queerly shaped covered box any more. They were big; so of course they liked to keep Kjersti in her place. If there had been something to play with, the *tinae* would not have seemed so hard, but just to sit still and not be able to see anything wasn't any fun!

Kjersti was back at the window. She simply had to see what was going on. The outdoors never said "Don't!" Kjersti had asked her sister where all the snow came from and had been told, "They are emptying feather beds up in the sky."

But she knew that wasn't true. Snowflakes turned to water and feathers were always feathers.

It had been snowing for two days. "The sky must be almost empty," she thought. The wind sent a cloud of snow past the window. When it cleared a bit, her big eyes grew bigger as she clapped her fat little hands and repeated, "Birds! all birds! two, four, two, four!"

When Far came in that night he looked like a snow man. As he shook and stamped the snow off, he said: "We are in for a Dakota blizzard worse than any we lived through in Norway or in Iowa. Flocks of snowbirds are fluttering near the haystack and stable; they seem worried and anxious. When birds seek shelter it is a sure sign of a coming storm. I have watered the cows and oxen a second time and given them extra fodder. I untied the calves so they can suck their mothers. I am worried about the ewe; she may get her lamb. The stable door is fastened tight. The storm will carry away anything loose out of doors."

Mor spoke in hurried tones: "I have brought in all the wood and put the dry saplings close to the house. The ax and saw are under the bed. I also brought in the barrel and the tub."

The children listened quietly for the coming storm. Far pushed more wood into the stove. Mor prepared the customary supper of bread and milk. Kjersti always enjoyed this part of the day because no one said "Don't!"

As Mor gathered the bowls and spoons after the evening meal she warned, "This storm may last for days; we must go to bed early to save wood."

Kjersti took off her dress and shoes. Her long chemise was underwear during the day and nightdress at night. She pushed a chair over to the bed and climbed in. She slept with Far and Mor and Tosten, the baby brother. Her sisters pulled out the trundle bed and prepared for the night.

The next morning they were awakened by a tremendous crash. Far explained that the storm had broken the big oak tree. Kjersti thought of the birds and their nests in that tree. She climbed down from the bed and slipped on her dress and shoes; then she stood in line to wash her hands and face. The small basin which served as family washbowl was filled sparingly with water. She had to have help to comb and re-braid her flaxen hair. She did not mind sitting on the *tinae* when she ate her breakfast of bread, butter, and milk, be-cause her sisters had to stand by the table while they ate. Mor buttered their bread and not a crumb must they spill.

How cold the room was! They had to huddle near the stove. Time and again the cabin shook; through every crack and crevice the wind whistled and screeched! Bang! the door flew open and sent in a wave of snow and cold air, which made them shiver. Far and Mor wrestled with the storm to close the door and put a brace on it.

All day long all hands were busy. No one spoke; they might have been a family of statues who had been granted life but denied the power of speech.

Kjersti was delighted when Mor polished the top of the stove; that meant *flatbrød*. She was told she might sit on one of the chairs and watch. Mor took coarse whole-wheat flour, a bit of salt, and enough hot water to make a stiff dough. This she made into a number of balls. With a grooved rolling pin she rolled each ball into a thin, circular sheet, the shape of a pie crust but as thin as paper and as wide through the center as two pies. She pushed a long, flat stick under the pie-shaped bread to lift it quickly from the table, and spread it on the clean, warm top of the stove. As soon as tiny bubbles were visible on the bread, she turned it over and baked it on the other side. Then she put it into the oven and baked it a light brown. As each circle was finished, she put it on top of the others to form a circular stack. If a tiny bit broke off, she gave it to Kjersti to munch.

In the fall Far had put a long piece of ash wood up under the rafters to dry. Now he took it down and began measur-ing, chopping, and chiseling till it took the shape of an ax handle, which he scraped and polished with the edge of a piece of glass until it glided easily through his hand. He arranged a bed of hot coals; then he thrust the ax and a part of the old handle into it so that the blade stuck out. Kjersti thought Far was playing when he kept a wet rag sizzling on the blade. Years later she was to learn that he had done this to keep the heat from destroying the temper of the steel. When the old handle had burned out, he drew the ax quickly from the fire and put the new handle into the eye of the ax. He had ready a small wedge that he drove into the cleft at the lower end of the handle until the eye of the ax was completely filled. Much later Kjersti learned that Far had hurried to put the new handle in while the eye was expanded by the heat.

The older children were crouched on the floor around the *tinae*, and with charcoal they drew pictures on its cover and its four sides. They dampened a piece of rag and erased their work, then drew again, each taking her turn. They went to bed by daylight, but for a long time they did not go to sleep. Far and Mor turned uneasily and sighed. The children asked no questions.

In the morning they heard Mor remark, "There is only an armful of wood left. I put the last dipper of water in the coffeepot." Far, who had been pacing the floor, stopped suddenly and reached for his cap and mittens. He buttoned his coat securely. "I will try to find the saplings you put against the house. If you will hand me the pail, I'll bring in some snow. Can you manage the door?"

An icy blast filled the room. Kjersti hid under the bedclothes. When Far came in again, he braced the door once more; then he steadied the saplings on two chairs, took the saw from under the bed, and sawed off lengths to fit the stove. Mor had filled several pans with snow and put them on the stove. Snow water did not taste good, but with a little soap it felt nice and slippery on the hands.

As soon as Far had finished his work, he resumed his pacing. Why did Far have to march all the time? The bed, stove, table, and three chairs took up so much room; the chest, the trunk, and the *tinae* had to have some space, too. Why was he so restless? Kjersti and her sisters had to sit and be quiet; why couldn't he? Why could grown people always do as they pleased?

Mor was different; her hands were always busy. "What will she do today?" Kjersti wondered. A kettle of tallow was on the stove. Mor found two sticks and fastened three little strings to each, leaving spaces between the strings. She put the kettle of warm tallow on the floor beside a pail that was filled with snow water. Then she seated herself on the *tinae* near by. She took one of the sticks and dipped the strings first into the tallow and then into the snow water. She did the same with the strings on the other stick. This she repeated over and over. Kjersti, crouching on the floor, watched the strings grow fatter and fatter as the dipping continued, until six nice plump candles were finished. This work completed, Mor put some melted tallow in a saucer and said, "We must have our shoes well greased when the storm is over." She gave each one a bit of cloth to be dipped into the melted tallow and rubbed on the shoes. If they rubbed the tallow in well, all moisture would be kept out.

Without pausing to rest, Mor pulled a bag of wheat out of the big chest, emptied some of it into a pan, picked it clean, washed it, and put it in a bread pan to dry in the oven. She freed the hand mill of coffee dust and bits of coffee; then she put some dry wheat into the mill and began grinding. She repeated this until she had a basin full of meal. When Kjersti could have plenty of milk, she liked the mush made from the meal Mor ground, but today she had to eat her mush with very little milk.

Was Far tired of marching? He reached up under the rafters for a piece of dry box-elder root, and again he started to measure, cut, chisel, and scrape. This time he produced a knife handle. What pretty figures it had! Box-elder roots have lovely designs. When Mor remarked that the *tvare* was worn out, Far glanced at her, reached for a slender piece of wood about sixteen inches long, and scraped and polished it into a smooth round stick. Then he took two pieces of oak wood, each about five inches long, an inch and a half wide, and an inch thick. He cut and fashioned them into a cross, polished the edges, and made a hole in the center of the cross into which he fitted the round stick. Mor smiled when he gave it to her. Now she could mix bread, churn cream into butter, stir mush, and beat anything else that a paddle or beater was used for.

Meanwhile, the other children were listening to Aagot studying her catechism; she was her own teacher, asking and answering the questions. How cold it was! They could even see their breath near the stove. And there were only a few sticks of wood left. Must they go to bed again so early? This time they took off only their shoes. How the wind howled, and screamed, and whistled! Didn't it ever stop? Didn't it ever go to bed, Kjersti wondered. That night they were too cold to sleep much.

On the third day the storm still raged. The bread and milk were gone. The children ate mush with a bit of butter and drank water. Far put the last stick of wood into the stove; then he broke one of the chairs into bits and slowly fed it to the fire. Why didn't they burn the *tinae* instead, Kjersti wondered.

As Mor took a sack of wool from a nail on the wall, she spoke: "Children, you may all help separate the long wool from the short. Then if you will untangle the long strands it will make the carding easier. I shall have to make some gray yarn; so you'd better mix half black and half white." They enjoyed working with the wool; they could pretend they were playing, and the work kept them warm. Mor carded a heap of wool into fluffy rolls the size and shape of candles; then she took the spinning wheel from the wall and began to spin the rolls into yarn, which later she would knit into stockings and mittens.

About the middle of the afternoon Far, who had been pacing again, stopped and listened. "The wind seems to be letting up. Every so often there is a lull in the storm." Kjersti hurried to the window. It was covered with frost. She could not see the outdoors, but she did see beautiful frost pictures. If her sisters would but let her draw on the *tinae* she knew she could copy some of them.

The lulls in the storm grew longer and longer. Far was donning his cap, mittens, and scarf. Then, taking the shovel from its place by the broom in the corner, he opened the door to see a wall of snow. While Far and Mor took turns shoveling, the children knew they were forgotten for the time being. They began a wild game of tag around the table and chairs. How they played and laughed as they grew warmer and warmer!

Far and Mor were gone for hours. They shoveled their way to the stable. There they found the cows and oxen warm but lowing for water. They gave each a shovelful of snow mixed with fodder. Later, when Far and Mor carried snow water to the stable, Kjersti understood why Far had kept on filling the barrel and the tub with snow. Far brought saplings from the stable and sawed them into stove lengths. Mor brought milk. They had a feast of bodily comfort, heat, and food.

When Far came in for the night, he had something in his hand. He called Kjersti. She came timidly forward with outstretched palms. He laid a snowbird in them. For a long time she stared, not daring to move.

"Far, why doesn't he fly?"

"He is dead."

"He is so cold and still; is that what 'dead' means?"

"Yes, it means that, and it also means that he will become a part of the ground once more."

"A part of the ground once more." Kjersti could not understand that.

Far took the dead bird and put it outdoors. Kjersti was never to forget her first feeling about death.

CHAPTER II

A Pioneer Factory

The children learned to look forward to blizzards because then Mor always seemed to find new and interesting work.

One day they heard her say, "We need soap. I have saved enough ashes from oak and ash wood." Far hewed off part of a hollow tree trunk about four feet long, and by using bark made a bottom in it so it would hold the ashes. Then he placed it on part of a tree stump in the corner, where it would be out of the way. Near it he set an earthen jar.

When the children saw Mor pouring water, a little at a time, on the ashes in the hollow tree, they wanted to help. But she stopped them, saying, "In order to get good lye we must soak the ashes of hardwood slowly."

After what seemed to them a long time, a slow drip came from the cracks in the bark bottom. Now they understood why Far had put a chip under one side of the stump, so it slanted. This caused the drip to go into the jar instead of on the floor.

When the jar was full Mor drained the lye into a large kettle with some tallow and put it on the stove, where it boiled and boiled. Finally she poured some of the mixture on a chip and let it cool. When she found it was stiff, she emptied the contents of the kettle into a trough that Far had made from oak wood. For a long time after that, there was

10

plenty of soap for washing clothes and bathing as well as for washing hands and faces.

Another stormy day she brought out some yarn she had raveled from old stocking legs. "Girls, you must learn to knit," she said. "From now on you must be able to make your own stockings and mittens." What a struggle! They knit and raveled and knit again. They would have enjoyed the new colored yarn, but they had to learn to knit well before they would be permitted to use that. Mor would never allow them to waste anything. Whatever they did had to be done right.

The winter months of the seventies and early eighties in Dakota brought many storms, but they also brought many sunny days. For weeks and weeks Mor had been carding and spinning until hanks of yarn, hung from nails, covered the wall above the bed. On a nail near by hung several small bags filled with moss, hulls of green hazelnuts, and several kinds of leaves and bark that she had gathered and dried the previous summer, together with some she had brought from Norway.

One day she filled the large kettle half full of water and put some of the bags into it. While it boiled she washed and rinsed a few skeins of white yarn. After removing the bags she put the yarn in, dipping and stirring while the water simmered. When she removed the yarn it was a soft green color. She kept on doing this for days, using different leaves, roots, and bits of bark until she had many skeins of red, blue, yellow, and green. Kjersti clapped her hands and called, "See the rainbow! The rainbow is on the wall. Mor, lift me up so I can touch it."

Mor just looked at Kjersti and thought what a queer child she was. She turned to Far and said, "Last summer Haldis Solheim promised me the use of her loom. I wonder if you would hitch up the oxen and fetch it."

While Far was gone Mor did the chores. Then out of the big chest, which had come with them in the covered wagon all the way from Iowa, she took skeins of cotton yarn and began to plan how to make cloth enough for two blankets and several dresses. She had to figure exactly the number of yards in length and the number of inches in width. A certain number of threads had to be counted for the width. The cotton skeins were used for this and were called warp.

There was great excitement when Far returned with the loom and the tools that belonged to it. The children, who knew they must not ask questions when grownups were busy, simply watched and wondered. For days they were satisfied to do just that.

A long board frame, eight feet high, was put up in the center of the room. On this the cotton yarn was first wound; next the yarn was transferred to a circular bolt and placed in the back of the loom. Then Mor finished the work by drawing each thread through three different implements and tying the ends to a bolt in front.

She used the spinning wheel to wind different colored yarn on as many bobbins, which she put in shuttles. Then she stepped up into the loom, sat down on the board seat, and began to work the treadles with her feet. Back and forth the shuttle flew from her right hand to her left and back again between the even threads of the warp. As the threads of the warp crisscrossed each other, the thread that had been sent through by the shuttle was caught fast and pushed firmly to the front by the hand bar.

Weeks went by, but Kjersti never grew tired of watching Mor's busy hands and listening to the thud of the treadle, the clack of the shuttle, the thump of the hand bar. By adding one thread at a time, Mor made inches grow into yards, and yards into a large bolt of cloth. The blankets were made of gray yarn only, but the dresses had different colored stripes.

Kjersti's fingers ached to weave. When Far and Mor worked outdoors each of the older sisters would weave and then take the threads out again. Kjersti made it plain that unless she were permitted to weave she would tell; so they had to let her. One would be on the watch for Mor while the others worked.

At last the yarn was all used up and the cloth was cut off the loom. While Far made the return trip to Solheim, Mor cut and hemmed the blankets. The children always remembered how warm they slept that night.

When the children saw that dresses weren't made so quickly as the blankets, they tried to help Mor with the work they were too small to do. She only looked at them kindly and said, "You will have to wait." In the night when all were asleep and the house was still, Mor's arm moved in rhythmic circles as she added stitch to stitch till each child had a new dress.

The children watched Mor measure and cut, and when they stayed up late they saw her sew; but the only thing they were allowed to do was to thread the needle for her. Kjersti couldn't count very well, but she knew that Mor had only one darning needle, one pair of scissors, two sewing needles, and four spools of thread. When not in use they were all locked in the big chest, and Mor carried the key. It happened that at times she forgot the key and went out to work; and then they watched their chance and used the scissors, but they never dared to take the needles.

Kjersti watched Aagot cut a doll from a piece of cloth and a chemise and a dress from another. Wondering why Aagot ran to the thorn apple bush under the hill, Kjersti followed. From the bush Aagot picked sharp-pointed needles and with the point of one of these made an eye in another for thread, which she raveled from a piece of cloth. There in the hot sun the two sat. The younger sister patiently watched the older as she wove the wooden needle in and out, breaking the flimsy thread again and again. It was hours before the sewing was done and the doll was stuffed with silky down from the milkweed. When, with a piece of charcoal, Aagot made lines for eyes, nose, and mouth and held the doll up for examination, Kjersti's eyes shone. Then she reached out her hands, only to be told, "The doll is not for you."

Because there were many things for which homespun could not be used, Mor was glad that flour could be bought in large cloth sacks. From them she made chemises, pillowcases, and sheets. Far, who could not wear wool socks during hot weather, used the remnants to swathe his feet. To obtain enough material for all these things, Mor hit upon a plan. Some of the pioneer women didn't use their flour sacks— they had money with which to buy muslin. On the other hand, they needed homespun yarn but they didn't know how to spin. With these women Mor exchanged yarn for flour sacks.

CHAPTER III

Birgit

Whenever Aagot was outdoors helping Far and Mor, Kjersti carefully unwrapped the rag doll and gazed longingly at it. She wondered if she would ever grow big enough to be able to make a doll all her own.

One day she was awakened by loud voices, followed by a squeaky cry. She sat up, rubbed her eyes, and saw a tiny bundle from which more squeaks came. Kjersti hurried out of bed, over to the tiny bundle, and exclaimed, "A doll! a live doll! Mor, it is my doll!"

Mor replied, "It isn't a doll. It is a baby, your baby sister." Kjersti never talked back, but no matter what anyone said, it was her doll anyway. She stroked the tiny hands tenderly and touched the soft cheeks. But what made the baby cry so much? Why did Mor look so worried?

As the days went by, Mor's face grew more and more tense. She carried the wee baby on her left arm while with her right hand she prepared the meals for her family. At last she said: "Go across the river and fetch Gamle Mikkel; the baby must be baptized. I don't think she can last till morning."

In silence Far went out. Mor left her work unfinished, sat down by the fire, and held the little twisted body close to her breast. The slanting rays of the sun fell through the bare

15

window and across the bare table. The children, wide-eyed, too awed to speak, sat down in their accustomed places.

Presently soft footsteps broke the stillness. Far and Gamle Mikkel entered. Without an exchange of greetings they removed their hats and set about finding a basin of water, a piece of cloth for a towel, and the hymnbook. The children gazed in silence as Gamle Mikkel dipped his hand into the basin of water and sprinkled the baby's head three times while he repeated, "Birgit, I baptize thee in the name of the Father, the Son, and the Holy Ghost." Taking the piece of cloth, he carefully wiped her head, and then he read from the hymnbook. When Gamle Mikkel folded his hands and bent his head to say the Lord's Prayer the children did the same but moved their lips in silence.

Slowly Mor sat down again in the same position, holding Birgit, who did not cry any more. Far reached out his arms but Mor shook her head as she said, "No! no! I must hold her myself now."

The spasms gradually ceased, the tiny form relaxed, a smile played on the tiny face; finally she breathed no more. Big tears trickled down Mor's cheeks. The children were awed; they had never seen Mor cry before. Gamle Mikkel went home, and after a while Far left once more. How long he was gone the children did not know.

The following morning a strange man came carrying an unpainted box, which was half filled with straw and covered with a white cloth. Mor washed Birgit, put on her little calico cap and pink dress, and laid her on the straw. Far took the box in his arms and Mor and the girls followed him to the empty dugout, where he placed the box on a bench.

Kjersti had not uttered a word until they all turned to go back to the house. Then she realized that Birgit was not returning with them. She clung to Mor's skirt and begged, "Take Birgit in again. It is cold here! Please, take her in again."

Mor's face was wet with tears as she lifted Kjersti on her

arm and let her touch the tiny hands, now so cold and stiff. Kjersti remembered the dead bird Far had once brought her and seemed to understand. With lagging steps they all returned to the cabin.

The children watched Far dig a deep hole near the large white poplar, but they did not know what he meant when he told them the grave was ready. In the afternoon a very beautiful lady, Hege Pladson, came to the house and tried to comfort Mor. Later two men came and carried the box to the grave, where they lowered it carefully. One of them read from the hymnbook; then all sang a mournful dirge.

While the men shoveled earth into the grave until it formed a mound, Kjersti hid her face in Mor's dress and refused to be comforted. When the children were once more in the house Aagot unwrapped the rag doll, looked at it a long time, then slowly walked over to Kjersti and said, "You may keep the doll now; I don't want it any more." That night Kjersti went to sleep holding the doll close to her face.

After that Mor often took time to hold the questioning Kjersti on her knee and talk to her.

"Birgit was sick from the first. The doctor might have helped her but we could not get him; he lives a long, long way from here and we have no money. If Birgit had lived she might always have suffered. She has it good now. She will never be cold, never be hungry; she will feel no pain; no one will ever hurt her. Death is not unkind; it is kind. We must not wish Birgit back. We miss her, but it was best for her to go."

Thus Kjersti gradually learned to feel happy about Birgit's leaving.

CHAPTER IV

Far and Mor

The children never dared to bother Far. He seemed like a
stranger whom they hardly knew. During the long winter
evenings he would fill the stove with wood, let it burn down a
bit, and then take off the large front door of the stove so he
could see the glowing embers. In his chair by the fire he lived
in another world. As the light flickered on his dark curls and
seemed to make his high forehead still higher, he talked softly
to himself, grew stern, then smiled, shook his head, rose ab-
ruptly, sat down again, and mused quietly. In such moods no
one dared to disturb him. Mor seemed to have the same feeling. He was not unkind nor severe. He was just Far.

Years later the children learned that he had been reared
in a home of plenty where the love of learning was of first
importance; that he had been graduated with honors, at
twenty-one, from Linnes School of Agriculture; and that he
had finished officers' school in Oslo with the same distinction.
They knew, too, that he had served in the king's army for
eighteen years, giving orders and drilling soldiers, and that
he had often acted as clerk for his uncle, Judge Sten Hamers-
boen. When they realized that this was his background, they
wondered how he had ever lived on that homestead in North
Dakota and kept his sanity. They understood, too, his dislike
for hard physical labor and his love of books and nature.

18

When a friend from Norway would come to the log cabin, Far was a transformed man. The children would hurriedly finish their work and sit at attention. They heard the names of Peter the Great, Napoleon, Alexander the Great, Diogenes, Socrates, Plato, Epictetus, and many others. Many things were discussed that they did not understand, but how they enjoyed the stories and the strange names!

No one was afraid of Mor. Her ruddy face, framed in flaxen hair, shone with good will even when she scolded. Mor had not gone to school much; she had always worked from the time she was a little girl. Sometimes when Far was away and she was knitting she taught the children to sing hymns. They loved to hear her rich musical voice. She told them stories, too. Kjersti knew every one of Mor's stories—they were so few—but she liked to hear them just the same. The one she liked best was "How Butterball Saved His Life."

Once upon a time there lived a fat boy who had a very round head, a very round face, a very round mouth, and very round eyes. When he cuddled down to sleep he might be mistaken for a ball of butter; so they named him Butterball.

One day he wandered into the woods, where he met a troll who had a large sack on his back. "What are you doing here in my woods?" asked the troll.

"I am picking berries."

"Don't you know you can't pick berries in my woods unless you belong to my family? Tonight I'll eat soup made of your bones." With these words he grabbed Butterball and thrust him into the sack. He gathered the ends together and fastened them securely with a strong cord; then he lifted the sack with Butterball in it on his back.

The troll walked and walked and walked till he groaned and sweated. Butterball, who was all doubled up in the sack, hardly dared to breathe, but he was thinking hard. Finally he said, "Have we much farther to go? Why don't you put me down and rest a while?"

The troll thought this a good suggestion; so, when he came to a big stone, he put the sack down. In the distance he heard the trickling of a stream—and he was so thirsty! He knew that Butterball would be safe in the sack; so he walked off to get a drink.

The troll was no sooner gone than Butterball took a knife out of his pocket, cut a hole in the sack near the top, and stepped

out. He hurriedly filled the sack with stones; then he hid behind
a big boulder. After a while the troll returned, picked up the
big sack, and walked off.

Butterball ran home as fast as his legs would carry him; how
he laughed when he thought of the troll and the soup he would
have for supper that night!

The children enjoyed hearing Mor read aloud from the
Bible because she always chose dramatic episodes from the
Old Testament. They enjoyed most hearing about the Israel-
ites in Egypt and their escape. Kjersti imagined she was in
Egypt and went through all the plagues; she even crossed the
Red Sea in triumph. Aagot thrilled to the story of Job. She
gloried in his ability to stand alone when he had lost all.
But how she wished he had not complained when at last he
fell ill!

During the gooseberry season, which opened about the
first of July and lasted some five weeks, Mor hardly had time
to sleep. Up with the dawn, she roused the weary children
from their slumbers. Each one had a set duty. Mor skimmed
the milk, warmed it, and put a certain amount in each of
four pails for the calves. Ragnhild brought the cows from the
pasture and Aagot milked. Kjersti had to help feed the calves.
She taught many a newborn calf to drink by holding her fat
hand down in the milk and letting the calf suck her finger
till he learned to drink properly.

After a hurried breakfast of bread and cream, with milk to
drink, each had to fasten a small bag to her dress front. Besides her small bag, Mor carried an extra large sack.

Across the footbridge they went, into the dark shady
woods, thick with underbrush. The grass was wet, but that
did not matter much, as they were barefoot. When nettles
burned their bare legs they never complained, only stopped
and scratched, and then ran to catch up with the rest. By
this time of the year the skin was thick on the heels and soles
of their feet, but burrs made their way through, and Aagot
had to help remove them. No one whimpered — there wasn't
time for that. The small sharp needles on the gooseberry

bushes stung and scratched their hands and arms, but that was to be expected.

When Mor and the children had filled the small bags, they emptied them into the large sack. By noon they returned home, hungry and scratched, but with the big bag filled. How good bread and milk tasted! And how good it felt to lie down and rest! It wasn't long, however, before Mor called again and they went back into the woods to repeat the work of the morning.

Gooseberries have tiny black tails that have to come off; so every berry had to be picked over by hand. They spent the evenings doing this. The children were not able to help very long; their eyes simply would not stay open. But Mor often worked all night, taking short naps by crossing her hands on the table and resting her head upon them.

The berry season was a time of plenty. It brought a pretty calico dress for each, an apron or two for Mor, shirts for Far, and many other things they needed; but most of all they enjoyed the sugar and the syrup, because during the winter months they often had no sweets. Mor made gooseberry sauce, too, when there was sugar enough.

By helping to pick and clean gooseberries and carry them almost six miles to market at a price of ten cents a quart, the children learned the value of money. To them money was a means to buy what they needed, not what they wanted. Ten cents seemed a great deal of money, and the spending of it had to be carefully planned.

When Far worked he never talked, nor could anyone interfere. Kjersti always managed to watch him from some place where she would not be noticed. One spring morning he took a knife and a small ax and went to a willow thicket. He selected slender willow branches with as few knots as possible, cut them into certain lengths, then pounded them carefully all over until they slipped easily out of their coverings. How white and slippery they were! He slit each one of them lengthwise through the center; then he crossed a certain number of slit branches and held them in his left hand, and with one branch in his right hand, started to weave. He did not stop working until he had finished four large white baskets. One was used for wool, one for clothes, one for wood, and one to carry fine hay to the calves.

Then he made something strange. This time he took longer willow branches and slit them through the center in the same way as before, but he did not remove the bark. He tied all the tapering ends as close together as possible, and then he gradually spread them apart and with a slit willow branch wove in and out, not very close. When he had finished he had a long cone-shaped basket that he called a *fisketeine*.

Below the house the beavers had made a dam across the Goose River. Far made an opening in the dam large enough to insert the *fisketeine*; then he fastened it securely, on both sides, to the dam. It was so arranged that the water flowed in through the large opening and out wherever it could. In those days there were plenty of fish in the river. But most pioneers had neither hooks nor nets; so they could not catch them that way.

The fish came gliding along in the water and were caught in the narrow end of the trap; they could not turn around and go back. About twice a day Mor would go down to the river, loosen the trap, carry it up on land, and pour the fish out. During the summer they had plenty of fish to eat and often shared them with the neighbors.

One spring a girl came to the neighborhood direct from Telemarken. Because she loved children, the day she spent at Kjersti's home was a memorable one. All day long she helped the children make baskets, told them stories, and in her mellow voice sang ballads about the goats, lambs, and children of her native land. Thus Kjersti's longing to learn how to weave baskets was satisfied.

When a footbridge across the river became necessary, Far picked out a long slender tree on the riverbank and chopped it down in such a way that it fell across the river with the tip touching the other side. When Far and Mor crossed on this footbridge they steadied themselves with long sticks, but the barefoot children skipped across like so many squirrels. Every spring, when the snow melted on the hills and in the deep gulches and ravines, and the rains set in, the river overflowed its banks and carried away the footbridge. Then Far had to do the job over again. There were so many trees that the ones he used were not missed.

For days Far had been walking here and there at the foot of the bluffs below the house; he seemed to be hunting for something. He finally said, "I have found a spring."

This time Kjersti could not keep still. "What is a spring? Let me see it."

Far took her hand and led her to the foot of the hill, where out of a circular hole, only two feet deep, the water bubbled. He had brought a pail which he filled with spring water and carried back to the house. How good it tasted! After that they never had to drink river water.

One winter, when a lone man in search of land came and asked for food and shelter in exchange for work, Far let him stay. For weeks the two were busy in the woods, Far directing, the man doing the work. Young oaks and ash were cut down, branches chopped off, and bark cleared away. With a broadax they chopped off pieces till the logs turned into planks about five inches thick. Using a stick for a measuring rod and a piece of charcoal for a pencil, they measured and marked all the planks. Each in turn was lifted upon two logs, and the men sawed along the charcoal marks till they had a certain number of planks the length of beds and the same number the width of beds. From the smaller poles they removed the bark only.

During the summer the stripped poles and planks were left in the sun to dry. When fall came Far smoothed all the planks with a plane. He had brought a turning lathe in his big chest all the way from Norway to Iowa and in the covered wagon from Iowa to Dakota. With the turning lathe and the tools that belonged to it he made legs and trimmings for tables, beds, and chairs. He had neither nails nor glue, but with his tools he fitted one piece into another so snugly that they stuck fast. The frames and legs of the furniture he made were fitted in this way.

The beds had the queerest springs. With a bit he bored small holes about eight inches apart in the bedframe; then he wove ropes in and out through these holes for the bottom or spring of the bed. Mor made ticks of heavy cloth and filled them with dry cornhusks or oat straw. When one of these ticks was laid on the rope springs it made a bed fit for a king.

Far made furniture for neighbors who did not have the skill for that kind of work. They in turn helped him with the rough farm work that he disliked.

Whenever we needed a new broom, Far chopped down some buffalo brush and cleared the main stems of tiny branches to a place about a foot from the tip; then he tied and bound many stems together to form a handle, leaving the loose tips to form the brushy part.

Mor was highly pleased when, with the turning lathe and its tools, Far chiseled grooves in a thin oak plank and made her a washboard. She didn't have to tire her back rubbing the soiled clothes on a stone any more. From wood he also made pretty spoons for the table and ladles, a potato masher, and scoops for the kitchen.

Because the children considered it an honor to be asked to help Far, Kjersti often wondered if he usually asked Aagot because she was big and strong or because she was named for his mother. Sometimes when he needed firewood he took a long saw that had a handle on each end, and called Aagot to help him. They put a log on two sawhorses that he had made. Then, with the log between them, each holding one handle of the saw, they worked up a slow rhythmic motion that they continued until there was no more log. When her arms and back ached, Aagot closed her lips and thought: "I must keep this to myself. Far says only weak people complain."

One crisp fall morning, Kjersti wondered why the big copper cauldron had been filled with water and heated. She heard a shot and hurried out to find the mother pig lying motionless on her side. Far came in for a bucket of hot water, to which he added some ashes; then he poured the water on the pig and called Aagot to help remove the bristles. When more hot water was needed, Far would fetch it. Aagot had a good time pulling and scrubbing till the pig's skin was white, smooth, and clean like her own. But until she was a grown woman she used to be teased for having helped butcher a pig.

When seeding time came, the children watched Far make a strong bag from a sack, fasten two strings to its upper edge, and tie it around his waist like an apron. He filled the bag with grain and walked over to the field; then, steadying the bag with his left hand, he scooped his right hand full of grain and walked ahead. As with rhythmic motions he swung his arm first to the left, then to the right, he gradually opened his fingers and let the seeds go. He kept doing this until wheat, oats, or barley had been scattered all over the field. The neighbors who did not know how to seed grain by hand, and had no machine with which to do it, were glad to let Far use their plow and harrow in return for his seeding their fields.

Kjersti watched all the changes in the wheat field and wondered: Why do grains of wheat swell when placed in the warm, moist earth? How do some of the tiny sprouts know they are to become roots and stay in the ground, while others rise up, push themselves through the earth, and grow into long stalks that again bear wheat? How can one grain of wheat grow into a whole handful of grains?

CHAPTER V

The Hen with a Shell on Her Back

The snow was still on the ground when the children had to take their shoes and stockings off to save them for the following winter. They liked going barefoot; they could run faster and see more. They were so busy that they often forgot about dinner and ate what nature had to offer — young shoots of grapevines, fresh sorrel from the ground, tender budding basswood leaves, and the bark of young branches on the chokecherry bushes. They made cups of bark and caught the sweet drips from the box elders; what a delicious drink after the sugarless winter! As the berries and nuts ripened, the children ate them too.

Kjersti's face was a question mark when she brought in the first crocus and the first buttercup. She was fairly bursting with questions. She wondered, "Why do grown people who know everything always say, 'Don't bother me. I am busy. Run along.' Why does everything happen all at once? The grass comes out of the ground, the leaves come out on the trees, and the birds come back. One just can't keep track of anything."

There were two things she simply had to keep track of, the berries and the birds. Time and again she ran to Mor and said, "The gooseberries have grown *so* much now," and measured off their length on her finger. She watched carefully because Mor had promised her a calico dress if there were plenty of berries that year.

The thought of a calico dress delighted Kjersti, who didn't like her homespun garment. Wherever it touched her bare skin it chafed and made tender sore spots. Sometimes she could hardly wait for evening to come so that Mor would take time to wash the raw spots and apply a little cool cream from the top of a milk crock.

A few weeks later Kjersti came running from the berry bushes. Her breath turned to gasps: "Come quick and see the queer hen! She has a head like a snake and four legs! She is making a nest in the sand!" Kjersti took Far's hand and led the way, followed by the rest of the children. When they came to a sunny spot not far from the river they saw a turtle that had dug a hole in the sand, where she laid one egg after another. Finally she covered them carefully and made her way slowly back to the river.

Far explained: "The turtle's body is covered with shell; so she cannot sit on her eggs to keep them warm till the baby turtles come out. The sun has to do that for her. When the eggs have lain in the sand long enough the baby turtles crawl out of the eggs and make their way to the river, where they take care of themselves."

Kjersti was pacified but not satisfied. She often returned and sat quietly near the place where the turtle had laid her eggs. Far and Mor were surprised some time later when she confessed, "I dug up one of the turtle eggs. I wanted to see if it was a real egg. I opened it and saw that it had a yellow center like a hen's egg. I saw a bird's egg like that, too. Why do chickens come out of some eggs, turtles out of some, and birds out of some? Why can't baby birds and chicks take care of themselves like turtles? Why does a turtle lay many eggs all at once when a hen or bird lays only one a day?"

But all Mor answered was, "The fire is almost out; do run and bring in some wood."

Anyway Kjersti had to leave the turtle and the questions

now, for the woods were full of birds. She liked those best that made their nests in low bushes or on the ground, where she could look at the eggs. But it wasn't long before she had a new question. "Mor, why do some nests have many small eggs all one color and the same size and one egg different in color and size?"

For once Mor was willing to talk. "Some birds are like some people; they hate to work. Such birds are too lazy to build nests and take care of their young; so they drop their eggs in other birds' nests and let the owners of the nests take care of them."

After that, when Kjersti saw a strange egg in a nest, she took it out and hid it in the sand. The sun could take care of it the same as the turtle eggs, she thought.

Kjersti felt it her duty to help the birds feed their babies; so when the mother bird was away hunting for food she found green juicy worms, stole up to the nest, and tried to call as the mother bird did. The little birds opened their mouths wide and Kjersti dropped a worm or a ripe berry into each mouth. The parent birds were so used to her that they didn't seem to mind. How busy she was! Every day she made her rounds, and there were so many nests!

Watching them, Kjersti decided that mother birds were not always kind. She noticed that when the baby birds were covered with feathers and could move around in the nest the mother bird gave them very little to eat. If the young birds didn't try to jump out of the nest and help themselves, the mother pushed them out. Kjersti thought they should have been fed and sheltered for many more days. She liked the parent birds when they taught their little ones how to fly and when they kept enemies away from them as they hopped in the long grass and among the bushes. To make up for what she thought was the mother bird's neglect, Kjersti shut the cat in the stable, and with her chubby hands full of worms and berries she followed the young birds, feeding them as best she could.

Far, who did his pacing outdoors now, often helped the children see the birds. He pointed out a tiny nest on the branch of a huge elm tree; then he brought a tall ladder and leaned it against the trunk and held it there. Each child in turn mounted the ladder and looked at the tiny eggs, the size of peas. Later they made another trip to see the baby birds, now as large as bumblebees. They were hummingbirds.

Kjersti and her sisters learned the language of many of the birds. Far had made a new dugout, where Mor kept milk and other foods during the summer. The children inherited the old one, which opened toward the woods. It became their Bird Home. Its earthen walls had many holes and its bark roof many crevices. Aagot took off part of the door at the top so the birds could come and go at will.

The girls learned not only the language of the birds but also their ways and habits. With crumbs and seeds in their hands, they would cautiously enter the Home, sit down on the floor, spread the food on their laps, and with half-closed eyes watch the birds come chattering, questioning, hopping all over them, eating out of their hands and laps.

Kjersti wondered why the birds were afraid of her when she stared at them. But what of that? With the help of little brother Tosten, a born mimic, she learned to imitate bird dialect so she could make the catbird, the owl, the whippoor-will, the robin, and the wren come up to the house. Even Mor had become so interested that she made some bags of old sacks and hung them in the poplars near the house, where the wrens liked to nest.

Kjersti, thinking of the hens merely as big birds, felt that Mor's treatment of them was so unfair that she had to speak. "Why do you take all the eggs away from the hens?"

"Eggs are good food. Don't you like them? We have to exchange eggs for other things we need, too. Besides, if we let the hens keep all the eggs there would be so many chicks that we could not take care of them."

"Yes, but you don't have to take all the eggs. Every day

when the hens return to their nests to lay eggs they find only the old nest egg. I know they feel bad to have their eggs taken."

To this Mor made no reply. Then something happened which made Kjersti quite happy. The hens did get tired of laying eggs and having them taken; so they went into the big woods and hid their eggs where no one could find them.

One day Mor said, "We are getting no eggs. The hens are stealing their nests; we must find them."

That night, after the chickens had gone to roost, she took a hen who had the habit of wandering off by herself and put her under a basket. The next morning she tied a string several yards long to one of the hen's legs, then, fastening the other end of the string to her own waistband, she let the hen go. The hen zigzagged here and there through the bushes and among the trees. Mor had to follow; but she did not mind because her hands were free and she could knit as she walked. When the hen was ready to lay her egg, she went straight to the hidden nest. Mor marked the place, let the string go, and, still knitting, returned to the house. Later that same day Kjersti saw Mor coming from the woods with her apron full of eggs.

After that, when Kjersti saw Mor putting a basket over a hen, she knew what would happen. But the big black hen seemed to understand that her nest was in danger. When Mor put the string on her she wandered here and there and finally dropped her egg in the grass. Mor started out with the black hen twice and then gave up.

One day the hen disappeared. Mor remarked, "The weasel got her." About three weeks later they saw the black hen coming slowly out of the woods. Following her, half hidden in the grass, were twelve fluffy chicks of various colors. Kjersti beamed and chuckled as she counted, "Two, four; two, four."

CHAPTER VI

The Lamb That Wasn't Wanted

When Kjersti heard that a lamb was expected in March she kept asking, "Is it March yet?" She had made several fruitless trips to the stable and had even talked matters over with the serious ewe, who was so patiently chewing her cud.

Mor said, "You must learn to wait; we all have to learn that."

One evening when the rest went to bed, Mor polished the lantern, took off only her shoes, and lay down on top of the covers. This made Kjersti so curious that she couldn't go to sleep. After a while Mor arose, put on her shoes, kerchief, and mittens, lit the lantern, and went out. She returned with some straw, which she put in the corner nearest the stove. She pushed the wood box and a chair in front of it, thus making a three-cornered pen.

Then she put more wood into the stove and set some milk where it would keep warm. After another rest, she went out again. She was gone a long time. Kjersti listened thoughtfully. At last there was a crunching sound in the snow; someone was running. Mor entered hurriedly with a bundle of sacks in her arms and set it on the floor. The bundle began to wriggle and cry, a lamb's head peeped out, and then his whole body came to view.

Kjersti sat upright in bed and stared. She was supposed to

be asleep; so she did not dare to speak. When another lamb came out of the bundle she had to pull the covers over her mouth to keep from shouting. Finally, when a third lamb appeared, Kjersti had lost any desire to speak or shout. She held her breath as she counted, "Two, four; two, four." She wondered if there would be many lambs, like birds. Would the room be full of lambs? How wet the lambs were, and how they wobbled! Mor rubbed them dry by the fire and gave each a few spoonfuls of warm milk; then she put them in the pen that she had prepared for them. Kjersti kept awake until she saw the lambs being fed again and covered with an old blanket.

When she awoke the next morning, two lambs were missing. Mor described how she had carried all three back to the mother sheep, how the mother sheep had welcomed the large lambs, but how she had chased the little one away. She did not want anything to do with her third child. Mor added: "Do not blame the ewe. Triplets are one too many for any mother."

To the children the lamb became their all-absorbing interest. They watched his every move. He was their first thought in the morning and their last at night. For some time he had to be fed by spoon; then Mor gave him milk in a pan. Kjersti put her hand into the milk and let the lamb suck her little finger. He continued to do this until he gradually learned to drink like a grown sheep.

The children named the lamb Truls. Often they carried him to the stable, where he played with his sisters. He never dared go near his mother; instead he made friends with Tafat (take hold), the dog. The two would play until they were tired; then they would snuggle down close together for a rest. The extra care Truls received made him as large and as strong as the other lambs were by the time he was six weeks old.

April brought longer and warmer days. The sheep were outdoors more of the time, as were Kjersti and her sisters.

Whenever Truls saw any of them he would come leaping and
bounding up, expecting to be given milk and to be petted.
He would follow them like a dog all over the woods and hills.
When they were sent on errands to the neighbors they were
sure to be followed by Truls and Tafat. Even after he was a
grown sheep, Truls seemed to think that Kjersti should hold
him in her lap.

As Truls grew old he became so fond of having his own
way that when he could not do as he pleased he would butt
any person he disliked and sometimes even those who had
been kind to him. He would back up, stiffen his neck, aim,
and come with full force. Because he was a big strong sheep
his butting became so dangerous that a piece of leather was
tied to his horns in such a way that he could look to the side
and down but not straight ahead. The leather blind kept him
from hurting anyone.

When Tosten, who was still a little boy, wanted some fun
he edged up to Truls. As he petted and talked he lifted the
blind so that the sheep could see Kjersti and Aagot. All at
once the air was filled with shrill screams from the girls, the
sound of their scurrying feet, and the echoes of laughter from
Tosten, who always managed to get the flap down again before Truls could do any harm.

Early one morning when Mor and the children were alone
they were awakened by a terrific thud on the door. Hurrying
out, they saw the panting Truls with his tongue out and his
blind off. By his side Tafat jumped up and down, barking
and yelping; then he started to run toward the pasture. Mor
and the children followed. From the distance sounded the
bleating of sheep and the bellowing of calves.

What a commotion! Calves, heads and tails in the air, ran
every which way to save their lives, and the sheep were following helter-skelter. A wolf was pursuing them. Suddenly he
halted, sniffed, looked up and saw the dog with his followers,
and instantly disappeared. Mor looked at the children and
said: "Truls saved the calves and the sheep. I don't know

how he got his blind off, but no one is going to put it on him again!"

As they were returning past the dugout where the food was kept, Tafat and Truls made another fuss. Mor opened the door and found that a hole had been eaten in the butter and the milk pans had been disturbed. When she saw a mound of fresh earth on the floor she knew that some wild animal in search of food had made a tunnel from the outside. That afternoon she said to the children: "Run and tell Vebjørn Søndreaal what has happened. He will know what to do."

It was dusk when Vebjørn came, bringing a trap and a strong chain. While he explained what was to be done, he placed the trap near the hole and fastened the chain to a pole near by. Then they all returned to the house to wait. After several hours of waiting, during which Vebjørn told many stories, the insistent barking of the dog sent everybody to the dugout. Noticing new, fresh tracks, Vebjørn whispered: "A badger. Look at the taut chain. But where is the trap?" They found that the badger had been caught by one leg, and in trying to escape he had pulled the trap up the hole as far as the chain would permit.

A tug of war began. Mor pulled at the chain with all her might while Vebjørn stood, ax in hand, ready to strike the badger as soon as Mor could get him out. Aagot held the lantern; Kjersti, Ragnhild, and Tosten kept back the sheep and the dog. Suddenly something snapped and Mor fell backwards, the trap in her hands. The badger had escaped, leaving the claws of one hind leg in the trap. "Never mind," Vebjørn said, "that badger will know better than to come back for any more butter."

CHAPTER VII

Ragnhild

When Ragnhild was a tiny infant her head was injured in an accident. After that she was never well. For months her pitiful cries sounded night and day. Nothing could be done because the nearest big town, Fargo, was too far away, and there was no money to pay a doctor. She did not walk until she was two years old and did not talk until much later. She always remained a child.

One spring evening, when Ragnhild was less than seven years old, a wandering tinsmith came to the cabin and asked for shelter. Mor, who never turned anyone away, permitted him to enter and gave him food and a bed in a corner on the floor. He stayed two days. By that time tiny pimples were breaking out on his face and hands. Mor became alarmed and told him he would have to move on to a bigger house where he could have more room and better care.

Ragnhild, who was a very beautiful child, was always noticed by strangers. During his two days' stay the tinsmith had held her on his lap and played with her. A couple of weeks after his departure Ragnhild was taken violently sick with vomiting and fever. Even Far became uneasy. He went to the people who had taken in the tinsmith and found the man of the house sick with fever and the tinsmith very ill, covered with blisters that turned to sores. Far had a long talk with the wanderer, who confessed that before coming to the neighborhood he had spent a night in a house where they had smallpox, twenty-five miles away.

Shortly before this, Dr. Faltin Bleckre, a young man who had worked as a helper in doctors' offices and had studied medicine for one year at the University of Minnesota, had come to Mayville, about eighteen miles away. Far hurried home and prepared to walk that eighteen miles. The following day he drove back with the doctor.

In each of the three families that had been exposed, one member came down with smallpox. The doctor could not do much for those who were sick, but he vaccinated the rest. No one in the settlement dared come near the homes where the smallpox raged. A man who lived four miles away brought a hundred-pound sack of flour and left it several rods from the Raaen house. Aagot had to open the sack and make many trips with a tin basin to get the flour into the house.

The doctor said Ragnhild could not live; pocks covered her whole body and she lay as if dead, barely breathing. Even though they had been vaccinated, Far, Mor, Kjersti, and Tosten had the fever and a few pocks, which disappeared in about two weeks. But Aagot escaped. She carried water from the spring at the foot of the hill and gave the sick to drink. Young as she was, she could milk well enough so the sick had milk; without it they could not have survived.

All that was done for Ragnhild was to give her water and milk to drink. After weeks of suffering, she began to ask for food. As the sores dried, her whole body itched. She was told not to scratch her face; Mor sewed the sleeves to the sides of her dress, but even that did not help much. All the sores finally healed, but the beautiful child had turned into a scarred girl with dim eyes who had forgotten how to walk and had to learn once more. When others were impatient with Ragnhild, Kjersti, who did not yet speak plainly, would take her by the hand and say, "Laddi, I will help you." From then on Ragnhild was called Laddi.

CHAPTER VIII

Making Primost

One cold rainy morning, the red and white cow was missing. Kjersti heard Mor say: "We must find Rølin; she has hidden away in the thick woods so she can have her baby by herself. A calf born on a day like this will never live."

As usual, Far said nothing; he simply put on his hat and coat and left. Kjersti had many questions to ask. Would Far never come back? Was he lost in the woods as she had once been? Would he find Rølin and her baby? The cold rain would hurt the little calf. Why couldn't it stop raining?

When Far finally returned, Kjersti thought he never would get through changing his wet clothes for dry ones. After he had dressed, he said: "Animals know much more than we think they do. I found Rølin with a white calf; they are both safe and dry."

"Dry?" Mor repeated, "In weather like this?"

"Do you remember the two large trees that the windstorm tipped over last summer and how the tops were caught in the branches of another tree, forming a kind of roof? Well, under this shelter I found Rølin and her calf. We shall have to leave them there till the rain stops." No one ever questioned Far's decisions, so nothing more was said.

Next morning the sun was shining. Kjersti was so excited she couldn't eat her breakfast. She watched Far take a bit of salt and a halter and start for the woods. She followed at a safe distance. When he arrived at Rølin's hideout he called her by name and talked kindly to her. Then he fed her the salt with one hand while with the other he fastened the halter on her horns. As he pulled on the halter, he talked soothingly and coaxed. Looking anxiously at her baby, Rølin started to follow Far. The white calf gazed bewildered at his departing mother; then he bounced like a rabbit through the long grass. In this manner they reached the stable.

Rølin was securely tied. The calf was captured and put in a bin. Poor bossie! She called and called for her baby and he answered, but to no purpose. At first, when Mor tried to milk Rølin, she withheld the milk; it took feed, salt, and more coaxing to make her give it. She was taken to the pasture where the other cows were grazing, and as the days went by she gradually forgot her calf.

Kjersti spent most of her time in the stable with the white calf. She stroked and petted her silent friend as she told him all her problems. When she asked questions she thought the calf nodded his head and seemed to understand. One evening she heard Mor say: "The calf is four days old tomorrow. I must have osteløpe [rennet] so I can make primost. If we wait longer the calf is going to eat hay and that will spoil everything."

The following morning Kjersti was taken to a neighbor. When she returned, the calf was nowhere to be found. Aagot pointed to a small grayish-white bag hanging from a stick and said, "That is the calf's stomach." Then she went on to explain that the calf had been killed and the stomach had been prepared and dried for osteløpe. Kjersti, whose heart ached for her pet, said not a word; she was learning to adjust herself to other people's decisions. But no matter how much they all coaxed she would not eat the veal that the rest of the family enjoyed.

For days Mor saved milk and kept it sweet in the spring

at the foot of the hill. Between times she polished the large copper cauldron till it shone like a bit of golden sunset. Then she put the bag on the stick in a little water to soak. When Mor said, "Everything is ready," the children hurriedly found three stones, each about a foot high, for the cauldron to rest upon. Mor filled it with milk and the children gathered dry branches to put under it. What fun it was to carry live coals from the stove and see the fire blaze under the cauldron and then to run in and eat breakfast while the milk was warming!

With the *tvare* Mor stirred the water in which the bag had soaked into the lukewarm milk. She let it stand for a few minutes, and when she stirred it again, the whole mass had thickened, and gradually it separated into curds and whey. The white curd, or cheese, was put into a mold and squeezed and squeezed until there wasn't a drop of moisture left, and then the mass was taken out and put on a shelf to ripen. By the time it had softened and turned a rich cream color, it was ready to be eaten.

The whey left in the cauldron underwent a different process. All day long some of the children were busy carrying dry branches, breaking them up and feeding them into the fire, while others watched to see that the whey did not boil over. Then came hours of constant stirring so that the thickening mass would not scorch. As it boiled, the whey took on a golden brown color and gradually became thicker and more difficult to stir. Finally Mor took over the work. When she was making extra good *primost* she added two or three quarts of milk mixed with cream. She kept the fire very low and stirred carefully until it was time to remove the kettle from the fire; then she kept on patiently stirring until the mass was cold and stiff. Then she molded it into a number of chocolate-colored *primost* bricks. This *primost* had a sweet nutty taste. Sometimes Mor made *primost* by simply boiling whole milk till it became brown and thick. She did the same with buttermilk, and *primost* made in this way had a tart taste. When immigrants from Norway came to the neighborhood they brought the rich golden brown *gjete-primost* made from goat's milk, which had a flavor different from that of any other kind.

When Kjersti was allowed to eat all the *primost* she wanted on her bread and butter she was so pleased that she gurgled with delight.

CHAPTER IX

Buck and Bright

Because of the white spots on his brown silky coat, Bright could easily be singled out among the other cattle. As he grew older, he became conspicuous for his size. His best friend, Buck, had a darker coat without any trimming and was smaller, but still resembled Bright; they were both active, patient, strong, and kind. Maybe that was why they were such good friends; the two were always together.

As they grew older they developed long pointed horns. Because they were very frisky and playful, they were likely to hurt each other; so Far sawed off the tips of their horns and pushed large hollow brass buttons securely on the ends. They enjoyed the buttons, for they could now butt each other in fun as much as they pleased.

When Buck and Bright were only two years old, Kjersti heard Far say, "Those steers will soon be oxen; they are as large as four-year-olds right now. They must be broken." She remembered the sheep who had broken his leg. She worried. What did Far mean to do? Surely he wouldn't hurt Buck and Bright? Whenever Far went to the pasture she was careful to follow. She noticed that he petted them a great deal, fed them salt, and talked kindly to them until, when he called them by name, they would come up to him. Even when they were in the pasture he could put halters on them and lead them around wherever he pleased.

The past summer Far had sawed off part of the trunk of a young ash tree, and then had hewed the bark from it and let it lie in the sun to dry through. During the winter he worked on this five-foot plank, measuring, cutting, and chiseling until he had two arches, the right distance apart. He was making a yoke. He also made two wooden bows.

He carried the yoke to the stable and put Buck and Bright side by side; then he laid it on their necks. Yes, the arches fitted. Around the neck of each he put the wooden bow; then he marked the yoke where the ends touched it. The next time he put the yoke on the oxen he had bored holes for the ends of the bows to slip through and had also made holes in them for the bow pins so they would stay in place. Underneath, in the center of the yoke, he had fastened a U-shaped iron or clevis that held a strong iron ring.

The bows held the yoke so that it could not come off, nor could the oxen pull apart. But Buck and Bright were such good friends that they did not mind being tied together hard and fast. Nearly every day Far put the yoke on the steers and walked them around. This became such a habit to Buck and Bright that they often came up of their own free will to get under it.

Far had once said that animals, like people, could learn only one thing at a time. After he had trained them to wear a yoke he taught them to obey orders. In gentle, firm tones he commanded "Gee!" and pulled them right, then "Haw!" and pulled them left. They made many mistakes, but he kept on repeating the exercise, never striking them and never shouting angrily. No matter how many mistakes they made, he was kind and gentle, only repeating the command.

Far prepared the wagon by loosening the wheels and greasing the axles. One day he yoked the oxen and backed them up to the wagon so that the tongue, which had an iron knob a few inches from the tip, was between them. In a twinkle he lifted the tongue and pushed it into the iron ring until there was a click of the ring against the knob. Then he hurriedly fastened a long iron chain to the bolt in the tongue close to the wagon and pulled it along the tongue. The chain ended in a large hook, which he snapped to the iron ring in the yoke. With the help of the chain the oxen could pull the wagon. The iron ring against the knob on the tongue held the wagon back when they were going down hill or backing up.

Far slowly led the oxen forward. How surprised they were when they felt the wagon following! The rumbling sounds it made were so close to them that they became alarmed and would have run away if Far had not been near. Every day the steers were hitched up to the wagon, walked to the road and back, and then unhitched, until that became a habit too and they no longer minded the rumbling sounds. They also learned to obey "Gee" and "Haw" without making mistakes. The children heard Far say, "Oxen must like and trust the one who drives them or they will be neither willing nor hard-working."

Buck and Bright became known as the best and strongest yoke of oxen in the settlement. During the winter they pulled huge logs for the new house; in the late spring they broke the prairie into fields where grain and vegetables were sown; and in the fall they made trips to the nearest town, where Far bought provisions.

CHAPTER X

Play

In those early frontier days there were no schools and few books in the upper Goose River Settlement. The only books in Kjersti's home were the Bible, the catechism, the hymnbook, and a book of sermons. An older child would teach a younger one to read. After that each one had to look out for himself and prepare for confirmation.

How Kjersti disliked Sunday! On that day she had to sit still and listen to Far read long sermons and long prayers. She also had to memorize much that she did not understand. Only the necessary work was done, and no one must play — that was wrong. One thing Kjersti did look forward to was Mor combing her hair, which she did only on Sundays. Kjersti always enjoyed seeing Mor undo her long thick braids, so tightly tucked away, and watching the comb flash back and forth till a mass of gold covered Mor like a silky cloud down to her waist. How she wished Mor wouldn't hide her hair again!

Kjersti began to live in her own thoughts. When those around her were doing things she could not understand nor take part in, her thoughts were busy with the big out-doors — the birds, the trees, the flowers, the river, the starry heavens, the wind, and the rain. As she dreamed and thought, she often chuckled quietly to herself.

On weekdays during the summer months when the children were not working they always played in the woods. One day Aagot ordered, "Pry loose as many dry stumps of trees as you can find, gather dry branches as even and as long as possible, and bring them all over here."

"Why over here?"

"Do you see the four large trees that make a square? The trees will be the four corners of a house. We'll fill the spaces between the trees with stumps and dry branches for walls." While Kjersti and Ragnhild gathered material, Aagot leveled the ground for the floor. Then the building began. Without tools or nails, how could they make the walls stand up? They had watched Far fence a pasture, using only wooden poles and rails. With what they had learned while watching Far and the ideas that came to them as they worked, they finally finished the walls, leaving an opening for the door. By common agreement they left out the windows. But what were they to do for a roof and a door?

Kjersti begged: "The leaf-covered branches are so beautiful; through them we can sometimes see the stars or a bit of red sunset. They keep out the hot sun, too. Please let the branches be the roof." After much discussion, they agreed to this. Two strong poles, placed across the opening, kept intruders out and served as a door.

Furnishing the house was more difficult. By searching the woods they found small trees that had fallen and dried out; these they sawed up for chairs. Bark from a dry tree they put on two tree stumps for a table. Hollow chips and queerly shaped bits of wood and bark served as dishes. It had seemed so easy when Far twisted a slender branch and tied it securely around a bunch of buffalo brush for a broom that Aagot felt sure she could manage that, but no matter how many times she tried, the branch would neither twist nor tie. A piece of string or rope would have done the trick, but there was none. The children had to put off sweeping until Mor discarded her old broom for a new one.

When they needed water Aagot followed Far's example and hunted and dug in several places at the foot of the nearest bluff until she made an opening where spring water bubbled.

There had to be a stable and cattle. They had seen Far make a dugout; so it was not difficult to scoop out an opening in the hillside, which they called a stable. Kjersti questioned, "But where can we find oxen, cows, calves, sheep, lambs, and chickens?"

Aagot replied, "Follow me!" To the prairie they went, where they found buffalo bones of many shapes and sizes. How pretty they were! The rain, snow, and wind had washed them clean, and the sun had bleached them white. Aagot sorted out two large bones that resembled oxen, and several a bit smaller that looked like cows. Ragnhild was given the care of the calves. Kjersti was delighted with the bones, which to her looked so much like sheep, lambs, and chickens that she insisted they moved. The play animals were put in their stalls, and the opening to the stable was closed. What good times the children had making a pasture, taking the animals out of the stable, and putting them back in!

Keeping the house in order was as much fun. There the children followed Mor's way of doing things, even to sprinkling the floor with water to settle the dust before sweeping. Several days later Aagot again gave commands: "Today we must make bread and cake. I have seen some light clay in the steep bluffs where the river makes a sharp turn; we must fetch some of it."

No one questioned the orders. Each set off with a large piece of bark on which she scooped as much clay as it could hold; then she carried it to the house and dumped it on the table. Mor lent them a wooden pail for water and gave them some old wooden spoons. With these they carried water and spooned it into the center of the pile of clay. With sleeves rolled up they stirred and mixed and molded the clay into stiff dough that finally became loaves of bread, round cookies, and many differently shaped cakes. The cakes were decorated with berries found in the woods. Bread, cookies, and cakes were left in the sun to bake.

Kjersti often had severe headaches, and she tired easily. When a growth appeared on her neck they called it a goiter. She learned to accept not feeling well, but she longed to do things like Aagot, who always seemed to find a way out. She was glad when the house was finished and she could sit there and breathe the good air while she wondered about the living, growing things of the woods. As she walked between the house and the stable, which held the pretty white animals, she whispered to herself: "I am glad everything is finished. Aagot can't find anything more to do now."

But one day Kjersti heard her say, "We must build another house."

"Another house?" Kjersti repeated. "We have all we need!"

"We must have neighbors, and neighbors mean houses."

Kjersti had many conversations with herself as she trudged and worked: "Why must we have neighbors? They will cause trouble. Why so much extra work when we have our own house to keep?"

Kjersti saw beautiful patterns in leaves and flowers, which she wanted to work out in clay. When Aagot had to help Mor, Kjersti and Ragnhild were busy making in clay what they saw in the things they loved.

As the summer months slipped by, the children completed four houses. "But where are the neighbors?" asked Kjersti.

"Come with me!" Aagot called, "We will find them."

Through the woods they scurried. What queer growths they found among the dry branches! "Yes, here is Knut, so small and bent. There is Andres, so big and strong. Tall lanky Jon is standing straight. Their wives, Guri, Kari, and Anne are not hard to find."

Knut and Guri were moved into one house, Andres and Kari into another, Jon and Anne into a third. The different neighborhood happenings that the children heard about lived again in the playhouses. There were church services, weddings, and baptisms. There was much visiting back and forth, with a great deal of merrymaking. There were also sickness, deaths, and burials — and a well-kept graveyard.

The children always thought of Ole Knudson, the Telemarkning peddler, as a playfellow. With heavy packs on his back, he trudged from settlement to settlement, bringing greetings and news from relatives and friends. When Ole opened the packs, work halted. Everyone gathered around him; the children gazed longingly at lace, ribbons, colored beads, and playthings, while Far and Mor enjoyed looking at furnishings and tools that they hoped some day to own. The children always hoped Ole would stay overnight, for in the evening he would relate funny incidents of his travels and the next morning he would leave something for each child in return for lodgings, a surprise package or two, a piece of ribbon, or a small bundle of decorated name cards to exchange with friends.

CHAPTER XI

Shadows

One Friday, late in the fall, Mor washed and scrubbed two dozen good-sized potatoes and boiled them with the jackets on in as little water as possible. After removing the skins, she mashed the potatoes and added a tablespoonful of salt and a cup of shortening. When the mass was cold she kneaded into it enough whole-wheat flour to make a stiff dough. The rest of the process was the same as that used for *flatbrød,* with the difference that this bread, though baked through on top of the stove, had to be kept soft and was called *lefse.*

That evening Kjersti heard Far say: "We must have some salt for the cattle and some new rope for halters. I also need a new ax, a pitchfork, and a spade. I shall have to leave early tomorrow for Grand Forks. It is a two days' journey."

"Yes," Mor replied, "the children all need shoes, too. The syrup pail is empty and there is no sugar. We have only a little coffee left. If you are leaving early I had better get your *niste* [food for a long trip] ready tonight."

With these remarks she laid a *lefse* on the table and spread a thin layer of butter all over its surface. She folded it, with the buttered surface on the inside, into a half circle so it looked like half a big pie and folded it again, making a triangle. She kept on spreading and folding until she had a good-sized pile. Into a box she put all the buttered *lefse,* a large piece of dried beef, a brick of *primost,* one of cheese, some ground coffee in a cloth bag, a cup, and the copper *kaffe-kjel* (coffeepot).

When Kjersti awoke the next morning, she heard Mor's anxious voice, "You will have to drive slowly. Rølin cannot walk as fast as the oxen." What were they going to do with Rølin? Kjersti dressed hurriedly and went outdoors. There were Buck and Bright hitched to the front of the sleigh, and Rølin with a halter fastened to her horns tied to the back of it. The box of the sled was full of hay.

Far put the *niste* box full of good food in the hay, buttoned up his coat, pulled down his cap, and drew on his heavy wool mittens. "I shall have to walk most of the way to keep warm." With this remark, he stepped in front of the oxen and called, "Come, Buck! Come, Bright! Follow me!" The strong oxen obeyed willingly. Rølin tugged at the halter, looked back and lowed, but that was of no use; she had to follow.

Kjersti was bewildered. She had to ask questions and Mor would have to answer. "Why was Rølin tied to the sleigh? When will Far bring her back?"

"Rølin will not come back; Far is taking her to town to sell her so he can pay for the things he is to bring home."

"Who will buy Rølin? Will they be good to her?"

Mor's face was serious as she said, "We do not know who will buy her, but unless they are good to her she will not give much milk and those who buy her will need milk. This winter you will have very little milk to drink; the black cow does not give much and the others are dry. But remember all the nice things Far will bring back from town."

"When will Far come back?"

"It will take him about a week to make the trip. It may start snowing, too."

Mor spent much of her time outdoors caring for the cattle and bringing in wood and water. The children had greater freedom; so they were busy and happy. Before they knew it the week was gone. Saturday morning Mor said, "Far will be back this evening. He and the oxen will be very tired. We must have everything ready."

While Mor did an unusual amount of work in the stable and at the woodpile, the children cleaned up the cabin and took their customary bath in the washtub. By sundown they were eating supper.

Mor put more wood into the stove. As it crackled and burned, the red flames played on the listening faces of the children. While she knitted she told again the stories they all knew by heart; then with Mor leading they sang all the hymns they knew. Kjersti's head began to nod and her eyes grew so heavy she simply could not keep them open. A stillness stole over the group. Even Mor laid down her work and sat listening. Then she arose and covered the dying embers carefully; there were no matches, so she had to save some live coals to start the fire next morning. Mor looked worried; the children felt that they should not ask questions. They slipped into bed, each busy with his own thoughts.

They awakened early Sunday morning, expecting to see Far, but he had not come. Many times that day they all ran to a hill beyond the house to look for him, but he did not come. Sunday evening there were neither stories nor songs. They just sat and waited. Monday morning came, and no Far — but on weekdays everybody had to work, and this kept them from looking for him so much. Evening brought the same lonesome feeling.

Tuesday came and went. Still Far did not come. Wednesday brought clouds and Mor prepared for a possible storm. Before evening, soft snowflakes began to fall. There was no more coffee; Mor cleaned and roasted wheat kernels, which she ground in the coffee mill and used instead of coffee. That night she put a candle in the window for Far.

On Thursday it was still snowing. Kjersti remembered the snowstorm of the year before. She was anxious for Far. "Why doesn't he come?" she thought. The candle was again set in the window. Friday dawned, cold and clear, and still. When Mor was through with the chores, she said, "Look after the fire and take care of things; I must go to the neighbors."

When she returned, she looked very sad and serious. In her arms she carried a bundle. She removed her wraps before she spoke. "Halvor Solheim returned from Grand Forks yesterday; while there, he saw Far in a saloon."

"Oh," Kjersti broke in, "where are Rølin and Buck and Bright?"

"Rølin was sold the first thing. The oxen stood tied to a post till a kind man took pity on them and put them in his stable, where they are cared for. We need not look for Far as long as the money lasts. Haldis Solheim let me borrow some food. When summer comes we must pick berries to sell so we can pay her back. Always remember to return a little more than you borrow."

From the bundle she took out a small pail of syrup, a bag of sugar, and a large piece of fat pork. The black cow gave so little milk that there was no cream for butter; pork drippings on bread did not taste very good but if syrup was stirred into the drippings, the children were satisfied.

Often after the children were in bed Mor would examine their shoes. This particular evening she opened a bundle in which she kept old stockings and patches. In the morning when the children reached under the bed for their shoes, each found instead a pair of *ladder* made of old stockings and soled with heavy sacking. Mor explained, "You will need shoes when the snow begins to melt; if you wear them now you will not have any then. The *ladder* will wear out, too, but you can learn to mend them. They will keep your feet warm."

As the cold increased, Mor was outdoors most of the time; when she wasn't caring for the cattle she was chopping wood. The children carried it in and fed the fire.

Far had been gone a month. After Mor's visit to the Solheims, no one asked questions. It was Saturday afternoon, and Kjersti was in the window looking for her birds, when she called, "I see a team!" All ran to look. How slowly the oxen moved! But where was the driver? The rig stopped near the house; it was Buck and Bright, gaunt and hungry-looking. With bent head, Far came slowly from behind the sleigh, unhitched the tired animals, and took them to the stable. As Mor poked the fire and put the coffeepot on, the children took their usual places and sat quietly waiting.

Far at last entered and without looking up removed his cap and mittens; then he mumbled something about being cold. Mor poured him a cup of hot wheat coffee; he drank it hurriedly and reached out for more. When he saw the children wearing *ladder* he shook his head and said, "The oxen are footsore." Then he reached for the tallow cup and went out again. Until dark Far seemed to think up excuses for being away from the house. When darkness came he sat down near the stove but was careful not to let the firelight play on his face. After all were in bed the children heard Far moan as he tossed about restlessly. Then all was quiet.

Next day life went on as usual, but there were no new shoes, no syrup, no sugar, no coffee, no rope for halters, no ax, no pitchfork, no spade.

Kjersti, who loved to watch the lights and shadows on the white walls of the log cabin, asked, "Mor, why do some places look light, and some dark, and some red? What makes them move?"

Mor, often very serious now, replied, "When you grow big enough to understand that wrong makes people unhappy and right makes them happy, and that we can make unhappiness and happiness move, you will be able to understand all about the shadows."

For a long time Kjersti sat lost in thought, and then she said, "Do shadows ever get anyone?"

CHAPTER XII

The New House

The early pioneers of the Goose River Settlement had to be sure of fuel and water, so they settled along the river. Those who came later settled on the prairie, where they built sod houses at first and often used dry sod for fuel.

A friendship soon sprang up between the farmers of the prairie and those of the river valley. Far, who had never become accustomed to hard labor, needed help; his prairie friends needed timber for houses and for fuel. To those who had little money and could not furnish labor he sold big trees for fifty cents apiece. As time went on, Far used and sold hundreds of trees, but the forest was so thick that they were hardly missed. When it was so cold that the snow felt like sand underfoot, his prairie friends felled trees. They sawed and split some into cordwood for fuel and cut others for lumber to be used for log cabins.

When Kjersti heard Far talk about building, she thought of a two-room house a neighbor had. Would Far build one like that? Buck and Bright pulled logs through the snow, across the ice-covered river, up the hill to a place near the cabin. By seeding time the logs had been cut into proper lengths, the branches and bark had been removed, and the two opposite sides had been cut down till they were flat and smooth. During the summer the sun and wind dried them through.

That fall a *tømmerman* with two helpers came to build the new house. The children spent all their spare moments watching how the ends of the logs were cut and shaped so that they could be fitted together without nails. Kjersti discovered with delight that the new house had two rooms, each twelve by fourteen feet, and that each room had two windows. Now she would be able to have one whole window to herself where she could see the big outdoors when it stormed or rained.

The house had a room upstairs, too, long and low, with a window in each gable. This attic was left unfinished; the rough studding and boards of the roof formed the ceiling and gables. Between the boards in the gables and around the windows were cracks where the wind whistled, rain dripped, and snow sifted through. For the upstairs Far made two low rope-bottomed beds, on which Mor placed straw ticks, home-woven blankets, and wool quilts. She also carried up the big chest, the flour barrel, a barrel full of wool, and the spinning wheel. There also Far placed his turning lathe and tools.

Up there the children slept the year around. And there they felt free to dream their own dreams and live their make-believe life. Only rainy days, however, found them upstairs. During the summer when they were not working they spent their time in the woods. Aagot, who had taken to wandering off by herself, spent much time alone, often weaving fantastic stories out of things she had seen and heard—she could easily make up the tales that Kjersti and Tosten begged for. Whenever Aagot returned from one of her trips there was great excitement and questioning.

"Where have you been? What have you been doing? What have you seen?"

"I have been 'way inside the big bluff where the mountain folk live. I helped them with their work and they showed me all their beautiful things."

Kjersti's eyes grew enormous as Aagot continued: "Every girl has a doll, and together the children have a box full of pieces, some thread and needles, and a pair of scissors so they can cut and make doll clothes. They have storybooks and even pencils and paper."

By this time both Kjersti and Tosten cried: "When you visit them again, take us along. Please take us along."

Aagot replied, "I can take you to see the mountain people when you are as big as I am if you do as I say now and help me with the work Mor wants done."

They kept their promise till they were big enough to understand that there were no people in the mountains. Then they laughed and said, "It was so much fun believing it — and we helped Mor and learned to work at the same time."

Tosten, the youngest in the family, was often not welcome in the woods and fields because he could not keep up with the others. To get rid of him Aagot would say: "There is a woman in the woods so big that she can hide you in her pocket. The wrinkles in her forehead are so deep that she can hide you in them, too." Tosten stopped teasing to go with them. When the older children returned he simply asked if they had seen the big woman and was told that they had and that she had asked for him. This continued until he was big enough to hold his own.

Rainy days in the attic room were not given over to stories only. Mor had said not to touch the wool, the cards, and the spinning wheel; but the temptation was too great. Wool carding made a scraping sound that Mor might hear, so they picked out the long wool and combed it as best they could with their fingers. On certain parts of the spinning wheel they put tallow, which softened the whirring sound when the treadle was used. This done, they all took turns at spinning until one day Uncle Nils, who had very good ears, called on Mor.

He remained standing by the door and said, "What strange sounds! Where do they come from?" Mor listened also. The two went upstairs. Mor looked at the lumpy yarn on the spindle; she took the wool out of the barrel and found more useless yarn hidden underneath.

As she removed the spindle and the thread belt on the wheel and locked them in the big chest, she said, "Now you must separate the threads of all the yarn you have spun and card them into rolls so I can spin them into yarn for stockings." They obeyed without objection, knowing that for them the spinning season was over.

Then something happened that destroyed all their interest in the new house. It was midwinter. Mor lifted and turned Kjersti, who was too ill to leave her bed. Far, who had little faith in doctors, said, "The fever has almost run its course; Kjersti will soon begin to mend."

A neighbor on his way to town stopped to see Aagot, who was working out, and brought a message that she would have to go home to help. The following morning was so cold that few ventured outside, but Aagot felt sure she could reach the log house with her bundle if she ran most of the way. The stinging cold that bit her face and chilled her whole body made her run like a wild thing. She felt a drowsy numbness creep over her and she wanted to sit down and rest, but she had heard Far say that that was dangerous, and she hurried on. When she reached home, they all exclaimed, "How white you are!" Hurriedly they thawed out her face, her stiff hands and feet, even her knees. The next day Aagot was unable to move her frost-bitten limbs, and Kjersti's fever had not left. Far went to get the doctor. In only a few weeks Aagot was up again, but spring brought the first crocus before Kjersti could venture outdoors.

Then Mor took to her bed and the doctor had to come once more. The children heard the doctor tell Far that she would soon be up again but that she had hurt herself by working too hard and that she must not lift anything nor do any kind of heavy work for many months. Watching over Mor and doing the work that she was not allowed to do, Kjersti and Aagot forgot about the upstairs and the big outdoors.

CHAPTER XIII

The Stars

Kjersti was sure Far knew everything. On a sultry August day when the yellow wheat field was so ripe that every stalk seemed to cry for help, a dark cloud showed just above the horizon; it grew, became restless, and moved, only to be followed by others like it. For some time Far watched the sky uneasily; then he came into the house long enough to say, "I am afraid both harvest and threshing are done." The clouds multiplied till they covered the heavens. How black they were! and how fast they flew! A storm was on the way.

Mor and the children hurried out to pick up and carry in chips and wood. It might rain so much that the outdoors would be dripping wet for days; and dry fuel was a necessity. As they hurried in with their last load, a cold wind came, so strong that it almost carried them away. A few big raindrops fell; then a white sheet of water, driven by a terrific wind, dashed against the windowpanes.

Far came in, all wet. The wind howled, the cabin shook. How dark it was! They could see each other only when the lightning flashed. Every so often the thunder made a tremendous crash. No one was afraid; Mor had said, "When it storms, God is talking to us." Far had not said anything, but he never was afraid.

Kjersti had reasoned that the rumbling sounds people call

58

thunder were only the noise caused by moving the chairs around in heaven. Maybe they were cleaning house or playing games. And how could anyone be afraid of anything like that?

As the wind eased and the rain slackened, the sky began to grow lighter. Then they heard a sound as if someone were throwing sand and small pebbles on the roof. "Hail!" they whispered. From tiny pebbles the hailstones grew to the size of hens' eggs that rebounded into the air, leaving deep dents wherever they struck.

When the deafening roar was over they opened the door and looked across the plain, to see yellow stalks broken and half buried in black earth where the wheat field had been. The children understood what Far had meant about the harvest and threshing being done, but they were too young to understand the full meaning of a lost wheat field. Merry laughter was soon heard as buckets full of hail were scooped up and emptied into a barrel; this would save many trips to the river for water.

Far never complained, and he frowned if anyone else did. The wheat field, which Far and Mor had hoped would bring so many things they needed, was never mentioned again.

Kjersti marveled so at Far's being able to foretell storms that she had to find out how he did it.

"How can you tell when a storm is coming?"

"By studying the sky and the way the weather acts."

"How did you know the storm was going to take the wheat field?"

"You are too young to understand that now, but you can learn anything from nature if you will take time to look, and listen to what nature has to tell you. But it takes time, a long, long, long time."

Kjersti remembered that Aagot always complained: "Time runs away. I just get something started; then time is up and I must do something else. If I could only stop time!" So what was Kjersti to do about time? She kept on repeating to herself, "It will take a long, long, long time." Mor had said, "We must learn to wait." If she could learn to wait, maybe time would come and all would be well.

Far made Kjersti a four-legged wooden stool that she liked very much and often carried outdoors with her, so that when she needed to rest she had a chair. Below the house was a large hay meadow. On warm summer evenings Kjersti would trudge off with her stool and put it in a special place on the edge of the meadow so that she could sit and look down into the hollow. On one of his walks Far stopped and talked to her.

"Why do you sit here in the dark?"

"I watch the stars."

"Wherever you see sky, you see stars. If you sit near the house you see the same stars that you see here."

"I have to sit here to see the stars dance and play. Look! the meadow is full of stars! See how they dance and twinkle! There is one, 'way up in the air! Now it is lost. There it is again! When the stars are through playing, do they return to the sky?"

Far stood lost in thought a long time before he spoke. "The lights in the meadow are not stars; they are fireflies. We will catch one and take it to the house with us."

Kjersti made a bed for the firefly by putting some green leaves in an empty matchbox; for windows she pricked some tiny holes in a corner.

The next morning she examined the firefly carefully, but she could not understand where the light had come from; it was gone. When evening came, she carried the fly back to the meadow, where it danced and played and twinkled as before.

Aagot explained that certain flies carried lanterns so small that no one could see them and that these lanterns gave light so that the elves, gnomes, and fairies could find their way in the woods and meadows after sundown. This satisfied Kjersti until she was able to understand more.

After this Kjersti became more interested in the sky. She

noticed that some stars moved and some did not. She thought, "The moon must be alive; she can change her face." Tosten said the stars that did not move were simply holes in the floor of heaven so one could see how beautiful everything must be on the other side. There were times when the stars seemed so near! If she could but go up there!

One moonlight evening Kjersti placed her stool carefully on the highest point of the hill beyond the house, then climbed onto it. She looked up at the sky, then steadied herself and jumped, only to come down on the hard ground and see the stars as far away as ever.

CHAPTER XIV

Haying in the Meadow

One summer morning Far's and Mor's conversation awakened the children.

"The grass in the meadow will have to be cut this week."

"The grass is tender yet; in another month it will be firmer and make more hay."

"Hay made from young grass contains more nourishment; besides, we must finish here before we can do any work on the prairie. Ole Swenson is to cut the meadow grass as payment for the trees he got last winter. I had better tell him to come. I shall be gone overnight."

Far had no sooner closed the door than the girls jumped out of bed and dressed. They knew it was going to be a busy day with lots of fun. Far wanted the house clean, orderly, and airy, but he did not like to be disturbed. They would clean house while he was gone. When the children were alone with Mor they felt free to laugh and talk and do as they pleased, so long as they accomplished their tasks and did them well.

Aagot laughed as she gave orders that morning. "While Kjersti and I milk, Ragnhild will feed the calves and Tosten will bring in wood and water for the day."

Far and Mor always worked a while before they ate breakfast; the children had to do likewise and learned to enjoy it.

They were through with their morning chores before the dew was off the grass. Mor had a jolly breakfast party. Kjersti and Tosten knew exactly what had been arranged for each to do, but they pretended they didn't.

To the merriment of the rest Tosten rose and said: "Kjersti, you help Mor make *flatbrød* and *lefse*. Ragnhild, you churn butter. Aagot, you take a bucket in each hand and keep on making trips to the river till the big copper cauldron and tub are full of water. It will take ten minutes to walk to the river but it is downhill and you can run, which takes only half as long; coming uphill with two pails of water is hard work but you have to do it. Now I shall have to rest because I got very tired making this speech." Even Mor joined in the laughter which followed.

An endless stream of warm water would be needed the rest of the day. Mor made a fire under the copper cauldron that stood in its accustomed place near the woodpile. It was good that the barrel back of the house was always kept full of lye water — it would all be used up today.

Tosten had a strange rest; he went in and out like a shuttle, never stopping until he had carried out all the bedding to be aired and sunned. He was such a little fellow that he did have to rest before he brought out all the chairs and other objects that could be scrubbed, and set them on the grass.

Kjersti's voice was heard: "Look at Aagot in Mor's cast-off dress! Are you going Christmas mumming in July?"

Aagot replied: "When I am through working I can shed this dress as a snake sheds his skin and put on my own, which will be fresh and clean. I look like a witch; I am a witch. I can make things boil without fire. You watch!"

As she talked she brought out a big wooden pail half full of large white lumps; then she filled the pail with cold water. The lumps began to sizzle, then to swell and boil and steam till all the lumps changed into a smooth, thick paste. Kjersti had to feel of the mess. Yes, it was hot! It had boiled, but the lumps had been cold. The water had been cold, and there was no fire. What had made it boil?

Ragnhild, who had been sent to the nearest neighbor to borrow a whitewash brush, returned. Aagot took part of the stiff paste and put it into another bucket and mixed it with more water until it was of the right thickness. Then she climbed on a high stool, dipped the brush into the lime paste and, with deft strokes from right to left and back again, kept on till the walls were as white as snow. Tosten mixed and thinned the whitewash and kept the bucket full so that she would not have to stop.

What was Kjersti doing all this time? She seemed to be waging war on all the wooden articles that had been carried out on the green. Her ammunition was a bucket of warm water, a small box of sand, and a homemade brush made from scouring rush that grew along the gulches. She scrubbed, scoured, soused, and polished until chairs, pails, churn, and bowls gleamed. All the woodwork, furniture, and floors in the house were unpainted; but they were kept a shining white, free from spots or blemishes. The wooden churn, milk buckets, and wooden bowls were kept that way, too.

The children wanted to finish before eating; so lunch was late. The feeling of satisfied hunger was good, but the feeling of tired limbs resting was even better. They talked of Ole Swenson and wondered where he was going to sleep — there was no extra bed. When Mor brought out a tick that she had made from flour sacks, the girls did not need to be told. What fun they had as they ran a race to the haystack near the stable! The fun increased as each tried to beat the other, filling her share of the tick. When the mattress was full of hay, the girls balanced it on their heads and steadied it with their hands. They marched forward, playing that they were carrying the sky into the house and upstairs. The hay mattress was placed in a corner on the floor for the girls to sleep on; Ole Swenson was to have their bed.

Both Aagot and Kjersti grew serious, thinking of the big

floor upstairs that had to be scrubbed before the cows were brought home from the pasture. As each went upstairs with a bucket of water, an ample floor rag, sand, and brushes, laughter and talking ceased; all that could be heard was the scraping of the sand and the brush and the swish of water. Every so often two red-faced girls, wet with perspiration, came running out to empty their buckets, fill them again with clean warm water, and hurry back to begin once more.

The afternoon wore on. Arms and backs began to ache; the high spirits and speed of the morning waned. Would they be able to finish that big floor in time? They strained every muscle and nerve to the utmost; their motions became jerky. They even grew so cross and impatient that they said unkind things to each other. When they reached the last space by the door they silently wiped away a few persistent tears and pretended that these were beads of perspiration; they felt neither relief nor joy in the completed work.

When Ragnhild brought the cows home to be milked, Kjersti and Aagot did not run, as usual, to get there to milk the cow each liked best. And when the cows came up to be petted they simply shoved the animals into place and milked so slowly that the cows became impatient. Mor had to finish the job.

Kjersti and Aagot did not want any supper. When they went up to bed they walked like old women; they thought of Far, who had twelve miles to walk that day. But Far walked easily; he had learned that when he was an army officer.

Next morning Mor didn't like to call the children—they were used to hard work, but this time they had worked too fast and done too much. Mor's voice had a kindly note when she called the first time. There was no reply. The second call had an insistent note. The children stirred. The third call had a note of command that brought a reply.

"Oh!" Kjersti moaned. "I am stiff! I can't bend! Don't come near me. My arms are sore. Oh! Oh!"

There was no pity in Aagot's voice when she replied, "I

simply hurt all over, but we'll limber up when we work, and we'll forget our hurts, too."

By the time they had finished the chores and eaten breakfast, they were quite willing to begin once more. Aagot scrubbed the floors downstairs; Kjersti washed, ironed, and put up again the white cheesecloth curtains. The last thing to be set right was the yard. Time and again while they worked there, Aagot made a trip to the house, opened the door, and peeped in, to return with a shining face. Kjersti did the same.

"All white! gleaming white, like a snow palace!" Kjersti said.

"The smell of scrubbed floors, aired bedding, and clean clothes is the best perfume I know," Aagot replied.

"It is beautiful! All so beautiful!" Kjersti exclaimed.

Order and cleanliness met the eye everywhere. The joy they should have felt the evening before, over work well done, came now.

It was two o'clock. Ragnhild returned from the hill, where she had been looking for Far, and exclaimed, "They are coming!" Soon a team of well-fed, spirited horses came prancing along; they were pulling a wagon to which a mower and a rake were attached. In a spring seat were Far and Ole Swenson. The two were in a merry mood; they had been chums in Norway and always enjoyed seeing each other. Ole Swenson endeared himself to Mor and the girls by telling Far he had never seen a cleaner house nor tasted better food.

Busy, happy days followed. The swish of the sickle and the fragrance of new-mown hay filled the air. Mor and the girls had much work to do before the hay was ready to be made into cocks. *Flatbrød* and *primost* had to be made, berries picked, clothes washed, patching done, and a dozen other things.

The children thrilled to any kind of hard work now, for in the evenings they could listen to Ole Swenson and Far talk about the big world across the sea. Ole Swenson had much to say about life in Madagascar, India, and China. His brother-in-law, the Reverend Ole Nilson, had interested all his relatives in mission work.

Tosten, Kjersti, and Aagot did not dare ask the grownups any questions, nor did they dare to tell what was going on in their own minds. But when they were alone they talked.

Tosten spoke first. "When I am grown up and have become a preacher I shall take a long, long trip across the sea to tell the heathen in China and India about Jesus. It is terrible for them to pray to wooden dolls — they won't do that any more when I get there. And when I come back you will wait on me and give me the best of everything because you won't know me."

Before he was through Kjersti was ready. "Oh, we'll know you! The way you strut around with your nose in the air — and I am sure you will always be scrawny." Then she sat lost in thought: "Tosten will go far away — but he has to; he must stop the heathen from praying to dolls." Her eyes shone with kindness as she added: "Tosten, you are good and kind even if you tease and argue. I am going to big cities; there I shall see wonders and learn all kinds of things. I must help Mor, but there are old people and sick people who need help, too."

Aagot kept most of her dreams to herself. All she said now was: "I shall keep my promise to Mor first. Then, some day, I shall stand on the highest mountain peaks in Norway and see all the rest of the world. After that I shall go to the pope in Rome and he will show me his palace."

The children were sorry when the sun dried the cut grass very quickly, because after it was raked into bunches Ole Swenson would leave. Much too soon came the day when Far went with him to the woods to help fill the wagon box full of choice oak and ash wood. Mor sent a flour sack full of gooseberries and a brick of *primost* to Mrs. Swenson. There was a big void in all hearts as kind Ole Swenson drove away.

Real labor began once more. Armed with pitchforks and

hand rakes, Far, Mor, and the children made the raked bunches into haycocks that would weather rainstorms and not take in water, which spoils the hay. Thanks to picking gooseberries in the woods, the children's arms and legs were so hardened that although they were barefoot they did not fare too badly in the hayfield.

Early in the spring Far had made a hayrack, which now replaced the wagon box. Far and Mor pitched the hay into the rack, Aagot and Kjersti arranged it and stamped it down, Ragnhild and Tosten did as many of the chores as they could, and the oxen pulled every load to a flat space near the stable, where it was unloaded and made into a stack.

The girls had to follow Far's orders carefully and put most of the hay in the center along the length of the stack and then walk back and forth to make a high, firm ridge, so that when the stack was finished, twenty feet long, fourteen feet wide, and twelve feet high, its top slanted on two sides like a simple roof. A stack of this type never absorbed water to spoil the hay. A load or two of coarse grass topped it off; and a network of large willow branches, weighted with stones, was spread over the entire top of the stack to keep the hay from being carried away by the wind.

Toward evening Far said, "We shall be through by noon tomorrow, which will give us half a day of rest." But the next morning it was raining. When the sun came out once more it was discovered that some of the haycocks that Kjersti and Aagot had put up had taken in water. The girls had to spread the hay to dry before it could be stacked. This experience taught them how haycocks should be made.

CHAPTER XV

Haying on the Prairie

The meadow did not furnish enough hay. Tarjei Jyrison, one of Far's friends who lived on the prairie two miles from the Raaen home, gave him the use of several acres of unbroken land in exchange for timber. Tarjei did the mowing and raking; all Far needed to do was to let him know when he wanted this work done.

Tarjei had been told. It was four o'clock in the afternoon. Kjersti scrubbed and aired the big *tinae*; Aagot helped Mor pack stacks of *lefse, flatbrød*, butter, *primost*, cheese, and dried beef. Far tightened the bolts in the hayrack, greased the wagon, and put some hay in the bottom of the rack, on which he laid the pitchforks and hand rakes. By eight o'clock all the chores were done and everybody was in bed.

Before sunrise next morning Mor called, "You must get up and milk before the cows leave the pen; there won't be time to go and get them this morning." There was a note in Mor's voice which told them they must rise at once. Because of the early hour, the cows gave less milk and the calves fought less for their drink, so that job took only half the usual time.

Breakfast over, Aagot helped Mor put the stacks of food in the *tinae*; Tosten and Ragnhild filled a gallon jug with sweet milk and a two-gallon jug with spring water; Far

69

hitched up the oxen; Kjersti closed all the windows. The lunch and jugs were set on the hay near the tools; and the door was closed, but not locked. Pioneers did not need to lock their doors.

Mor and the children seated themselves on the hay near the *tinae*, jugs, pitchforks, and hand rakes so that they could keep them in place. Far walked ahead; the oxen followed. How the hayrack shook and pitched as the wagon rolled over the uneven ground! Whenever the wagon passed over a gopher hill, Aagot had to grab the *tinae*, Ragnhild and Kjersti each held on to a jug, and Tosten laughingly handled the rakes and forks, playing that they were so many oars on a boat. Mor had brought her knitting, and through all this she kept right on with her work. When they reached the hayfield the labor of the meadow was repeated.

By the time the sun was well up in the heavens, the children began to think so hard about food that it interfered with their work. The sun seemed very hot; the sharp grass and stubble hurt their arms and legs. As an excuse to rest, Aagot and Kjersti made many trips to the water jug, which stood in the shade of a haycock. Far noticed that they began to lag; he looked at the sun and said, "It is only about eleven o'clock, but we had better eat."

The children did not have to be told to fetch the *tinae* and the gallon jug of milk, which had been hidden in a haystack, and put them on the shady side of the stack. How they ate of Mor's *lefse, flatbrød, primost*, cheese, and dried beef! They were so hungry that they would have swallowed everything whole, but Far was eating slowly, so they had to also. The sweet milk tasted so good they simply could not drink it fast.

When the meal was finished, they all stretched in the shade for a much needed rest. The children, fed and rested, felt contented, and the discomforts of the forenoon seemed to disappear.

They started work again full of life and vigor, but by the

middle of the afternoon they again suffered the discomforts
of the morning. Mor got out the copper coffeepot. But where
was the coffee? She had forgotten to put it in! The children
were never given coffee, but Far and Mor must have theirs.
Aagot took the coffeepot and started for the Jyrison home.
When Tarbjør, Tarjei's wife, saw the bashful Aagot with the
coffeepot she called, "Come on in. I know your mother sent
you to make coffee. I'll start the fire while you fill the pot
with water."

The sod house was dark and cool. Aagot, coming from the
bright outdoors, could see little at first, but she found the
pail of water. Then, becoming accustomed to the darkness,
she discovered in one corner a pretty white pig; in another,
some little chicks.

To find that people and animals could live in the same
room surprised Aagot so much that she forgot what she had
come for until Tarbjør called, "The water is boiling; where
is your coffee?"

Aagot had to say, "Mor forgot it this morning, and she
wants me to ask if you would lend us some till we come back
tomorrow morning."

A smile played on Tarbjør's rugged features and showed a
row of even white teeth. "Sure, I can trust your mother with
anything; here, child, take as much coffee as you need." It
would have been fun to visit for a while, but Aagot knew
that could not be done now — maybe tomorrow; she must
hurry back because she had to prove to Far she could be depended upon.

Far and Mor drank the hot coffee, the children enjoyed
the milk, and all ate what was left over from the noon lunch.
The sun's rays began to slant and the air was cooler; no one
cared to rest now. They must get as much done as possible
and get home to milk the cows and feed the calves before
nightfall. When the rack had been filled with hay for the trip
home, Mor and the children climbed on top. How restless the
oxen were! Far once more started ahead; the oxen followed

willingly, eager to get home. The rhythmic swaying of the
load relaxed tense muscles, and by the time they reached
home the children were so rested that they did not mind
helping with the chores.

They repeated the trips daily until there was a huge stack
of hay on the prairie to be hauled home during the following
winter.

Haying on the prairie was much fun, at first. In the morning they played they went to a picnic; in the evening they
returned. And didn't they have the best picnic lunch in the
world! The birds and insects of the prairie were different from
those in the woods. One noon when they were supposed to
be resting, Far took the children to a large anthill. For a
long time they watched the busy creatures at work. When
they returned Far said, half aloud as if speaking to himself,
"Go to the ant, thou sluggard; consider her ways, and be
wise." The children did not understand what Far had said,
but they remembered the words, and years later the meaning was clear.

Kjersti, who wasn't very well, half scolded as she nursed
her scratched hands and feet before going to bed. "The cows,
oxen, and sheep must have hay. Haying is hard work but
then it lasts only a few weeks. Carrying water from the river,
washing clothes, scrubbing furniture and floors—that is
much harder work and it is never done; it lasts the year
around and year after year. It feels so good when everything
is clean, but couldn't we just live outdoors and not have all
this hard work?" Then she shook her head, "No, not in
winter."

One summer while they were haying, they saw smoke in
the distance. They had seen many fires, so they did not wonder at this. But when the smoke came nearer and they saw a
huge black something moving forward, they stood rooted to
the ground. They had heard talk of a railroad and trains but,
never having seen them, they could not understand about
them. That night Kjersti awoke in a nightmare; she thought

she saw the huge black mass coming toward the woods and she could not get out of the way.

The very next morning after the haying was finished, Aagot said: "I have to go to find out about something. I'll be back by noon. Don't tell Far."

Tosten and Kjersti wanted to go with her but they said nothing. They could not keep up with Aagot on the road and they knew they were not welcome, but they watched for her return. After five long hours they saw her coming and ran to meet her. "Where have you been? What did you do?"

"I have been to where they are building the railroad. First they scoop the earth into a high solid ridge. On top of this they put heavy wooden planks quite close together. On top of the planks they nail down long iron rails that look something like raised wheel tracks. The huge black thing they call a train has wheels that fit the iron rails; the train cannot move unless it is on these rails."

When Kjersti understood that the train could never come down the path toward the woods, her fear vanished.

Growing Up

CHAPTER XVI

The Burden

Spring came again. The hard frost was slowly leaving the land. The greening hillsides were sprinkled with pasque-flowers and buttercups. Valleys and gulches were knee-deep with mire.

Kjersti had a new interest; she was keeping watch on Per Stake, the hired man. One day she came hurrying in so fast she was hardly able to speak: "Buck! you must come to Buck!"

Mor and Aagot, who were baking *flatbrød*, replied, "Buck is big and—"

"Oh," Kjersti broke in, "Buck is in the mire!"

The three hurried to the far pasture, where they knew Per was hauling hay. In the distance they saw the big load and heard Bright lowing. Faster and faster they ran. They heard whiplashings and the answering moans of Buck. Then there was a splashing sound of something sliding, followed by the terrible groan of an animal in pain.

As soon as Bright saw Mor, Aagot, and Kjersti he began calling as for help. Buck was down; he was so covered with mud that it was hard to see what position he was in. Per, trembling, mud-stained, and pale, stood near by.

Mor looked at the oxen and then at Per, who spoke at last: "Buck stepped off the hard trail and sank into the mire. I

77

tried to make him get out again but he wouldn't mind. Then I freed him from the yoke and used the whip on him; that did not help either so I took him by the horns and turned him over. I guess he will be glad to get up now. Ha! Ha!"

Buck did not move. Kjersti made her way up to the load for a wisp of hay. Remembering how Far had treated the oxen when he had taught them how to be useful, she stepped up to Buck, patted his muddy head, and held out the hay. Buck looked at her as if he begged to be let alone, but finally he stretched out his tongue for a few straws of the green hay and began munching. Kjersti petted, coaxed, and fed him till he looked at her with love and trust in his eyes and seemed to understand that he had to try to move.

Kjersti brought more hay and stood farther away as she coaxed. Buck began to move; then he groaned pitifully. They soon saw that he could not use his hind legs. With a terrible effort he dragged his body out of the mire onto dry land. They unhitched Bright and let him loose. Per slunk away without a word.

Kjersti stayed with Buck the rest of the day. Some kind neighbors came and helped Buck to his feet. Moaning, he moved slowly forward, half dragging his hind legs.

Before Kjersti would go to sleep that night, Mor had to answer some questions. "Mor, why did M——— bring Per Stake to us?"

"He came to his house from Norway. He could not employ him and Per had no place to go; so he brought him over here to work for us."

"But Per hurt the black cow when she had her baby calf and now he has hurt Buck. Why does Far let him stay here when he does such things?"

"The day Per was brought over here Far was in the Shadows; he was in them when the black cow was hurt, and he is in them now."

"Why does everything go wrong when Far is in the Shadows?"

"Because then he neither knows what he himself is doing nor what others are doing to him."

The following morning Kjersti awoke early from a troubled sleep and hurried to the pasture to help Buck. As the weeks went by, Buck was given the best of care. He ate and drank but grew thinner and thinner. One day when the children returned from town there was no Buck. When they were told he had been shot they were glad because they knew he could never be hurt any more.

Far got along without a team; he rented the land to one of the neighbors and when he needed any hauling done, he paid for that by selling trees. But M—— began mentioning the value of owning a team of horses and of replacing the old rail fence with barbed wire and having some ready cash. M—— and his son-in-law had a team to sell and cash to be invested — at a high rate of interest. Mor saw that horses, a pasture fenced with barbed wire, and extra money would be fine things to have if you could pay for them with the fruits of your own labor, but she also saw the danger of getting these things by borrowing. She made Far see that too, but when those who had an interest in the matter were able to lead him into the Shadows he saw no danger. On one side were able scheming minds bent on regaining what they had lost in Norway; on the other, a trusting, hard-working mother trying to save her home.

Time seemed to stand still, but it had moved a long way when one morning M——, his son-in-law, and a well-dressed stranger entered with Far, who was in a merry mood. The children stared as they saw M—— and his son-in-law put a pile of gold, silver, and paper money on the table and heard them say that they were leaving the extra team they had brought. Some large papers were spread on the table and Mor had to sign them.

The children could not understand how the signing of a paper could change everything, but it did. Far was away a great deal more and Mor was very different. She went about as if she were carrying a burden. She often sat lost in thought, and she took more time to talk to the children. When alone, they asked, "Mor, what was that paper you signed?"

"They called it a mortgage; it gives those who left the horses and the money the right to take our home unless we can pay them so much money every year for a certain number of years, besides paying the value of the horses and the money they left."

A chill stole over them all. Mor and the children had barely been able to live before. How could they take over this new burden? They had been glad of the barbed-wire fence, which kept the cows from breaking into the fields, but they wished the old fence back, even if that meant herding the cattle. They did not like the frisky horses, who never could take the place of the faithful oxen.

"Mor, let us give it all back; then you take your name off the paper and all will be as it was before."

"When you sign your name to a mortgage or other piece of paper you take on a burden that you will have to carry until you pay in full."

Kjersti and Aagot stole up to Mor and touched her hands as they whispered, "We will help you carry the burden."

The children noticed that whenever Mor could sell a pail of gooseberries or a few pounds of butter for cash she put the money in a little box that she kept in the big chest. One day, after weeks of doing this, she put on her red plaid shawl, tied the box in a kerchief, and left the house. Kjersti followed. They walked for an hour until they came to the house of M———'s son-in-law, who held the mortgage. There Mor emptied fifty-cent pieces, quarters, and dimes out of the box to the amount of twenty dollars. In return the man gave her a slip of paper to which he signed his name. On the way home Mor, who seldom sang any more, hummed as she walked. This surprised Kjersti into talking: "I thought you had forgotten to sing. Why are you so happy? Is the burden gone?"

"No, the burden isn't gone but if we can keep on putting money in the box it won't grow any bigger. We must pay the ten per cent interest."

After that Kjersti saved for the box many a dime or quarter that came her way. Aagot, who was older and of a different temperament, brooded over the burden until she sometimes thought of nothing else. While the other children played, she would sit hidden by some low swinging bough and stare at the river; she watched the water bugs in their hopeless struggle against the swift current of the stream.

It was a relief to all when a poor homeless family with many children moved into the neighborhood. They homesteaded forty acres of leftover slough land and stayed at Kjersti's home until their dugout and lean-to were ready. After they had left, Mor said, "The best way to forget trouble is to do something for others."

CHAPTER XVII

School

Aagot, who was sent out to help the neighbors when someone was sick or when a new baby arrived, came home in a
great hurry one Sunday, all out of breath. She called Kjersti
and Tosten outdoors and whispered: "Do you know something wonderful is going to happen? Last night I heard two
men say they are going to begin hauling lumber and —"

"Oh," Kjersti broke in, "hauling lumber isn't anything
wonderful."

"Don't interrupt. Just let me talk and you shall hear.
They are going to build a big house only fifteen minutes'
walk from here; it is going to be a schoolhouse. There will be
a teacher and books, too. Anyone can go there and it won't
cost anything! You two must go; Ragnhild will be at home
with Mor, and when I am needed I will come home. I am
going to get a new calico dress and shoes for the work I
am doing now, but I shall have to stay a long time yet to
earn them."

Monday morning two loads of lumber arrived, and after
that many more. From that day until the schoolhouse was
finished, Tosten, who was fleet of foot and as curious as
Aagot, was a daily visitor. Every evening he reported to the
other children on the growth of the big house. Late in the
fall of 1886 the roof was on, the six windows were put in,

and the whole building was painted white. How beautiful it looked, standing on a bluff against the big woods!

To the great disappointment of the children, there was no school that fall. Later, after the stormy winter had set in, they heard that a teacher from a school farther south was coming to teach for a few weeks. Because of the severe weather and because they had no suitable clothing, none of the children in Kjersti's neighborhood attended.

On a warm Sunday afternoon in the following spring, groups of neighbors gathered to discuss various problems. So many new things were happening; life was not simple any more. On August 17, 1874, only a few weeks after the first pioneers had arrived, they had gathered under the big oaks at Halvor Berg's home and, with the aid of Student Ny-kreim, had organized Hol Congregation. For years services were conducted in farm homes. But the school district, organized on June 21, 1879, had grown very slowly. With pioneer Ole Arneson, a Luther College man, as teacher, there had been school for a few weeks in three different log cabins. Then a schoolhouse was started in the southern part of the settlement; it took two years to complete. The land these pioneers lived on had been in dispute among three counties; this was costly both in ill feeling and in money. In 1883 Steele County became independent. In 1885 the neighbors agreed to organize a township; they named it New Berg, in honor of Halvor Berg, who had come from Iowa on a scouting trip in 1873 and in 1874 had returned to show other pioneers the way. When the legal papers were drawn up, the Norwegian settlers were disgusted to learn that the Yankees had written "Burgh" for "Berg" and had made the name all one word — Newburgh.

Now there were rumors that a young girl was coming to teach in the new schoolhouse. Where was she from? Who was she? What did she look like? What could she teach their children, in a language they did not understand? The Newburgh pioneers had come from rural districts in Norway, where they had had stern men teachers. The children listened to the talk of their elders and felt uneasy about what might be in store for them in the new schoolhouse.

Monday morning found Kjersti and Tosten up with the sun. Outside next to the wall was a tub full of water, plenty of soft soap, and a wash basin. As they splashed and scrubbed, they talked:

"Look to see if my ears and neck are clean."

"I'll help you. They shine now. You braid my hair and I'll part yours on the side like Far's. Your hands are clean, but look at your feet!"

"My feet are sore; the skin is covered with cracks that are full of dust."

"Mor says that every night before you go to bed you should soak your feet and wash them clean, then rub them with melted tallow or cream from the milk. I do this; my feet feel good and look clean too. The best thing you can do this morning is to wash your feet and walk, not in the dusty road, but in the clean grass all the way to the schoolhouse."

Kjersti and Tosten were too excited to eat breakfast; they only drank milk. With bread, butter, and *primost* that Mor had wrapped in a piece of clean cloth for each, they hurriedly left.

They were the first to reach the new building, but they soon saw children of all sizes and ages coming from every direction. An hour before school opened, dozens of children had assembled. So serious and quiet were they that they might have been mistaken for a crowd of dummies. All eyes were strained down the road to watch a moving speck. Yes, it must be the teacher. She came nearer and nearer. The children didn't move; they only stared. When she was within a few feet of the door she stopped and said, "Good morning, children."

Just a few dared to reply, "Godmorgen." As she unlocked the door, she nodded her head and smiled.

Left alone, everyone looked at everyone else as if to say:

"Have you ever seen anyone as beautiful? And dressed all in white — like an angel!"

When the teacher came to the door again, she was ringing a small bell. The children understood that they were to go in. They crowded into seats, most of them three in each. The teacher made a speech and wrote a long list of words on the board. Beata Mark, who had been to school in another district, understood English. At recess she tried to make the following points clear to the rest:

1. Anyone who whispers will stay after school.
2. Anyone who laughs out loud will stay in at recess.
3. If you have to talk to anyone, raise your hand and say, "May I speak?" If you are thirsty, say, "Please may I get a drink?" If you have to go out, say, "Please may I leave the room?" The ones who never ask these questions will get better marks than those who do.
4. Anyone who speaks Norwegian in the schoolhouse or anywhere near it will be punished.
5. My name is Wilhelmina Hildebrandt. Call me Miss Hildebrandt.
6. The schoolhouse is on Edward Mobeck's land; it is the Mobeck School.

The pioneer children knew how to work with their hands. They lived an active life in the house, in the fields, in the woods. Even though they worked hard, they had much freedom and few restrictions. School was very different. The school day began at nine in the morning and lasted till four in the afternoon, with fifteen minutes' recess in the middle of the forenoon, an hour for lunch at noon, and ten minutes' recess in the middle of the afternoon.

To sit still, in an unnatural position, on a hard bench, staring either at the blackboard or at a book, trying to learn a new language, was a hard task that made heads ache and limbs stiffen. On the way home from the first day in school, Kjersti and Tosten had very little to say to each other. In the evening they went to bed quietly without being told.

As the children began to understand English and as they became acquainted with one another and with the teacher, who was strict but fair, they were happy in this school. Beginners, large or small, who did not understand English were taught to read from a chart fastened on a tripod that stood in front of them.

A month passed by quickly. The chart class was so large that those who understood most were promoted to the first reader. Kjersti sat with Mina Berg, who owned a reader. When they were studying, Mina would turn over a page, whether Kjersti was ready or not. So, in order to learn her lesson, Kjersti had to learn to manage Mina. At first this was not easy, but after she learned how she did not mind; and by learning to handle Mina she learned to handle others. With Tosten it was different; he could not study with anyone — he made everybody laugh. Something had to be done about getting him a book.

When Aagot, who was again working out, came home, Kjersti made it plain to her that Tosten had to have a book. Aagot gave him the money she had earned for a new calico dress and returned to work a few weeks more. By the time she had earned enough for her dress, there were only a few weeks of school left. Kjersti and Tosten were using many words she did not understand; they were also talking about what the other children had told them and how differently they lived.

One Sunday Aagot read Tosten's reader through; with the aid of the pictures she understood a good deal. She decided that she must go to school to find out about this new life, but the busy season on the farm had set in, when the children were needed at home. The three got together and planned. By getting up early they could get the cows, milk, feed the calves, bring in wood and water for the day, and still reach school on time. This work made Kjersti and Aagot so tired that they were not able to play at recess time, but they watched others play, and that was fun too.

After school they did much the same work and picked over gooseberries besides. When the hay was to be made into cocks they stayed out of school to help with that and later with stacking it.

Aagot, too, had to get her lesson from another girl's book; she had trouble because she was not so diplomatic as Kjersti. She soon noticed that many of the girls who wore shoes and stockings and pretty ruffled dresses, trimmed with lace, made fun of Kjersti's homespun dress and bare feet. Aagot suffered much more from this than Kjersti, who kept in the background most of the time and seemed busy with her own thoughts.

On the way home from school one day the girls with the ruffled dresses jeered, "Look at the ends of Kjersti's braids; they are tied with thread. Ha! Ha!"

Aagot had heard Far talk about the justice of the peace and his duties; so she threatened, "Say that again and Far will report you to the justice and you will be sent to jail." The jeering stopped! The threads on Kjersti's braids were never mentioned again.

They made fun of Tosten's homemade clothes, too, but he had the gift of turning the laugh on those who made fun of him in such a way that he soon became everyone's favorite.

Aagot developed a feeling of resentment. "Why can't we go to school like other children?" she questioned. "Why can't we be dressed so no one could make fun of us? It is all because of the burden. It was awful of those people to talk Far into borrowing money, but Far didn't have to be in the Shadows; he is to blame as much as those who talked him into it. I must help Mor pay back that money because it is right. But why should there be Shadows? Why should there be a burden?"

Aagot won the respect of many children by making them believe that she knew a third language as she repeated strange words found in Mor's old hymn book: "Kyri eleison, Sexagesima, Litaniet, Septuagesima, Fastelavns Søndag."

The Newburgh pioneers were well satisfied with Miss Hildebrandt. She had kept good order in school and the children all liked her. She was hired to return the following summer. One thing the parents did not like, however, was the changing of their children's names. Tosten Raaen became Tom Rouen, Lars Moe became Lewis Moon, and others' names were changed. But when they were told that they had to do this to be Americans, they accepted it. Aagot was the only one who refused — when called by a changed name she never replied. Some grownups adopted the idea and changed their names of their own accord. Gjermund Haugabak became John Hogen; Laverans Fjelstad, a Telemarking, who became the first postmaster of Hatton and one of its saloonkeepers, was known as Lewis Fisk.

When the short summer term was over the children went back to their homes to help their parents wrestle with the soil and to look forward to the opening of school again the following summer.

The schoolhouse became the center of religious, social, and political meetings. Religious services were conducted there instead of in the farm homes. Debates were organized in which adults as well as children took part. But what they enjoyed most were the "socials," when beautifully decorated baskets, each containing lunch and the name of a girl, were sold at auction to the highest bidder. The money obtained from socials was used not for school improvements but to help furnish the new church being constructed. When, in the summer of 1889, a cyclone destroyed the half-finished church, those who were not in favor of socials said, "God let this happen as a sign that socials are sin!" In spite of the disputes, however, the church was rebuilt and later was well furnished.

CHAPTER XVIII

Dreams

A few weeks of school had opened up a new world of interests for Kjersti and Aagot. When they passed their playhouses they stopped and put back things that were out of place, but they never went into the houses to play again. Ragnhild, who was ever a child, took over the care of their neglected rag dolls.

The girls had dreams of their own now, which they wanted to make come true. There were so many things they wanted to do; but they had promised Mor to help carry the burden. The struggle between their desire to live their own lives and their feeling that they must do their duty by Mor made the girls old for their years. Birthdays were never mentioned; the life of each was divided into periods of accomplishment, not years.

In school Kjersti had hoped to find answers to her numerous questions, but instead she found even more to ask. She longed to do so many things that her dream grew bigger and bigger. She could talk to Aagot now about some of the things that bothered her:

"Did you see the white bread, jelly, and cake the Mobeck and Berg children brought to school for their lunches? Do you think I will ever be able to cook and bake things like that? And I want to learn to sew a calico dress with ruffles

89

and lace and make other pretty things with crochet lace and embroidery."

"Don't you remember we heard that the Yankees in Fargo and Grand Forks live on bread as white as snow and on cake, pie, pudding, and jelly? They dress in such beautiful clothes that they can't work with their hands; they all have hired girls to do that. The Yankees know everything; they have lots of books and speak English only. When you grow bigger you can hire out to the Yankees and learn all kinds of things."

Kjersti was used to not having her own way. She remembered Mor had said, "You must learn to wait; we all have to learn that." But it was getting harder and harder to wait. The other girls in the neighborhood did not have to wait for things; why must she? If she could only get rid of the growth in her neck, then maybe her head wouldn't ache nor her heart beat so fast; then maybe she would be able to run swiftly and work so fast that she wouldn't have to wait so long.

Tosten had been so young when Kjersti and Aagot had promised Mor to help carry the burden that he did not understand the meaning of it, and later they never told him. When he was still so small that he wore dresses he used to climb up on a chair and play that he preached a sermon. His sisters were the audience; they had to sit at attention and say "Amen" every little while. As Tosten grew older the dream of his childhood remained with him. He felt and saw the trouble and poverty at home, but he was left free to choose and work out his plans for the future as best he could.

Because of the work and responsibility that she had, Aagot in her early teens was a grown woman. She shared the dreams and longings of her sister and brother only to the extent that she wanted Kjersti and Tosten to amount to something. Aagot knew what she liked best — school and books. She felt sure, however, that she could never have them. The promise to Mor must come first. Her aim was to learn to work so well with her hands that she could earn the highest wages. She felt that she must learn to speak and write English, but perhaps she could do this while she was earning money and learning to become skillful with her hands. The only place where this could be done was in the homes of the Yankees, who spoke English only; and they lived far away.

Kjersti and Aagot thought much and talked little. They were troubled; there seemed to be no way out. Then something happened. Lars Solem, one of Far's good friends, lived in the hills about five miles west of the river. He got his wood from Far and paid for it with labor in the field and forest. A week before he was to start working in the field he came. The children listened carefully to what he said.

"I don't think I can work for you this spring. You know we have three little children; the youngest is only a few weeks old. My wife can't leave them to take care of the cattle, and the potatoes and the garden must be planted."

Before Far replied Aagot rose and passed so close to them that they had to look at her to see how big and strong she was. As both became aware of her, they looked at each other and smiled knowingly. Far spoke, "We will send Aagot to stay with your wife while you are here!"

When Aagot went off with her bundle, she felt so important that she fairly flew; she was going to do a man's job. While Aagot was gone, Kjersti had to work much harder at home, but they proved that Mor could get along with only one of them for long periods of time. The girls then planned to take turns and hire out to those who needed help but to be near enough to home so that they could be called if necessary.

At first Kjersti could only take care of babies and wash dishes, but as she grew in stature her work grew with her. After a while they discovered that both girls could work out at the same time if they took turns going home every week to wash clothes and clean the house.

The first year they had to work a long time for a pair of

shoes or a calico dress. Later they received twenty-five cents
a week, still later fifty cents a week, and finally a dollar or a
dollar and a quarter a week! Even if they worked all summer
or all winter they were seldom paid until after threshing.

It was a Sunday noon in the month of November. Mor,
Aagot, Ragnhild, and Tosten were listening to Far reading
the text and sermon for that day from *Lars Linderots huspostil*. Tosten sat so he could look out of the window when
Far did not see him. Down the road came Kjersti; she was
carrying something tied in a bandanna. She came slowly, as
she always did; but this day she stopped often, opened the
handkerchief and fumbled with something, looked at it, then
bundled it up and started walking again. She finally entered
the house and sat down with the rest.

As soon as Far was through reading he went for one of his
long walks. The rest gathered around Kjersti. No one spoke
as she put the bandanna on the table, undid the knots, and
slowly, caressingly laid a big round silver dollar on the table,
then just as tenderly laid another by its side, then a third, a
fourth, a fifth! She looked at Mor, at Tosten, and at her
sister; then she laughed. This was her big day. Hadn't she
dreamed and planned all summer about this day and how
she would surprise those at home! When she had felt home-
sick and had almost given up she had thought of this day
and of all the things she would buy. One day she had planned
to buy a lovely white hat with red roses, a white dress, and
dainty shoes and stockings. The next day she knew this
would not be wise; so she decided on pretty underthings with
lace and embroidery. When the third day came, she knew
this would be just as unwise. She knew she could not choose.

She ceased laughing as she spoke. "Oh, I want a new calico
dress with ruffles; I have been dreaming about it all summer.
But I must have shoes and that will be two dollars." She
put two dollars back in the handkerchief. She took the next
two dollars and pushed them over to the edge of the table
where Mor stood. "Mor, you must have shoes, too."

She looked at the dollar left on the table and added, "I have to have two aprons. And, oh, I must have a crochet hook and some thread." She added the last dollar to those already in the handkerchief and tied several knots in it.

Ragnhild had come closer; Kjersti took her hand and said, "Next time I'll get two calico dresses with lace and ruffles, one for you and one for me."

When Aagot's turn came, she had earned more; so after she had bought the necessary clothes for herself she had more money to give Mor.

One day the neighbors were gossiping. "Why has Mor sent for Kjersti and Aagot to come home? Why are they hurrying so?" The neighbors all knew that Mor often sent for the girls when Far went into the Shadows. But one of the men had seen and talked with Far that very day. "What can have happened?" Kjersti and Aagot knew less than the neighbors. When Mor sent word for them to come home, they never questioned.

A cold fall wind was blowing; they kept warm by running; Aagot was far ahead and called back to Kjersti, "Hurry up! I see them carrying a coffin into the house!"

"Wait for me! See that bent old man with the long white hair; he is taking things out of a wagon."

When they came nearer they recognized Gamle Aslak, who had often visited them. Far and Mor had talked a great deal about him lately. Gamle Aslak had no place to live, and that would be terrible when the long cold winter set in. Mor met the girls outside the house and explained that Far had gone to see the old man that day and had returned with him.

Aagot and Kjersti joined in the work of moving Far's and Mor's bed into the kitchen so that Gamle Aslak could have the inner room. There they put up his bed and an old stove. They also arranged his clothes, his dishes, and a box in which he kept his food. The old man was to do his own cooking, but Mor and the girls had to supply him with wood and water, keep the room clean, and do his washing.

All the time the girls were working they kept on thinking about the coffin. They were almost bursting with curiosity, but they had to hold it in check till they could get Mor alone. When evening came she went to the stable to milk; the girls each took a pail and followed.

"Mor, we saw two men carry a coffin into the house. Where is it? Who is going to use it?"

"The coffin is in a corner upstairs; Gamle Aslak is going to use it."

"But he is alive, and he is going to stay with us all winter, isn't he?"

"Gamle Aslak is old and poorly. You have heard Far say, 'Young people may die, old people must die.' A snowstorm may set in any time when no one can get to the nearest neighbor; besides, it takes many days to get the lumber and make a coffin. It is a good thing to be ready when death comes."

When they went upstairs to bed the girls took a good look at the coffin. It was a long, low, unpainted box; they opened the lid and saw that the box was half full of straw, on top of which were two sheets and a straw pillow. The coffin was always in sight; whenever the children were conscious of it they thought, "This is the room in which Aslak will rest when he is through with his wanderings." Soon, however, they thought no more about the coffin than if it had been a trunk put aside for future use.

That night the girls snuggled together in bed, but not to sleep. Aagot spoke first. "I wonder why so many homeless people come here to spend the winter? It is queer Far lets them; he likes it quiet so he can read and think. Now he has to march outdoors again."

"The winter Lars and Sennev were here they were waiting for their house to be finished. Lars helped with the chores, and Sennev was so neat and clean that Mor did not mind cooking on the same stove with her. Lars and Sennev were full of fun, too. And didn't you love the baby girl that came?

I always used to run home and play with her as often as I could."

"Yes, but the winter Mikkel and Astri spent here wasn't so good. Astri didn't know how to work, and Mor had to pick up after her and do cleaning that Astri should have done."

"But they were kind folks. If Astri had only let us play with her baby boy! Don't you think she should have, when he was born here?"

"Yes," Aagot said. Then she added, "It is going to be hard to keep Gamle Aslak. He is neither cleanly nor orderly, and there are times when he isn't a bit nice."

"Mor says that we are all going to be old some day and may need help and that a good deed returns to the doer. We must be kind to Gamle Aslak."

By this time Far was pounding on the ceiling, which meant they must go to sleep.

During the winter Gamle Aslak fell ill. The girls had to take turns staying home to help care for him. When the warm weather set in he became well enough to go to a relative to visit. In a few weeks, however, the queerly shaped box was sent for. Gamle Aslak had ceased his wanderings.

That same spring Martha Larson, a good neighbor, took to her bed, never to rise again. She had a three-months-old baby, whom Mor took and kept most of the summer; the girls had great fun taking care of the baby during the day, but Mor had to keep him at night if he was cross and restless.

About this time a mission society was organized. The pioneer women became greatly interested in foreign missions. They were eager workers and criticized severely those who did not join the society or take part in it. It distressed the girls to hear Mor censured; they were at the age when other people's opinions meant a great deal. Aagot and Kjersti began to develop a feeling of shame about many things at home. They were too young to reason and understand real values. But being busy from morning till night helped them get over this, as they did with so many other troubles.

Heavy work was beginning to tell on Mor; she often complained that her back ached. Kjersti decided that something must be done about it. One morning she put on her sunbonnet and said she would be back by noon. The other children asked where she was going, but she wouldn't tell.

When she returned she had the mysterious look of one who is hiding a happy secret. Tosten, who was the pet of the family and generally got what he wanted, thought he could worm it out of her.

"Where have you been?"

"I have been to Lars Solem's."

"What for?"

"I bought a well."

"You can buy a pump, but you can't buy a well."

"Yes, but I bought a well just the same! When Aagot and I are away working Mor won't have to carry water up the steep hill."

Tosten laughed and teased a great deal about Kjersti's well, but she didn't mind; she only kept on looking happy and mysterious. A few days later Lars Solem came to the house and explained to Far and Mor that his wife needed help in the house and that Kjersti had offered to stay as long as they needed her if he would dig a well for Mor. Far gave Kjersti a long look and then walked out. Mor's eyes were wet; the rest turned to their work to hide their feelings. Tosten relieved the tension and brought laughter as he remarked, "I wonder what the new water will taste like."

Lunch was prepared and Kjersti's bundle was wrapped. Lars Solem stayed until the well was completed, but Kjersti stayed at his house much longer. After this, when Kjersti, Tosten, and Aagot had arguments as to which had accomplished most, Kjersti always won because she had dug the well.

CHAPTER XIX

The Machine

In the years that followed the coming of the railroad to Hatton in 1884 and Miss Hildebrandt's arrival at the Mobeck School, changes took place so fast in the Goose River Valley that they were nothing short of miracles. Settlers came from all directions; even the poorest land was homesteaded.

Far, who had never become accustomed to hardship, was glad when small towns sprang up along the railroad like toadstools overnight. A trip to Grand Forks or Fargo had taken about a week with oxen; now he could walk to Hatton or Northwood and back in a few hours. Ole B———, their nearest neighbor to the south, was also pleased at having a market close by. But his pretty young wife, Anne, wanted nice things for her girls, and he was not pleased that the nearness of the stores made it easy to spend money.

One morning Anne came to call on Mor, as she often did. While visiting over a cup of coffee, Anne said: "I am expecting another baby; I must have some pretty muslin, lace, flannel, and other things for little garments. Gro Mark will lend me patterns. Her little girl, Beata, has beautiful dresses; Gro knows how to sew and she has only one girl, so she can keep her looking nice. I could take a jar of butter to town and buy what I need most, but I don't like to go alone."

Mor hesitated and then replied: "We are almost out of sugar and coffee. I could take a pail of eggs and go with you." It was settled.

The next day found Anne and Mor on the way to Hatton.

"Doesn't it seem good to be able to go to town and pick out what you like? The men mean well, but what awful-looking things they bring home, when pretty things don't cost any more!"

Mor trudged along in her homespun skirt and calico basque, her face beaming with the carefree feeling of freedom. Anne was a friendly neighbor who enjoyed giving and helping. Mor loved to listen to her kindly voice as it rattled on, but she was thinking of her own children. Only Aagot had been baptized in a white dress; the godmother had insisted on lending it to her. The other children had been christened in pink calico dresses. Well, what difference did it make? They hadn't known.

Aloud she said: "You know we have a mortgage. If the ten per cent interest isn't paid on time, we have to pay twelve per cent compound interest. After a few years, if we can't meet the payments at all, they can take our land and our home. I did not understand this when I signed the papers, but it is only right that we should pay back the money we borrowed. If we can do this and have something to eat while we are doing it, I won't mind about clothes or anything else. It isn't hard to be poor and get along with little if you feel sure you can keep your promises. But I worry so! When Far isn't himself he takes anything and everything and spends it."

Ole B——— was a man of the soil who took all the responsibility and spent all his time caring for his family; so it was hard for Anne even to grasp what Mor said. But she took hold of the handle of Mor's egg pail; her eyes shone tenderly and her voice had a troubled note as she replied: "The saloon, the open saloon! Isn't there any way to stop it?"

They had reached the big general store. "Hegge and Nelson" was painted in large letters across the front. Mor and Anne joined a group of women who had come to town on much the same errands as they had. Hege Pladson, the dark-eyed beauty of the countryside, stood smoothing the folds of her black cashmere dress and pointing to the pretty wearing apparel so cleverly displayed as she remarked, "Oh, we all ought to have new hats and new summer dresses." Several glanced at Mor, who wore a kerchief instead of a hat.

Olaug Aasen, with her practical turn of mind, spoke up. "Yes, that would be nice! But look at those handy tools, and those interesting things for the house! If I had one of those high chairs I could at least rest while eating; I wouldn't have to hold the baby."

Many of the women had come to town with their husbands, but where were the husbands now? The men were gathering near the depot. Olaug led the way over; the rest of the women followed. The train had just come in, and a crew was unloading wagons, buggies, plows, harrows, seeders, mowers, rakes, binders, and even threshing machines. Another group of men were busy arranging the things that were unloaded. But something even more interesting was going on. "Who are those well-dressed men?" Anne asked. "They are telling stories to make everyone laugh."

Olaug replied: "Haven't you heard about the agents sent out by the company that sells the machinery? See, they are treating to drinks. They'll get the men to buy."

Seeing and hearing all this, the women forgot the finery they had come for.

The flashy agent mounted a box. He grinned and laughed as if he were there for the sole purpose of displaying his even white teeth. He rubbed his hands with satisfaction; then he preached: "You farmers work too hard and suffer too much. I have seen enough to know that if you keep on this way you will be old long before your time. Yes, and you will be crippled. What we have here will save you from all this." He pointed to the grand display. "Let the machine work for you!"

The pioneers had often suffered and worked beyond their strength, but they had accepted hardships as part of the payment for owning a home and a quarter section of land. And hadn't they overcome one obstacle after another? That in itself was a miracle. The sympathy and pity expressed by the agent attracted only the weak, but it set the strong thinking. They had become so used to getting along with little that they had grown contented with simple living. Now the hard-won contentment began to change to discontent. Arne B———, a farmer who was easily persuaded, spoke up: "We need the machine. We want the machine. But we haven't the money to pay for it."

"Oh, money!" the agent shouted, "That's nothing. All you do is sign a paper and pay so much every fall when you market the grain. These prairies that stretch beyond the horizon hold an endless amount of wealth. Gold mines can be drained of their wealth, but these prairies never can. Break up the soil! Seed it in wheat, and your fortune is made!"

Mor listened wide-eyed. "All you need to do is to sign a paper and you can have anything," she kept on repeating to herself. Aloud she said: "It isn't true! It isn't true!"

Who spoke? The men turned to look. Only a woman with a kerchief on her head and a red plaid shawl over her shoulders.

The pioneers, by nature cautious, hesitated. But this was a new country. They began to debate with themselves and one another. "Haven't we seen miracles all along the way? I was eight weeks on the ship from Norway to New York; it took some of you thirteen weeks, and others even sixteen; there were times we were sure we could never make it, but we did. In New York we lost heart again. We could not speak the language. We were driven like cattle onto trains that took us to Wisconsin and Iowa. We still remember those sweltering foodless days when some of us almost perished, but we arrived.

"We came from Wisconsin and Iowa to Dakota in covered wagons; we came through a country that had no bridges and no roads; we often traveled for days without seeing anything but bare prairie. But we again arrived. Empty-handed, we started to work; today we own our homes. The agents come from states where great wealth has been made; maybe they know best what we ought to do."

Before the day was over, much of the machinery was sold. Arne B——— had become the owner of a threshing machine; Ole B——— had bought a binder; of the rest, each had bought what he believed he needed most.

Lumber companies had their agents out, too. They offered the same easy terms as machine companies. Osten Pladson, who was a master builder, bought lumber and built himself a large eight-room house. Three other prosperous farmers, Nick Berg, Lewis Thompson, and E. M. Sondreaal, did the same, hiring Osten to do the work. Lars Mark had a frame addition built onto his spacious log house. Frame buildings became the usual thing and with them factory-made furniture. It became almost a disgrace to live in log or sod houses. There were those who signed mortgages in order to build themselves houses so they could live in style.

There were still other agents, who traveled in pairs. One day when Aagot returned from Haldis Solheim's house she had much to report. "I was helping Haldis churn butter while she was washing clothes, when there was a knock at the door. Haldis opened it and there stood two men who smiled and shook hands with her, though I am sure they had never seen her before. They asked if they might tie their horses and come in to rest a while. Haldis was glad to have them come because they were jolly and full of fun. So much noise woke the baby, but that was no trouble because one of the men picked her up. He said he had never seen a baby so wonderful; Haldis' baby cries a lot and is hard to take care of; is

that what wonderful means? The other children were outside playing; Haldis called them in. The men said they were
the best looking, cleverest children they had ever seen. Is
that so, I wonder?

"Haldis gave them cookies and milk; they drank so much
that I am afraid she won't have enough for the calves this
evening. They told her they had never been in a house so
well-kept and that her husband was lucky to have such a wife.
Then they asked: 'And where is your sewing machine? You
haven't a sewing machine? Surely your husband wants you
to have one.' The agents went to their rig and fetched a machine. They showed Haldis how to run it by sewing up a
dress she had cut for the baby. They said they would call
again to see her husband about paying for it."

"Yes," Mor said, "but Halvor Solheim hasn't any money.
Buying a machine would mean a mortgage. I must go and
warn Haldis."

The agents went blithely on their way, making friendly
calls at every house. They left sewing machines with many
families that could ill afford them. Aagot and Kjersti had
already learned the full meaning of buying things with other
people's money; they never even thought that there ought
to be a machine in their home. They were so eager to learn
to sew, however, that they made a nuisance of themselves at
the houses of neighbors who owned sewing machines.

When book agents called to take orders, Far sold trees
and subscribed liberally to whatever they had to offer. Weeks
later, *Lars Linderots huspostil, Laakes husandagtsbok,* and
books the children could not understand arrived. Tosten
and Aagot were always to remember their disappointment, and
later they could not understand why the agents could not
have taken orders for books with stories of faraway lands.

The general stores also did big business; by giving credit
they enticed the farmers to buy much that they could have
done without. The wheat fields would pay in the fall.

The settlers became intent on gain. As a spirit of rivalry

developed, the helpful friendly pioneer spirit disappeared. Each had a homestead of 160 acres and everyone had the right to take a tree claim of 160 acres, provided he planted and cared for a certain number of trees, and to take a third 160 acres by pre-emption. A man who had some means and was aggressive enough could thus become the owner of 480 acres of land. Railroad land sold for ten dollars per acre. Sections 16 and 36 in every township were set aside as school land and could be bought for a small sum of money. Most of the pioneers wanted wealth for their children; many of them imagined that possessions would bring happiness, contentment, and ease.

CHAPTER XX

Kjersti and Tosten

Many of the pioneers prospered; others eventually failed. When the field work began in the spring, single men hired out to the farmers by the month and stayed until the work was finished in the fall. They were called hired men. What did they do the rest of the year? Some went to the big cities and spent their money; others went to the logging camps in Minnesota and Wisconsin, earned more money, and saved what they had already made. A few stayed at farm homes and were glad to do chores for room and board. Kjersti, who worked out a good deal, saw and heard much that gave her wisdom; she hit upon a plan which she talked over with Tosten.

"I have heard we are to have winter terms of school now; children have warmer clothes, and they can stand to be out in the cold more."

Tosten chuckled: "Then the big boys can go to school, too! Won't that be fun? But every seat is taken in the Mobeck School and there is no room for more seats."

"They are going to make the schoolhouse longer by building onto it. There are already three windows on each side; there are going to be five. Ours will be the only schoolhouse so big that it has ten windows. And, listen! I am going to school, too. I know of a good hired man who wants a place

104

to stay this winter. He can help with the outdoor work, and you and I can help in the house mornings and evenings and week ends. I am going to tell Mor about it right now. I shall not let her have peace till she tells Far."

The hired man came, school opened, and Tosten and Kjersti enrolled. But Kjersti soon found she could be in school only part time. She liked to help the neighbors when they were in need, but being out of school made lessons difficult. It felt good to earn a little money, but she would rather have been in school every day. Tosten was so quick that he took only a third as much time as she needed to complete a task; he could do almost any housework as well as Kjersti, and so Mor usually let Kjersti go when a neighbor asked for her. During these years Kjersti was far from satisfied; she looked like a little old woman trying to solve a puzzle.

There wasn't much fun in Kjersti's life, but she often felt a great contentment that partly made up for the lack of play and of freedom to do the things she liked. She felt uneasy about Tosten; from the day he entered school it seemed as if he were constantly on top of a bomb that might explode at any moment. Every moment of his waking hours he was up to something, and he even walked and talked in his sleep.

Kjersti began writing down things that happened.

Tosten laughed out loud in school today; he had to sit in at recess. Maria made fun of him; he didn't mind, but I was ashamed. I talked to him about it on the way home; he said he couldn't help laughing when funny things happened. I told him to shut his eyes when he saw things like that, but I suppose he won't be able to—he is so curious. Besides, he makes funny things happen himself. . . .

Tosten brought the skis he has made out of barrel staves and an empty sack for a sail; at recess he stood on the skis and held the sack above his head with both hands; the north wind sent him a long distance south across the snow; I was worried almost sick for fear he wouldn't get back by the time Teacher rang the bell. He barely made it.

Tosten played a trick on a boy who could not speak enough English to explain to the teacher; the boy had to sit in the corner, and it should have been Tosten. After school Tosten gave the boy his pencil. . . .

We have had no school for two weeks. It snowed and blew for months till the valleys and gulches were almost level with the bluffs. Far said, "If it starts to rain when the thaw begins there will be a flood." And now the flood is here. A warm wind melted the snow; then it rained for days. When we heard a roar like many thunderstorms, we ran to the edge of the bluff, where we could look down on the river. There it foamed, with muddy water 'way up on the trees. Big cakes of ice were floating in it, even trees. Oh! and a poor calf; he was dead.

I am glad we live on a high bluff where the river cannot reach us. Gamle Mikkel lives on the lowland near the woods. The river kept on rising till the water came into his house and stable. His son, who has horses, had to come and take his father, mother, grandmother, and the two children away. The chickens were put in the wagon with the family; they made an awful racket and tried to fly away, but they had to return to the wagon because there was water everywhere. The cows and calves followed the wagon, swimming when they had to.

This morning we heard shouting from a place where the river is deep and narrow. We ran as fast as we could, and there on the other side stood Arne B——— with a letter in his hand. He called, "The flood has swept all the bridges away. How can I get this letter across?" Mor told him to take his shoestring and then tie the letter to a heavy stick of wood, and throw it across. Arne did that, but the stick landed in the water. Stick and letter started to float downstream; we snatched up long poles and followed. At last we were able to get hold of the letter. Mor is drying it in the oven. Far is going to Newburgh post office to mail it tomorrow.

We can hardly keep track of Tosten; he wants to go sailing on anything that moves downstream. He took the big box that Mor puts the milk cans in when the weather is warm; he uses the box for a boat. One day when he got out far enough the stream took the box, and off they went. Tosten caught hold of some branches; the box tipped over, but he saved himself. We did not dare to tell Far. Tosten put his shoes in the oven to dry quickly; when he remembered the shoes, they were dry and shriveled like leaves in the fall. I had to walk to where Aagot works, and she had to walk to town to buy Tosten another pair of shoes. . . .

When Tosten runs fast he can get through the woods to Vesle Mikkel's in ten minutes. Far likes him; so Tosten can go over there as much as he wants to. Vesle Mikkel cannot do the things Tosten likes to do; he is not strong enough. When he was a small boy he was sick for two whole years; nobody thought he would live. His grandfather even brought home boards to make the coffin. Vesle Mikkel got well, but he is thin and small. He is very smart in school, and he is full of fun, also. He and his sister Birgit used to get clay from us to make cakes and bread for their playhouses until they found that there was some on their own land.

Vesle Mikkel and Birgit live with their grandparents; their mother died when Birgit was born. At first the old grandmother had a lot of trouble with Birgit. During the day she fed her milk and water with a spoon; she even stayed up late to feed her just before going to bed. To quiet her in the night the grandmother let Birgit suckle her breasts. In time there was plenty of milk for Birgit both night and day! Mor says children should suckle for a year only, but Birgit kept on till she was three years old.

The footbridge across the river is just a long, uneven tree. When Birgit comes to see us we help her across, even if the river is shallow and there really wouldn't be any danger if she fell in. One day Tosten was going to do this; when they were halfway across he hopped to make the bridge shake; she fell into the river while he skipped across like a cat. Her grandfather scolded when she came home wet and muddy. . . .

It is again winter and we are in school. I am glad for Tosten now; he is at the head of his class. One day we had a long poem to memorize; Tosten was the first one in the whole school to learn it. . . .

We have debates in school. Today the question was, "Which is better, money or learning?" Tosten believes it would be better to have learning, but because there were some big boys on that side that he wanted to beat he tried to prove that it would be better to have money. He said so many funny things that he made even the teacher laugh. . . .

I was so frightened today that I could not speak nor move. During the noon recess while the teacher was away, Tosten, with the help of the big boys, climbed on top of the schoolhouse. Then he walked all along the ridge of the roof. The children all cheered, but when he finally stood on one leg no one spoke. I closed my eyes. Tosten likes to walk on the railings of bridges, and he climbs to the very top of the tallest trees. I wonder if he shouldn't have had wings. . . .

Tosten likes to play; in the evening he sometimes goes to a neighbor's where there are many boys. Far thinks that Tosten might learn things he ought not to, so he goes after him. Far never scolds nor preaches, but we can tell by his face when there are things he does not like. . . .

Aagot is so important now. She is a hired girl and makes two dollars a week. She is away nearly all the time and comes home only when Mor needs her badly. Aagot is so different from what she used to be that we children often wish she wouldn't come home. She never tells us stories any more, and she hardly ever talks to us. She doesn't laugh either. In the morning she gets up before anybody else and cleans and scrubs all day. She begins upstairs and never stops until the whole place has been gone over, even the cellar and the yard. She simply drives us all to work, carrying water, running errands, and what not. We never feel free when Aagot is at home — I believe Far feels it too. She thinks that if we all work hard and save everything, we can soon pay the mortgage. It would be good not to have the burden.

Every time she goes away again, she tells Tosten and me that unless we go to school every day, and help Mor a lot besides, all kinds of things are going to happen to us. What does Aagot know about school? She has only been there a few weeks. And she ought to know we do all the work we can at home. When Mor tells Aagot about things that bother her, Aagot thinks we should help more. I wonder what she will do when she gets to heaven. Everything is beautiful and clean in heaven; she can't scrub, and scrub, and scrub when she gets up there. . . .

I have been working for a lady who has lots of beautiful things; she taught me how to crochet and embroider; now I shall have nice underthings like Mina's. I hope this lady will want me to work for her again so I can learn to sew. . . .

Tosten teases me about being slow and calls me a snail. I don't think he will do it again because I have a good one on him. When we were little children, I used to take Tosten along to pick black haw. In the woods were some poisonous berries. Aagot looked at Tosten's berries and said, "Those aren't poison berries, are they?" This frightened him and he answered, "Kjersti gave me and I ate. I suppose this is the last song I'll sing." Then he hummed a sad tune. I do not get far retelling this happening, however, before he comes after me. This ends his teasing.

Tosten spent the day with Uncle Nils. When he came home he shouted over and over, "See what I got from Uncle Nils!" It was a big book full of all kinds of pictures; the name of it was Catalogue. Uncle Nils had told Tosten that he could send for anything pictured in the Catalogue but that he must send money along. Tosten says he is going to save any money he makes because there are so many things he wants to send for. I am glad he got the Catalogue; now he will let me have the Almanac. I like to learn some of the big words in the Almanac, such as Sarsaparilla, Hoffmandrops, Painkiller, Hostetters Mavebitters, and many others. Tosten likes the funny pictures and jokes best. . . .

I don't think debating is good for Tosten; he is growing so contrary that he argues about everything. The hired man gave him a harmonica, which Tosten says cost two dollars. I know very well it doesn't and had almost proved it when Tosten said, "The Bible says the harmonica costs two dollars." Far too proves many things by the Bible. It is a big book and has many hard, long words, but I am going to keep on reading it till I find out about the cost of the harmonica. . . .

We learn in our catechism that if we only have faith we can move mountains. I had a big wart on my left hand; Aagot had heard that drawing a circle with a coffee bean around the wart three times would make it disappear; while she did this to the wart on my hand, we both repeated, "I believe, I believe, I believe." This was a month ago; now the wart is gone. We tried to say "I believe" about some other things, but it didn't work. . . .

Far has been away for a whole week; Aagot had to come home. She and Tosten filled some sacks with wheat, and harnessed and hitched up the horses. It was bitter cold and Tosten had such thin clothes; Aagot took Far's old heavy coat, German socks, and overshoes and dressed Tosten up good and warm. He went to town with the load. When he returned, he was rather cross and said, "I'll never go to town dressed like this again! People made fun of me and said, 'That boy must belong to a family with big feet.'" . . .

I have learned to make *fattigman bakels*. They taste so good they almost melt in your mouth. I'll write down the recipe so I won't forget it: Beat three eggs to a froth; add three teaspoonfuls of sugar, one tablespoonful of cream, and a pinch of salt; put in flour enough to make a stiff dough; roll as thin as paper; cut into any shape you like; fry in hot lard like doughnuts.

I can make *rømmegrøt*, too. There are few who can do this; it is very difficult. You take a pint of whipping cream and let it stand till it is thick but not sour; put it in a kettle and boil a while; add flour slowly, stirring all the time till you see yellow butterfat coming; then do not stir any more. Keep the kettle on a very low fire and more and more butterfat will come, which you keep pouring off into a bowl. When all the butterfat has come out, stir in more flour till the porridge is very, very stiff. In another kettle have a quart of boiling milk, and stir this slowly, little by little, into the thick porridge until it is the right thickness. When this is done, pour the porridge into a large bowl and pour the yellow butterfat on top; sprinkle sugar and cinnamon over it. This makes enough for five people. It is eaten with milk like any other porridge. When I eat *rømmegrøt* I don't want anything else; it is the best food I know.

Something else I like very much is *klub*. You can have *klub* only during butchering time because the blood must be fresh. When Far drains some of the blood into a pan he adds some salt and stirs the blood till it is cold, to keep it from clotting. This is the way *klub* is made: Take five cups of grated raw potatoes, mix in one cup of blood, three cups of whole-wheat flour, one half cup of suet chopped fine, and salt to taste. Pour this mixture into small cloth bags and put them in a large kettle of boiling water. Let them boil for an hour and a half. Eat the *klub* with butter or fried salt pork.

CHAPTER XXI

Christmas Mumming

Kjersti continued her writing.

We have a new church. It is so big that there are seats for everybody, and it isn't a bit crowded. Osten Pladson built it. He must be smart to be able to build a house like that! Last night we were in church to see the Christmas tree. It was the first one I had seen, a big evergreen that stood 'way up in front of the church. Chains made from red berries and colored paper were hanging from the branches; on the twigs were many, many candles that twinkled like stars.

Some children spoke pieces and there was singing; then the minister preached, but I don't remember much of that because I was watching the candles twinkling and twinkling. Under the tree were many packages with people's names on them. Bernhard Tollefsen, our new minister, read the names aloud. Each one went up to get a package; some got many packages. It was fun to see them being opened. Some people were glad, some surprised, and some looked displeased; I think they didn't get what they wanted. Some day maybe I'll get a present on the Christmas tree — I wonder what it will be!

It was so cold last night that on the way home I froze my legs; they are red and swollen now and, oh, how they hurt! I shall have to stay in the house till they are healed. But I am glad I saw the Christmas tree with all the candles that twinkled like stars. . . .

111

Last night was New Year's Eve, and we went Christmas mumming. No, you can't go on Christmas Eve, because that is Christ's birthday, but you can begin in the evening on Christmas Day and keep on every evening till New Year's Eve. The neighbor's children came; so there were six of us, all dressed as crazily as possible so that no one would know us. Aagot dressed Tosten and me. She put a long white dress of her own on him and tied a cord around his waist. She made a mask out of part of a flour sack — I wonder what Mor will say when she sees that a flour sack has been cut up. Such a looking mask! There were holes for the eyes and nose, charcoal marks for eyebrows, and a stiff paper rolled to look like a long nose. She cut an opening under the nose and sewed some red cloth on for lips; it was an awful-looking mouth, so crooked! After she put the mask on Tosten, she put Mor's old black hood on his head. Tosten was a witch.

She fixed me up so they would think I was a boy dressed like a girl. I had Far's old coat, cap, and mittens, Mor's old skirt, and Aagot's old shoes, so large they looked like boys' shoes. Aagot did not make me a pretty mask at all; she took flour sacking and cut openings for the eyes and nose and then put it on me. She tied a red kerchief on my head. It was good that we had so many clothes on outside our own, for it was a cold night.

We always have a good time at Even Midboe's, so we decided to go there; he lives about a mile from us, but we didn't mind the distance because we had so much fun on the way. We fell down in the snow and rolled over one another; then we got up, and a little farther on we did it all over again. Before we knocked at the door, we decided that only Tosten should talk, because he can disguise his voice. Even must have heard something; he opened the door and saw us before we had a chance to knock. How his dark eyes twinkled, and he laughed so hard that he could hardly tell us to come in! It was so warm in his house that we thought we would melt. When the children saw Tosten they were scared and began to cry. Even talked to them, but I could see they were afraid anyway. He asked us where we came from and where we were going. Tosten said, "We come from east of the sun and west of the moon and we are going to a place where the sun never sets." He must have read that in a book.

Then one of our party began to cry — she always spoils everything by crying — and Even knew who she was. His voice was very kind when he said, "It is nice of you to come and visit us on New Year's Eve. Take your masks off and we shall have something to eat. You must be hungry, you have walked so far." Ingeborg, Even's wife, brought cookies, apples, and candy, and a glass of Christmas mead for each. We could not eat with our masks on; so we had to take them off. How surprised they were when they saw that the witch was Tosten! The children all came up to us and helped eat the nice things Ingeborg had put on the table. Then we played games. Even and Ingeborg laughed and laughed and told us to play more. When we were ready to go, they helped put our things on. It was a good thing they did, because we were so full of food and so tired, it took us a long time to get home. . . .

Tarjei Jyrison and his brother Halvor have violins, and when they play you can't sit still — you just have to get up and keep time to the music. When Halvor works for us, he brings his harmonica along and in the evening he plays. Aagot goes outdoors where she can hear the music and there she hops and skips and twists and whirls. I wonder what Far would say if he saw her! He thinks dancing often makes people go wrong — anything that does that is sin, the Bible says so. I have looked for it, but I can't find either that or the cost of Tosten's harmonica. But when Far says so it must be there because he doesn't lie.

Tosten would like to play the violin, but Mor thinks that would be wrong. When we were small, Tosten sometimes would sit on the wood box by the stove, take a long stick of wood for a violin and the stove poker for a bow, and sing, pretending he was playing the violin. He used to tell my sister and me to stand in opposite corners of the room and slowly move toward each other until we met, then put our arms around each other and keep on whirling as long as he played. Sometimes I got so dizzy I fell over; then he would laugh. But we were never allowed to laugh all the time we were moving. We had so much fun dancing when Tosten played; I wonder if that was sin? Maybe the sin is in real violin music. . . .

Mor always goes to church early because she likes to visit the graveyard back of the church before the minister comes. I enjoy going with her because she knows all the people who lie buried there. She reads the name and verse on the tombstone; then she tells me some interesting story about that person. We keep on going from one grave to another until the bell rings and we must go in. . . .

We have been to Per Gulbrandson's funeral. He was a big strong man who had been in the war to help set the Negroes free. He wasn't afraid of anybody or anything. He always did what he thought was right and said what he pleased. A long time before he died he suffered terribly with cancer, but he never complained. When he was buried, some soldiers dressed in uniforms came; they carried flags and made speeches — and a gun was fired over his grave. . . .

Two weeks ago Tosten was away for several days. He walked many miles to a place where they needed help to dig a well. He got a mandolin as pay; it had been used a good deal. A book of notes came with it. Tosten looks so funny when he stares at the black dots in the book and uses his fingers on the strings. But sometimes when he plays it sounds so good that Far and Mor listen.

Last night when we came home from a neighbor's it was so dark that we couldn't see the road. When we were halfway home we saw a ghost, a real one that moved slowly along the edge of the woods. Ragnhild and I were so afraid we could hardly walk. Aagot went on ahead; then she said, "Oh, it's that awful boy!" Then we heard Tosten's laugh. I think Tosten tries to pay her back for things she made us believe when we were small.

We used to go through the big woods to Kari Lee's house. She told us stories and treated us like grownups, and that was such fun! Once it was more fun than usual, and we forgot to go home. It must have been very late when the door opened and there stood Aagot, looking so terrifying that everybody stopped talking. We got up and went home with her. On the way she pointed to the sky and said, "See the sunrise! You have been out all night." Tosten felt so bad; he thought he had done the unforgivable. Well, we found out later it wasn't the light of the sun we saw in the sky but the moon. We never stayed out late like that again. But Aagot can't made us believe things as she used to. . . .

Mor has been to visit her mother, Grandma Ragnhild Berg Rødningen. She brought back a book called *Hjertespeil*. It has pictures of Jesus, and of the devil, and of people. On some pages there are large pictures of hearts. It shows how one devil can get in and how other devils follow; then Jesus, who was in the heart when they came, looks very sad and has to leave. Then there are other pictures where all the devils have to leave; then Jesus returns and looks so happy. Mor explains that devils come into our hearts when we are angry, envious, mean, unforgiving, or unkind, or if we lie or don't keep our promises — and, oh, there is no end to the list! I don't want devils in my heart; so I shall watch myself, but it isn't going to be easy when there are so many of them. Aagot says she is going to put up an awful fight. Everything is so easy for Tosten that I don't think he will have any trouble. And Ragnhild is like a little child; so they won't bother her. . . .

We have had another snowstorm that lasted for three days. On the second day Aagot and Tosten bundled up and each took a pail; they knew that the cattle must be driven to the river for water. Far warned, "Walk close to the fence, and you'll find the stable." I wanted to go too, but I get so out of breath that I couldn't. When Aagot and Tosten returned their cheeks were as red as fire, but the rest of their faces was all white. They told how they had untied two cows that went to the door and looked out, but mooed and returned to their stalls. The cattle were thirsty, but they wouldn't face the storm. Aagot and Tosten put some snow on the hay in the cribs; then, with their pails, they waded in the loose snow in the woods 'way up to their armpits till they found the old drink hole in the river. Aagot carried one pail of water for each cow and Tosten carried one for each of the two horses. Then they milked the cows, gave some milk to the calves, and brought the rest of it to the house. Mor heated milk and toasted some bread, on which she put plenty of butter. My! it was good food.

Aagot doesn't like to play games; she thinks she must work all the time, but when Tosten brought out the cards he has saved from Arbuckle's coffee packages, she had to play with him. I guess it is a queer game — Tosten made it up himself.

Uncle Nils has given us his *salmodikon*. It is a hollow box-like case which is placed upside down on the table. The box is six inches wide, four inches deep, and thirty-six inches long. In one end there is a wooden plug; in the other, a wooden screw. To these a heavy violin string is fastened. All along the center of the box, beside the string, are marks and numbers. You put a finger of your left hand on the string opposite a certain number; then with the right hand you use a violin bow on the string, at the right end of the box. You have to have a book full of numbers correctly arranged for each song; then you can learn any tune.

Troubles, and Solace

CHAPTER XXII

Destruction

All day long Kjersti had been trying to tidy the house. When she mopped the floor she stopped and rested her tired arms on the long mop handle. The sadness on her face deepened as she thought of all the tragic happenings of the summer and fall. She thought how hard every one had worked and how Far had sold the grain as soon as the threshing was done, intending to pay the money on the mortgage. Instead he had gone away and had not returned until all the money was used up. Then he had sold three steers and two cows and used that money, too. The worst of all was when he took the cream checks. Kjersti shivered as she remembered how angry Aagot had been as she threatened, "After this I'll milk the cows onto the ground; I'll not carry those heavy milk pails up and down that steep hill for the saloon!" But Aagot had not carried out her threat.

All through the settlement the feeling against the saloon was growing. Stalwart men were often heard to say, "Something ought to be done," but no one was brave enough to take the lead. Beneath the surface, however, strong forces were at work.

Every time Far went away some women from near Hatton visited Mor. One day Olaug Aasen and her sister-in-law, Thea, came. Olaug preached like a minister. "Hatton has one

general store, one post office, two elevators, and six saloons.
I know three of the saloonkeepers: Fisk, Gunderson, and
Bry. They were poor when they came here a few years ago;
they are rich now, and we all know where they got their
money. The saloons are kept warm and cozy so the farmers
will want to come in when the weather is cold. I have often
seen the saloonkeepers on the streets begging men to come in
for a hot drink before starting on a long, cold drive home—
only to keep them there until their money was gone. There
are men in the saloons who do not drink; they buy liquor and
treat until they get the farmers drunk; then they take their
money. The saloonkeepers get half. Those who have formed
the drink habit can't stop when things are bad. There are
others, also, who did not drink before but who are drinking
now.

"Are we going to stand by and see all this destruction and
not lift a hand? My husband does not drink and I have no
son, but I am heartsick over what is happening to other
women's husbands and sons and to their homes. We live in a
sod house, but we owe no one a penny. Many families will
have to suffer because they bought machinery and mortgaged their farms; others, because they built frame houses
they could not afford; and still others will have to pay dearly
for all the things they bought on credit at the stores. But all
that is nothing in comparison with the suffering, shame, disgrace, and loss brought on by the saloon!"

During this long speech Thea, who was a dignified lady,
kept nodding her head. When they were ready to leave, she
said very quietly, "We must keep everything a secret from
the saloonkeepers."

As the weeks went by there were many other callers,
among them being Pastor Grønlid, the minister from Hatton.
He hated the saloon and had the courage to say so. As he
spoke his florid face grew redder and his keen blue eyes
flashed steel. Mor was so awed that she was hardly able to
reply to his suggestions.

On the morning of January 10, 1890, Mor tied her best kerchief on her head, wrapped her red plaid shawl snugly around her shoulders, pulled on her wool mittens, took a hatchet, and started off. Far must have suspected something. When he saw Mor leaving, he called, "You had better leave the hatchet here." She had to go without it. When she reached Hatton, she joined a mob of women who had gathered on the outskirts of town. Some were armed with hatchets, some with hammers, and some with long sticks. After an exciting talk Olaug and Mor took the lead; the rest followed. Everybody from far and near was in town that day; there were teams and people everywhere. The saloonkeepers were doing a grand business raking in money, never dreaming what was in store for them. They were so busy that they hardly looked up when Olaug and Mor opened the door; but when they did, they couldn't move from sheer surprise or fright.

The women rushed in and madly chopped, smashed, and raked down liquor bottles so that the whole floor was soaking wet in a minute. Mor was strong as a bear, and since she had no hatchet she took chairs and benches, lifted them, and hurled them at the shelves full of bottles, at windows, and at big mirrors. The crowds in the streets cheered. Pastor Grønlid was taking care of Mor's red plaid shawl so she could work better. Wherever the battle waxed hottest he could be seen. He was of great help to them all because he kept near by and encouraged them, "Keep on! keep on! good work! good work!"

One saloonkeeper stepped up close to Mor and yelled, "You'll pay for this, you wildcat!"

But Mor kept right on with her work, and without looking up she replied, "I am not destroying more than I have already paid for."

When there was no more to destroy they went down cellar, where kegs and barrels were kept; they chopped at spigots until streams of liquor flowed and their shoes and long skirts were wet. An old drunk dipped up some of the liquor in his cap for a last swallow. He tried to push some of the women away; there was a scuffle, and his head was cut so that it bled. The women carried their work of destruction to the rest of the saloons. When they got to the last one, owned by Lewis Fisk, he stood outside, sneezed, and said, "*Ver saa god og gaa ind*" (Please go in). They rushed in, to be met by a smell of burning pepper so strong that they too sneezed, coughed, and gasped for breath. Fisk had been warned; so he was ready for them. His saloon was not raided. The women went home that night rejoicing in their achievement. The news of the raid spread like wildfire. From then on, the saloonkeepers in neighboring towns, as well as in Hatton, were very careful to have the appearance of living within the law.

The old drunk whose head had been gashed did not keep the wound clean. It got so serious that he died about a month later. As a consequence a trial was held. The saloonkeepers and their friends claimed that one of the women who had a hatchet had caused the man's death. She had had to defend herself, however, and she had not hurt him much; drink and neglect had aggravated the infection that finally resulted in his death.

It was the month of May. Mor and the children were in the churchyard when Sven Heskin, the Traill County sheriff, served papers on Mor to appear at a trial. Aagot felt ashamed of this. Kjersti did not mind, though, because all who had taken part in the fray, no matter what weapons they had used, had had papers served on them, including Pastor Grønlid. They had to go to Caledonia, the county seat, for trial.

Mor was gone over a week and the children had to do all the work. They were glad when she returned. She said, "We had such a good time listening to all the funny things the witnesses said and the speeches of the lawyers and the judge! We had good food and slept in good beds. I had a real vacation." On May 20 the women won the case, and the saloon-keepers learned a lesson.

Kjersti thought, "Per Gulbrandson was brave when he helped free the slaves, but I think Olaug Aasen is just as brave for what she has done."

Other tragedies, aside from the saloon brawl, made deep impressions on the children. They couldn't forget the day when Arne B———'s wife, Kristi, sat visiting with Mor over a cup of coffee. Kristi, starting to cry, had said: "I won't be coming here many more times. We shall have to move away. You know Arne and I can't understand English. When Arne bought that threshing rig the agent had us sign a mortgage and give the rig and a quarter section of land as security, but he said that we could have as many years as we liked in which to pay for it. Arne also bought a binder and gang plow and mortgaged the horses and cattle. The last three years the grasshoppers, hail, and drought have taken most of the crop. We could not pay the interest, and now the machine companies are going to take everything. A man brought a lawyer yesterday, and he explained that even if the land and cattle are worth many times as much as the machinery we bought, the law gives them the right to take all. If I had only known what I was signing!

"Arne says there is some cheap land near Larimore, twenty miles from here. But it is going to be hard to start all over again on the bare sandy prairie, and in a Yankee settlement, where we don't know anybody."

There was a long silence; then Mor spoke. "I have signed a mortgage too. I am afraid we too shall have to move. Maybe we shall be neighbors again!" Then she went to the big chest and took out the blue-covered Bible history; she returned to her chair by the table, opened the book, and began to read the story of Job, the upright man. Mor had read this to the children many times, but every time it seemed more wonderful.

Kjersti thought to herself, "Job had so much that I don't

see how he could keep track of it all, even with his ten children to help him. Just think, he had seven thousand sheep, five hundred yoke of oxen, three thousand camels, and lots and lots of other things! Then things began to happen. A messenger came running and told Job that all his sheep had burned up. This man was no sooner gone when another messenger came even faster to tell him that the robbers had taken his camels. The messengers kept on coming until Job learned that he had lost everything. The last messenger said that a strong wind had blown down the house and killed all his children. Job must have felt terribly bad, but he never cried nor complained.

"Then he was taken sick; sores covered his whole body. He was so poor that he had no one to take care of him; he sat outdoors in the sun. He began to feel sorry for himself — Mor says self-pity is the worst thing there is! Job's friends came to talk to him, but that didn't do any good. When Job got through feeling sorry for himself, God helped him so he got well and became richer than he had been before; he even got ten other children."

Kristi and Mor did not talk for a long time; then Kristi wiped away her tears as she said: "Job did what was right and still all that trouble came to him! We did wrong when we borrowed. We should not blame others because of the troubles that have come to us."

"Yes," Mor answered, "borrowing is a great mistake. We did wrong; so we must expect to suffer for it until all is paid back." When Kristi got ready to leave, Mor put her kerchief on to go part of the way with her; they both seemed more cheerful as they walked away.

Kjersti looked at the other children and said, "I shall never, never, never borrow any money."

CHAPTER XXIII

The Grandest Thing

Kjersti's diary continued to picture life in the old neighborhood.

Tosten has built a granary; it is about as big as half of our house; he hauled the lumber and did all the sawing and hammering. Far only planned it and helped put up the frame. The neighbors say it is wonderful for a boy twelve years old to build a granary; I think so, too. But I wouldn't tell Tosten that; he says he has me beat now, even if I did dig a well. Of course I didn't really dig a well — I paid Lars Solem for doing it by working for his wife.

We have some new neighbors — old man Erickson and his wife Caroline; they made themselves a dugout and lean-to on Ole B———'s land a short distance from here. It is fun to help Caroline because she is so grateful. Nearly every day Ragnhild goes over there and washes dishes; every so often I wash the floor for her. When Caroline was growing up she always worked outdoors; she just doesn't know how to work in the house. When she comes to see us we always give her a cup of coffee and something to eat; then she laughs and tells us what happened when she was young. Her face is one big wrinkle, her skin is all yellow, and she has no teeth. It is hard to believe she was ever young; but Mor says she was, so it must be true.

There was such excitement yesterday! Martha Larson, our nearest neighbor on the east, who has been sick a long time, came and asked Mor to go with her to Mayville. Dr. Boeckmann from

125

Minneapolis is there, and they say he can cure anything. Mor didn't think she could go, she had such a backache; but after much talking she got ready, and they walked to Hatton, where they took the train. Mor is back now, and she says they really had a good time. When they got to Boeckmann's office the crowd waiting to see him was so large that it was dark before Martha and Mor had a chance to go in. The doctor told them to go to a hotel and come back next day, but they didn't have enough money to do that. He examined Martha and told her she had to take medicine and maybe have an operation. Mor said she couldn't pay him but would like to know what to do for the backache she had had since Tosten was born. He told her to go home and not work so hard. But how can Mor do that when there is so much to be done?

Dr. Boeckmann is a kind man. When they asked him if they could sit in the office overnight, he told Martha she could lie down on the office couch, and he put a blanket on the operating table for Mor to sleep on. They were so tired that they soon fell asleep and didn't wake up till the next morning.

Mor has a cousin in Mayville who has a boarding house; they went there for breakfast. Mor wanted to see the town, but because Martha can't walk much they sat in the depot until the train came and took them back to Hatton. . . .

So much has happened that it is a long time since I wrote anything. Last week Sennev Solem was here for several days and didn't want to go home; she said she just couldn't stand it any longer. There must be some awful trouble in her family. The roads are covered with ice and so slippery that you can hardly go anywhere, but Mor had to go with Sennev to Northwood to see a lawyer. After Sennev had told her troubles, the lawyer said she could claim all the property and get a divorce from her husband besides, but when he found out she didn't have any money he told her to go home, tend to her housework, and obey her husband.

Sennev has nowhere else to go; so she had to do as she was told, but it must be terribly hard. She has to live in a tiny dugout, and her four children are all babies, only a year apart.

So many people are sick and so many can't get along with each other; and when some people grow old, they can't take care of themselves. There are young people who are helpless, too. It would be nice if there were a big house where they could all be cared for. . . .

Oh, but the grandest thing has happened! Far doesn't go away any more on those trips to spend money; he doesn't work, but he plans what is to be done and he is kind and helpful. Mor is happy; she sings while she works. The mortgage is just as big as it was and there is much interest and compound interest to be paid, but when wheat and cattle are sold this fall, all that money can be paid on the mortgage because Tosten, Aagot, and I earn our own clothes and dress Mor and Ragnhild. The cream and berries pay for food and many other things. If we keep on doing this every year, we'll soon be rid of the burden. Then we can all go away to school and we can have nice clothes.

Aagot has gone to Hope to work for Attorney C. J. Paul and his wife; they are Yankees and pay her three dollars a week. She sent Ragnhild and me red pincushions, Tosten a card, Far a black tie, and Mor a large white apron with beautiful crocheted lace. Mrs. Paul showed Aagot how to make the apron. These were the first Christmas presents we ever got. We sat and looked at them a long time before putting them carefully away. When I go to church to see the Christmas tree with the candles that twinkle like stars, I'll tell those who wonder why there are no presents for us that we got our Christmas presents in the mail! . . .

The growth I have on my neck is called a goiter; a man told Far that iodine will take it away. I use that every day now. When the goiter is gone perhaps I won't have any more headaches and my heart won't beat so fast.

After being away nearly a year, Aagot came home for a visit. She says she hasn't talked Norwegian since she left home and she has read many English books. There is no Lutheran church in Hope; so she hasn't been to church. Hope has a Congregational church; the members dance and play cards when they want to. The Lutheran church believes that is wrong; so Aagot would not go to the Hope church.

Aagot says most of the women in Hope don't work; the hired girls do that. The women do things they like and they visit one another a lot. If I could do as I like I wouldn't go visiting; I would go to a big city and learn to make beautiful clothes, fine lace, and embroidery. I would learn how to prepare the best food and how to take care of children and sick people.

Aagot says she is going to learn the dressmaking trade; but she has to go back to Hope another half year and earn more money first. She gave Mor enough to pay for a share in the Hatton Creamery; she will have to save the rest so she can pay for her room and board while she is learning to sew. . . .

I am sure, now, that Far is very smart. We used to hear the story about Asgrim Rud, a man in Norway who lived a wild life and spent so much money that he was about to lose his farm. He took out as much insurance on the houses as he could. One night there was a big fire that burned up nearly everything. The insurance company sent a man to investigate; there was a trial. It was proved that Asgrim had set fire to the buildings to get the insurance money to pay his debts. He was put in prison; his children and wife came to America to her brother, Ole B———.

Last spring she and her brother came to Far and asked him to write a petition to King Oscar II of Sweden and Norway, asking him to let Asgrim out of prison so he could come to America to his family. Far wrote and sent the petition. Today there came a reply from the king that he will grant the petition, providing money is sent for Asgrim's passage. Ole B——— is going to send the money right away.

The neighbors cannot understand how Far dared to write to ask the king for anything. They don't know that Far and his brother Sander used to bring old relics to the university museum in Oslo, which pleased the king so much that he wrote and thanked them; they don't know that when Far was an army officer he often talked with the king! Once Far and his brother hunted in the woods until they found twigs and branches resembling different letters of the alphabet. They cut these out and put some of them together to spell "King Oscar II" and framed them. This pleased the king very much.

CHAPTER XXIV

Disaster

Kjersti found relief in putting her thoughts on paper.

Aagot spent four months in a dressmaking shop learning to sew. I know she doesn't like to make dresses. I asked her why she did it. She replied, "So I can make more money; we must get that mortgage paid." But she isn't dressmaking now. Everyone wanted her for a hired girl, but not everyone wants her for a dressmaker. I guess she isn't very good. Tosten doesn't find fault with the way she patches his trousers now, though, and people don't make fun of the way she makes our clothes; so she has learned a lot anyway.

Uncle Nils sent for a sewing machine and Aagot got it at a low cost. When she is away Tosten sews all kinds of things on the machine; he even patches heavy wheat sacks and overalls.

After trying to be a dressmaker for six months, Aagot gave it up and went to Grand Forks, where they pay good wages for hired girls. She walked from house to house and asked if a hired girl was wanted. One woman said, "Yes, if you can wash clothes." Aagot replied, "Let me try." She stayed. Since the minister said it would take time to study nursing but would not cost much and would pay well, she has been thinking about becoming a nurse. But when she thinks of sickness, death, and sorrow — and remembers the cold little body of Sigri Midboe, whom she helped to prepare for burial — she knows she had better not try that.

No one can make fun of Mor any more for wearing a kerchief

on her head; Aagot sent her a black hat with two feathers on it. She sent Ragnhild one, too, but Ragnhild's has red flowers. This morning Far had a letter from Aagot saying that the people she works for are going to Winnipeg and that they will pay Aagot's fare if she can go along. She asked Far what to do. He answered, "That will be for you to decide." . . .

Aagot is in Winnipeg. She sent home money for us all to buy new shoes. She says she is going to keep on working until she gets enough to buy some books and to pay tuition; then she is going to attend school for a few months. The lady she works for is going to let Aagot work for her board and room while she goes to school.

Far took us to town today with thirty quarts of gooseberries, which we sold to buy sugar, coffee, a pail of jelly, and a pail of herring.

It has been just terribly hot for a long time — 103° in the shade — and no rain. It is July; the grass is turning yellow and the wheat stalks are wilting. Far says there will be hardly any crop this year. But we don't mind much because Far is at home and we can all work.

At E. M. Sondreaal's they have diphtheria; people are so afraid that they do not dare to go into the house to help. First one of the boys died, then the oldest girl. Far went over to see if he could help; he was in the house but we didn't get sick. . . .

Things are not so good at home now. Ragnhild is so sick that she does not know anybody; Dr. Wadel says it is brain fever. She has been in bed four weeks and she isn't any better. Mor thinks we must write for Aagot to come home, but Tosten and I are going to help all we can so she won't have to come. . . .

Far has been fine for three years and all has been well. Now the most terrible thing has happened. Last week a man came and talked and coaxed till he got Far to go to town. We haven't seen him since, but we know where he is. My catechism says that we should forgive those who do us harm and be kind to them. If that man should ever need help I'll try to be kind to him but I can't forgive him. Oh, I don't know what to do! Tosten has written and told Aagot everything. She has attended school in Winnipeg a month; she will have to give it up and come home. . . .

Mor is all worn out. It was a good thing Aagot came. She is taking care of Ragnhild and doing all the work. But our house is like a funeral; everybody is glum; no one talks or laughs; I am glad I can leave home now.

I am working for the Hoyts in Northwood, about six miles from home. They are Yankees. It is a big house full of beautiful things. When I told Mor about the rugs and carpets on the floor she wouldn't believe me. The food is all different, too. I didn't think I could learn so many new things, but Mrs. Hoyt worked right with me the first three weeks. Yesterday I made a cake; it did not turn out right. When Mrs. Hoyt saw I felt unhappy about it, she said, "You are clean, orderly, and careful, and that is worth much more than being able to make cake."

She is very kind; when I have headaches she helps me with the work. I get two dollars a week; as soon as I can do every-thing alone she will pay me two dollars and a half, and if I be-come very good I'll get three dollars, later maybe more. I have been here a month and have eight big round silver dollars. I wonder if I have done enough work for all this money!

I have bought the finest coat for Mor! This is the way it hap-pened. Mrs. Hoyt is very stylish; so she buys new things to wear every spring and fall. I heard her say to her husband, "I wish I could sell my last year's coat." When she came into the kitchen I asked her how much she wanted for her old coat. She answered, "You may have it for two weeks' work." The coat is made of black broadcloth and lined with black satin. My! Won't Mor look nice in it! No one can make fun of her red plaid shawl any more. When Mor was young she worked a long time to save six dollars for a coat, only to have the money stolen; now she will forget this experience she has so often told us about. I am going to buy a screen door and screen for the windows at home, too. . . .

One year has gone by, but so much has happened that it seems like many years. Aagot had some money left that she gave Mor for a trip to Minnesota; Ragnhild got better so she could help with the work; the harvest was good; and Aagot milked eight cows and sold cream. This fall Far sold the grain, took the cream checks, and went away. I had to come home, and we sent for

Mor. When Far returned the money was all gone. He feels so bad over what he has done that he can't stay at home this winter. He sold some cattle to get enough to go to his brother Sten, near St. Peter, Minnesota. . . .

As soon as Far left, the man who has the mortgage on our land foreclosed it. He started to help himself to trees in our woods, but Tosten hurried to town and found out he has no legal right to do that. Upon his return Tosten went to the woods and threatened the man with the law; so he did not dare to take more. One year from now we will have no home. If we hadn't worked so hard and paid so much interest we would have lost it long ago.

Aagot has been at home a year now. Her clothes are worn out; taxes must be paid; those who stay at home must have food and clothing. Mor and Tosten say that if we get a man to chop wood they can do the rest of the work and take care of Ragnhild, who is in bed most of the time again. Aagot and I are going to town to earn the money needed. . . .

It is spring once more. The winter wasn't so bad. Mor and Tosten did their share. Aagot and I paid the taxes and gave Mor the rest of the money. The ladies we worked for let us go home every other week to wash clothes and clean house for Mor. Thursday was my day at home because I had to wash, iron, bake, and clean for Mrs. Hoyt before I could go. I left Wednesday evening after supper and got back late Thursday evening. It is strange how much farther one place is from another when you are not feeling well or when you are tired.

Spring brought Far back from his trip to Minnesota and Iowa. As soon as he found out what had happened while he was gone, he walked to Northwood to see Lough, the banker, where Aagot worked, and talked to him about the foreclosure on the farm. The banker explained that if a new mortgage was made out it would have to include interest overdue, both simple and compound, the cost of the foreclosure, and a judgment. Mor called Kjersti and Aagot home. The three talked and worried about things they could not understand. All they saw were the big figures of the new mortgage and all they understood was that they would never be able to pay it. Mor

did not sign until she was told that she had to sign or move
— and where could she go, with a sick girl on her hands?

Aagot spoke up, "The new mortgage will give us the right
to live here for a few years; we will work and save so we can
take care of you and Ragnhild after that."

Kjersti had much to think about. "I love a beautiful
house, nice clothes to wear, and good things to eat," she
mused, "but I'll never borrow money to get them!"

CHAPTER XXV

To Make Dreams Come True

When many of the girls in the neighborhood married young, Kjersti began to wonder why she and Aagot were not popular with boys. She thought maybe it was because they were not beautiful and because their clothes were so old-fashioned. She knew that one man liked Aagot and that she liked him, because whenever they had seen each other Aagot would be unusually good-natured and would laugh and sing.

One evening when Aagot put on her best dress and walked toward the poplar grove, where she and the young man had their meeting place, Kjersti felt that something unusual would happen. She found a hiding place where she could listen. It wasn't long before she discovered them, standing tall and erect as though ready for battle. When he spoke his voice had a note of command, "Have you decided to marry me now?"

Aagot wasn't afraid of anything, but her voice shook as she replied, "Can't we keep on being friends?"

"I have said many times that if we can't be married we can't keep on seeing each other," he almost shouted.

"Time passes quickly," she pleaded. "We could wait a long, long time, but it really wouldn't be long until we could marry."

"I have waited as long as I am going to. It is now or never!"

When no one spoke for a long time, Kjersti knew that Aagot was thinking of the burden and trying to find a way out.

"You know," Aagot pleaded, "I have a promise to Mor. If I marry you now, will you let her and Ragnhild come to live with us in the same house when this home is lost?"

"You know my people will not hear of that. You have to choose between your promise to Mor and me."

Aagot walked away; then she returned and asked slowly, "Must I decide tonight?"

"Yes; tonight and now."

Their faces looked so white in the moonlight that Kjersti was afraid. When Aagot spoke her voice was low, "I have to keep my promise to Mor. I cannot do otherwise."

He just stared at her until Kjersti began to count on her fingers; then, without a word, he turned and walked swiftly away. Kjersti ran into the house and went to bed.

The next morning Aagot returned in time for the milking. Mor wondered why she was so pale and quiet, but Kjersti did not dare to tell, nor did she dare to tell who had put the big stack of split wood into an orderly pile that night.

A week later Kjersti walked slowly toward the poplar grove, her thoughts working fast. "Oh, I don't want to come here this morning. Good thing I am first; I can't be scolded for being late, anyway."

She seated herself on the stump of a tree and dug her toes into the cool moist earth as she continued, "There is no breeze and still the poplar leaves go click, click, click as if something is being nailed up."

She rested her head in her hands. "Disagreeable things make my head ache so. Why do people bother one another? Why couldn't we just live and let live? When I was a little girl I wanted to be grown up so I could do as I please. Now when I am almost grown I see that people who want to do right must do certain things not because they want to but because they have to."

Tosten changed her mood. "Why do you sit all doubled up like an old woman? How thin your hair is! Your braid isn't any bigger than a pig's tail. You run barefoot almost the year around; that will make your feet as big as Aagot's, and you won't be able to get shoes large enough."

Kjersti raised herself, pulled down her dress to hide her feet, then looked up and smiled. Tosten could move shadows even when he teased. He glanced toward the house and continued: "I wish the preacher would come. You know Aagot is a preacher; she is always telling us what we ought to do and what we ought not to do. I wish she would hurry up; I want to go swimming this hot day. I heard the scrubbing brush going and—Oh, here she comes."

A few long strides brought Aagot to the poplar grove. Tosten frowned as he looked at the tattered dress that she always wore when doing rough work. But this time she wasn't conscious of his glance. The large hands whisked the remaining soapsuds off her arms, then stroked back an unruly strand of hair that had somehow come loose from the tight knot at the back of her neck. She moved over to a newly made gopher hill; as her hot, tired feet sank into the good earth, so soft and cool, she breathed her relief.

Then she began to talk. "The new mortgage is good for several years, but it is so large that we can never pay it. When the time is up the land will pay—until then we must pay the taxes and interest, which will be a lot more than it used to be! Earning three dollars a week isn't going to make it; we must do something else. I asked the teacher if she was sure I could pass the examination if I attended school three winters, and she said she was sure I could. I shall work and save every cent to go to Concordia College, where so many grown-up people go who haven't been to school much.

"Kjersti, you will be able to do anything you like for a

long time. I hired out to Pastor Bernhard Tollefsen and his wife for the summer. They live only three miles from here, so I can come home to do the washing and cleaning. When I am a teacher I'll earn thirty-five dollars a month, almost three times what I earn now. Then I can take care of everything at home so you will be free, and —" She didn't get farther; Tosten sang out, "And I shall be right here to help outdoors and indoors and go to school when there is any."

"Yes," Aagot said, "but when your turn comes to go away to study for the ministry you will have to have money. You'd better begin to save. We have to make our own dreams come true. No one must help us; that would be a shame."

"Oh," Tosten broke in, "Aren't the services over? I don't like sermons." He pushed Kjersti from the stump, climbed onto it, and began singing, "A-a-a-a-a-amen!" as they did in church. That made them all laugh.

Kjersti chuckled to herself, "I thought it was going to be some more talk about doing more work at home and, oh, I can't work harder. Instead of that, I can do as I please for a long, long time."

She again listened to the click, click, click of the poplar leaves as she mused, "You dear leaves, are you busy nailing up trouble?" Her eyes shone and the chuckle grew into a deep gurgle of satisfaction as she kept on repeating: "I can do as I please for a long, long time. I shall learn to make beautiful dresses, with ruffles and lace! In Grand Forks there are shops where you can learn to cut and fit and sew all kinds of dresses. I must go to Northwood first to make enough money to get to Grand Forks. I'll be a city girl, and after a while I'll have lovely things to wear." Click, click, click, went the leaves, and to Kjersti they said, "Yes, yes, yes, your troubles are over."

Before many weeks passed, a letter came from Kjersti:

DEAR BROTHER,

I am in Grand Forks learning to sew. I work for my room and board at the home of a very nice family. The dressmaker is

French; her name is Madame Pirette. Her shop is full of beautiful dresses made of silks, velvets, lace, and other kinds of cloth.
I only baste and overcast as yet, but after a while I'll be making
dresses. I am going to make myself one, too. You won't know me
when I come home; I'll look as nice at Beata Mark.

Have the wrens come back to their nests in the poplar trees?
How many new calves have we? What colors are they?

Truly,
KJERSTI

That summer Far bought a binder. Tosten felt grown-up;
he arose at five in the morning without being called, and he
sang as he fed, curried, and harnessed the horses. Seated on
the binder, he was so eager to see the ripe field cut into
bundles that he drove too fast. Far had to watch so he didn't
overwork the horses. A man was hired to do the shocking.

After the shocks had dried in the sun and wind for three
weeks they were ready to be stacked. Tosten and Mor went
to Hatton; he to hire a man to pitch bundles, she to buy provisions. They spent most of the day trying to find a man, but
it was too late in the season, the workers had all hired out.
Tosten suggested, "We'd better go by Reverend Tollefsen's
home and see Aagot; she will know what to do."

They had a short consultation with Mrs. Tollefsen, who
decided, "Aagot, if you bake bread, wash clothes, and clean
the house first, I can do the rest of the work for two weeks
while you go home and help."

Two days later, when Tosten was eating breakfast, Aagot
opened the door and called, "I beat you this morning; I have
had my breakfast and walked three miles besides."

"Why did you bring a pitchfork? We have two. You'd
better put on some shoes; there won't be any time to nurse
sore legs."

"Reverend Tollefsen told me to take this fork along; it
has four tines and is light and will make it easier to pitch
bundles. My shoes will wear out if I use them in the field. I
can nurse my legs when we are resting, so that won't take
up any time."

Stacking grain was a novelty that first day. It was great fun to have Far bring lunch in the middle of the forenoon. And to sit down to a prepared meal at noon was something new. In the middle of the afternoon Far repeated the visit and at night there was another of Mor's good meals. As the sun was setting it was fun to ride home on the horses.

The next morning Aagot was frightened—she tried to jump out of bed and couldn't. The new task of pitching the heavy wheat bundles as fast as Tosten could stack had done it. She had to crawl slowly out of bed and dress as slowly. She couldn't keep up with Tosten that day or the next. Stacking grain was easy work, but you had to know how. Tosten had learned the trick from Lars Solem. Aagot wished now she had been as wise. Then, to tease, Tosten made the stacks tall; he laughed when Aagot sometimes missed the stack as she tossed the bundle up high.

In work Tosten and Aagot were well matched; they enjoyed working together and planning ahead. Still, when Mrs. Tollefsen came to get her, Aagot was glad to go. She would rather work in the house than stack grain.

When threshing was done the stacks had yielded 1,300 bushels of wheat and 300 bushels of oats.

CHAPTER XXVI

A Wonderful Secret

Kjersti moved slowly along the sun-baked sidewalks of Grand Forks; heat, hurry, and hot stuffy air dogged her steps no matter what she did. Mrs. Brown's house seemed to be made of work. So much company and so many parties! Shouldn't Kjersti be glad to have a chance to work for her room and board at a place where she learned to prepare all kinds of foods and where she learned to do things properly? Oh, yes, she was; but it made her too tired for work in the dressmaker's shop. When she tossed on her bed in the hot, stuffy room over the kitchen, she was longing, ever longing, for one night's sleep in the loft of the log house, where the cool wind flowed in through the cracks.

The hard, hot sidewalks burned through her shoes. At home, the green grass among shady trees would soothe and comfort hot bare feet; she would sit on the footbridge and dangle her feet in water that felt soft as velvet. The sheep would come and rub their cool satin noses on her hands and arms. Then she would sit in the shade and help Aagot shear the sheep as they used to do.

Her goiter was growing, but a high collar would hide it. To sit still and bend over made her heart pound and her head ache. She couldn't sew for a living, but she must stay long enough to learn to make her own clothes. She knew she could do housework even if she didn't feel well; she could forget herself when she moved around. Mrs. Brown had said that a good cook could earn five dollars a week. Kjersti decided to go home for a while and then hire out as a cook, but she must stick to her job a bit longer. Every Saturday found her saying: "Tomorrow is Sunday, a whole day of rest. All I have to do is to cook the meals and wash the dishes; then I can lie on my bed and read and sleep all the rest of the day. When I was a little girl I used to hate Sunday, but now I look forward to it all week. Strange how things change!"

The day finally came when Kjersti packed her new dress and her patterns and said good-by to Madame Pirette. Mrs. Brown filled a large tin breadbox with odd dishes and kichen utensils, which she gave Kjersti. There wasn't room in the trunk so Kjersti decided to carry the huge bundle in her arms. How surprised and glad Mor would be to get all these things!

One of the neighbors who had gone to Northwood drove Kjersti home. Mor helped to get the big box into the house. Kjersti changed her dress, took off her shoes and stockings, and hurried outdoors. As she went to the woods she breathed deeply. Yes, the birds were back. How the lambs had grown! So many new calves — they were afraid of her, but she would soon make friends with them. The river was the same — cool, clear water, moving, ever moving. When she came to the spring, she took a hollow reed and drank deep of the good water. Then she heard Mor calling, "Come to lunch!"

When they were through eating, Kjersti explained as she unpacked: "Look at these flowered curtains! They aren't new, but they will look beautiful when we get them up. Two nightdresses for Ragnhild; and see this piece of carpet! Isn't it pretty? And here is a dress for you, a tin box with a cover to keep bread in, and two waists for me. I got all these things from Mrs. Brown; she bought new ones for herself. I am going to fix up one room for a parlor. We can all sleep upstairs.

My! won't Aagot be surprised when she comes home! And here is a package of yeast; you won't have to save some of the bread dough for the next baking any more."

Mor usually baked after the rest had gone to bed. When Caroline Erickson brought flour Mor felt she had to bake *flatbrød* for her. She didn't mind so much when Kjersti was at home because she could bake as fast as Mor rolled. This evening, talk and laughter accompanied the thud of the rolling pin, far into the night. A good thing Far slept upstairs so he wasn't disturbed!

Whenever Kjersti had been away, Mor looked forward to her return because she took time to tell Mor about the things she had seen and heard and learned. Kjersti made the first pie Mor had ever tasted, and she showed her how to make cookies and rice pudding. During the day Kjersti cleaned the house, cooked the meals, and fixed up the parlor. Mor enjoyed working outdoors at light tasks. When they were through they both rested while they pieced a quilt, and chatted as they cut, matched, and sewed.

Kjersti was again growing restless; she knew she had to be moving on—this time far away. Maybe Mor wouldn't like it, but she had to tell her.

"Mrs. Brown said that it is easier to breathe where it is high and dry and that a change often cures sick people. I asked if she knew of a city in a place like that and she told me about Helena, Montana."

Mor looked worried. Kjersti hastened to add: "It is far out west, but it doesn't take long to get there on the train. They pay more for cooks out there. Maybe I can work and get well at the same time. Cooks don't need many clothes. I'll stay a whole year and bring back nearly all the money I earn. I'll write as soon as I make enough to pay Aagot for my ticket. When I return I'll be well and I'll have money besides; then I'll do something that will give you all a surprise."

The same neighbor who had brought Kjersti home took

her back to Northwood, where she boarded the train for Helena.

In due time a letter came:

DEAR MOR,

Give the money in this letter to Aagot for my ticket.

You like to ride on the train. You should have come with me; this is so different from going just to Grand Forks. There are small towns all along the railroad, and the train stopped at every one; they are so much alike that I could not tell one from the other. At every station the people were doing the same thing; a depot agent helped to load and unload boxes, a postmaster put a bag of mail on the train and took one away. Among the group were a drayman, some hotelkeepers, and crowds of people of all ages and sizes, who must have come just to see the train and what would happen, because they left when the train did.

We rode all night; I tried to sleep but couldn't. The next day I was so dizzy and my head ached so that I wished I had stayed at home. Through the train window we saw hundreds of sheep. We got to Helena in the evening the second day. I left my suitcase at the depot and went uptown to look for a place to work. I walked from one hotel to the next till I found one where they needed a second cook. They let me rest for two days; since then I have been working. I'll soon be first cook and make some more money. I feel much better, too.

It is late. Good-by.

KJERSTI

Tosten wrote regularly and reported on everything. Kjersti always kept the following letter from him:

DEAR SISTER,

You ask about Aagot; she has been at Pastor Tollefsen's almost a year. She still wears old dresses and goes without shoes to save money. One day the minister came into the kitchen and saw her bare feet. He asked, "What did you pay for those shoes?" She replied, "*E fek dei atpaa handeln.*" [They were thrown in for good measure.] He laughed and walked away. She is so stingy that she saves almost all she earns.

You must be rich by now. Why don't you send me some money? When I fish, hunt, or swim, time runs away and makes me late. I need a watch to keep track of time. I also need lots of other things.

Ragnhild has been in bed for many months. Aagot washes and cleans as she used to, but it got too much for Mor anyway and she wanted Aagot to come home. Instead of that, Aagot hired a newcomer girl to help Mor; she is going to pay this girl by sewing

for her. The newcomer girl isn't very clean. I couldn't tell her
how dirty her neck and ears looked; so I took a rag and plenty of
soap and water and washed my own real well while she watched
me. The next day she did hers. She can scrub but she doesn't
know how to rinse; so I washed the floor one day, saying I knew
she was tired. It helped, but the floors aren't as white as they
used to be!

You ask about Far. He hasn't been away for a long time. He
walks to Hatton for the mail and comes right back. He bought
many books from an agent; he reads nearly all the time.

Lars Solem has chopped a pile of wood so high that I am
sure we will have enough till next winter.

I am in school most of the time; I am in the highest class now.
Excuse my poor writing. Good-by for this time.

TOSTEN

Living in a different climate was good for Kjersti, but after
she got used to it her old ailment returned. She longed for life
in the open and for home. In her thoughts she was ever with
those who had been closest to her. She often wrote in her
diary.

Aagot is going away to school this fall. She can never leave
books alone. The summer she was fourteen we all had the
measles. Far hung blankets over the windows because the light
hurt our eyes. Aagot was preparing for confirmation; so she was
all the time studying the large catechism. Far hid the book but
when he and Mor were outdoors, she got out of bed and found
it. She studied all she wanted to, because as soon as she saw Far
coming she hid the catechism in the straw mattress and when he
went away again she dug it out. Far used to say that we should
go to bed to sleep but Aagot would wait till Far was asleep and
then get up, light the lamp, and hang some blankets so that Far
could not see the light if he should wake. Then she would sometimes read till dawn the next morning. Someone told her it was a
sin to read novels. This made her terribly unhappy. She bought a
book, *The Royal Path of Life*, and read and read and tried to
live by it. She made the rest of us unhappy, too. When she is a
teacher all her work will be with books. She will be happy then.
She wants to be a teacher so she can make more money, but the
main reason is that she loves books more than anything else.
When Tosten and I were small Aagot taught us to read. I guess

she likes to be in the schoolroom. She wanted to learn to be more patient with children; that was one of the reasons she went to Pastor Tollefsen's, where there are many children.

I wonder what Aagot will say when she hears about Tim, but I am not going to say anything about him for a long, long time. Funny the way we met; he came to board at the hotel. One day he said he wanted to see the cook who could make such good bread. When I saw him in the door I thought he was a town official come to hunt for some wrongdoer. He looked at me and laughed as he said, "So you are the girl who can cook." After that he often came in for an extra piece of pie that might be left over. Tim used to live on a farm, too; we never tire of talking. He says we ought to do something else besides make money, dress, eat, and drink.

I have the biggest, most wonderful secret in the world. Tim has asked me to marry him and he will wait for me as long as I want him to. He isn't like Anton, who wouldn't wait for Aagot. Tim is a carpenter but he is going to keep on till he becomes a builder who can draw plans for large buildings. I am going to keep on, too, because I am going to be a nurse. Then we are going to build a great big house with many, many rooms so we can take in sick people, old people, and children who need care. I want it to be called "The Tim House" but he says we will call it "Kjersti's Home." It will take many years to become a nurse but I won't have to pay out money for room, board, and clothes while I am training.

Tim is going farther west, where a new town is being built, and I hear that Aagot is away at school. I think I will go home for a while and help Mor. I must send my money to the North- wood bank; I don't dare carry it. Mor will be in the cook shanty when I arrive. I'll open the door and say, "Are you going to make *flatbrød?*"

The evening Kjersti came, Mor dropped all work. The two sat by the old stove and talked until after midnight.

CHAPTER XXVII

Sun, Stand Thou Still upon Gibeon

Kjersti did not rest long; the threshing season was at hand. In the past Aagot had made a name for herself by doing double duty, cooking for threshers and keeping house in homes where mothers were all but worn out. Now it became Kjersti's turn. It was hard work, but the season was short, and a dollar a day was big money. Kjersti soon became known for the good food she could prepare. Tosten was much concerned about what Kjersti was going to do with her money.

"Why do you put money in the bank? The bank doesn't need it."

"I am not giving it to the bank; it is safe there till I need it."

"But you could let me use it till you need it."

"Let you use it till I need it? If you can't make money to buy the things you want, how do you plan to make money and pay me when *I* need it? You had better learn to earn your own money before you spend it. I am going to leave my money in the bank. You are going to be a minister, Aagot is going to be a teacher, and I am going to be something just as important—but I am keeping that a secret. I know I will be able to do things now because iodine is reducing my goiter and I feel much better."

146

It was Aagot's last day at the minister's home. She was leaving for the winter term at Concordia College. The Reverend Bernhard Tollefsen stopped his pacing and handed the baby to Mrs. Tollefsen. Then he spoke to Aagot, "It is a year and a half since you came to us; what do we owe you?"

"Subtract the days and weeks I have worked at home; then give me two and a half dollars a week."

"You had three dollars a week before. It wouldn't be fair for us to pay you less. You have often done work for two, keeping house, taking care of the children, and helping my wife with the sewing."

"I shall have two and a half a week, anyway. We have attended your church; you confirmed Tosten, Kjersti, and me. We have never paid *presteløn* [minister's salary]. I would feel I had done wrong if I had charged more."

The Reverend Mr. Tollefsen waited a while before he spoke. "I have enjoyed having the three of you come to my classes. We don't expect children to pay a minister's salary. Your father never came to church. I don't know that you should do this. But if you will have it so, I will do something else; I will pay you interest on the money you have coming from us since the first summer; you will need it when you get to school."

Aagot felt that she couldn't contradict the minister. She was silent when he handed her an extra ten dollars, but in her own mind she decided, "I shall give it back, in service, twofold."

During the two years that followed, Tosten, Kjersti, and Aagot found themselves repeating the lines from Joshua, chapter 10, verse 12: "Sun, stand thou still upon Gibeon; and thou, Moon, in the valley of Ajalon." When Mor had been so busy that she had worked almost night and day she had often told them the story of Joshua — how he had prayed for the sun and the moon to stand still so that he could get his work done, and how God had done as Joshua asked. Kjersti pondered much over this.

"Why couldn't we ask the sun and moon to stand still so we could get our work finished? Work! so much work, and so many things to be done! So many babies are born; Aagot has been in fourteen different homes when babies have come. When Lewis Huus was a wee baby she had to buy the material and make the christening clothes and even take him to church to be baptized. Another neighbor, Mrs. W. Olson, had been so busy when her baby, Clara, came that there were no baby clothes for her; Aagot had to make them—a good thing she can sew. She even had to give Clara her first bath. Oh, well, I have twelve babies to my credit already, so it won't be long till I have many more than Aagot!

"Yes, I must go where there is sickness and death. Those who take care of sick people can't stay up all night; others have to take their turn to help. Sometimes I have to stay many days. When the soul leaves, the body turns cold and most people are afraid to touch it. But I don't mind; I wash and dress the body and help put it into the coffin. The Bible says heaven is a beautiful place, where no sickness, sorrow, or unhappiness can enter, where everybody is happy all the time. Then why are people afraid? And why do they dress in black and sing sad songs, and cry and cry when anyone dies? We ought to sing songs of joy and be happy because a person can't be hurt any more! Of course some people don't believe in the Bible, but those who say they do cry just as much as those who say they don't.

"Oh, so many want me to keep house; often they send for me to cook at weddings, too; and I have to help at home during the winter months when Aagot is away. If I could stop the sun and moon so that I could help everybody who needs help, it would be wonderful; then I could make more money, and go away. I am going away, but no one knows that now.

"Aagot says if we plan well and work fast we can get everything done without asking the sun and moon to stand still, but she is getting so old and knows so little that I feel sure she would like to stop time. But she can work faster than anyone else I know; so maybe she'll get everything done."

There were times when Kjersti told Tosten her worries, but he only laughed and said: "When I hear of anyone who wants a well dug, if I have time, I go and do it; when I hear of some fencing to be done I do likewise; the same with butchering or any other work I can do and get paid for. If I should worry about all the fences and wells in the country I would soon have to dress in sackcloth and ashes. I think you had better do what you can and forget the rest. Here comes Aagot. You sit around and sew for the neighbors all week; then you almost kill yourself on Saturday, cleaning house, baking, washing, and ironing. No wonder you don't get through till midnight and have to stay in bed all day nearly every Sunday."

"Oh," Aagot replied, "but I earn money sewing. I must have money."

"Money, money!" Tosten taunted. "Dress in rags, and ruin yourself!"

During the years Aagot attended school, she felt it her duty to spend the summers in the old neighborhood so she could help at home when that was most necessary. Through the influence of Pastor Bernhard Tollefsen she sometimes secured a six weeks' term of parochial school. This was a big advantage because she could work at home mornings and evenings and week ends, and still earn twenty-five dollars a month. Often she had to spend most of the summer with Mor; then she used odd moments and evenings to earn money by making clothes for women and children. There was no style to the dresses Aagot made. But the people she sewed for were satisfied; she used every bit of cloth and did the work well. Besides this, she earned money by getting in a few days' cooking for threshers in the early fall, and often several days or nights of nursing.

Every time Aagot went back to school, Tosten and Kjersti

were instructed to write often and report everything. When things happened that would have brought her home, Tosten generally waited until they were over before he mentioned them. One day a letter arrived from Tosten:

HATTON, NORTH DAKOTA
Dec. 26, 1897

DEAR SISTER,

Many thanks for your letter. I suppose you have been looking for a reply, but we did not want to write till we got the mail in hopes that there might be another letter from you.

We are all fairly well except Ragnhild, who is in bed, as she was before you left.

I have had diphtheria but I am almost well again. We were afraid Ragnhild might get it so I lay on the sofa in the kitchen. I had the medicine bottles on a chair by the sofa so I could take the medicines myself. Mor had all she could do to take care of Ragnhild.

You remember how much fun we used to have Christmas mumming at Even Midboe's? Well, there is only sorrow at Even's house this Christmas. His two boys, Torger and Ole, died from diphtheria. Ole died Christmas Eve. While they were sick, they kept on talking about Far and calling for him to bring spring water. I don't know what caused their deaths; they seemed to be over it and started to eat when they suddenly took sick again. I have been very careful about eating. I had Dr. Peterson three times; it isn't going to cost much because he was down at Even's anyway. I am over it now and have had the bed-clothes in the sun all day. I put some Dr. Ward's liniment on the pillows; so I guess no one will catch diphtheria from me.

Diphtheria is raging in many homes. Both Dr. Peterson and Dr. Carr are busy. At one of our neighbor's everybody is taking medicine; the sick to get well and those that are well to keep from getting sick. Such doings!

You ask about Far; he walks to Hatton after the mail and comes right back. Otherwise he is at home all the time.

This will have to do now.

TOSTEN

N.B. The minister has typhoid fever.

At Concordia Aagot was as big a problem to the people she met as her own problems were to her. Carrie Moen, her roommate, took her to task. In her good-natured way Carrie, who was an experienced teacher, would tease her. "When in class don't lean 'way forward and stare so at the teachers! You can hear just as well sitting upright. Don't hold your handkerchief in your hand all the time; notice Mrs. Bogstad, our history teacher; you never see her handkerchief. You have beautiful hair when you let it loose so it can be seen; but you pull it back so straight and do it up so tightly that it looks as if it hurt."

Aagot set about following Carrie's instructions. But how could she loosen her hair? The pins might fall out; her hair might come down. What a disgrace! She stood in front of the looking glass, combed, pushed, and pulled at her hair; then, in disgust, she followed the habit of years, and did it up so she would not have to think about it all day.

Aagot had come out of the field and the kitchen, where she had been a leader, into closed rooms with benches and books, where she yet had to find herself. Life became a hazy mixture of *do's* and *don'ts*, rules and regulations, that hammered at her brain night and day till she sometimes broke loose and stormed.

"Carrie, you simply have to teach me the Roman numerals this evening. I gave the wrong number when I read a chapter in Bible class today. The girl who has always whispered the numbers to me had it wrong; I can't depend on her any more. Why do they use Roman numerals anyway when the others mean the same and take up so much less room?

"I can learn the multiplication table by myself if they would only give me time. But I have to get the other lessons. Fractions? There can't be any use in fractions. Who wants $1/31$ or $1/157$ of anything? And I don't believe the teachers themselves know the meaning of $13/219 \times 5/87$ or $19/21 \div 1/37$. Yes, and they want us to find the least common multiple and the greatest common divisor! When the teacher kept on explaining for me, one of the smart boys looked at me and said, 'Maybe you can find them in the woods.' The woods haven't anything so useless; woods are full of beautiful live things that have meanings. In Fargo I found a building called a public library; it is full of books about the most interesting things. Why couldn't we read them instead? Oh, there must be houses and houses full of books in the world; and here I sit, trying to divide 19/21 by 1/37!"

Soon after this, she made the wonderful discovery that most problems in fractions could be solved by rules. She could now use her energy for other subjects.

Going uptown took time because the school was some distance from the business section. Aagot always went when Carrie did. She felt she was not wasting Carrie's time when she could get information while they were walking.

"Now listen, Carrie; see if I know my geography lesson. The three rivers of Maine are the Penobscot, Kennebec, Androscoggin; and they flow into the Atlantic Ocean. The lakes are Moosehead, Rangeley, Sebago. The capital of Maine is Augusta, and the large cities are Bangor, Portland, Lewiston. In history we have a long list of dates of battles to memorize. I hate dates; I hope there won't be any more wars! Well, I don't know them; so I can't have you check me. I'll learn them tonight. Oh, but there is something else! I know the earth is round because Columbus proved that, but I simply cannot understand why all the water in the oceans, lakes, and rivers doesn't run off into space, and why the people on the other side of the earth don't stand on their heads. I asked Betsey Stavens, who has gone to school a lot, and she laughed and laughed. If she knows, why didn't she explain?"

"Well," Carrie replied, "you have so much to learn that I believe the best thing for you to do is to study the things that you have to know to pass the teachers' examinations. You can't take time, now, to dig into the causes and reasons for everything; many of the questions and problems that bother you will solve themselves later on."

After a walk with Carrie, Aagot attacked her lessons again with renewed courage. Studying far into the night during the winter months wasn't difficult; the cold kept her awake. But when warm evenings came, she fell asleep over her books. As a remedy she generally resorted to putting her feet in a bucket of cold water.

Aagot seemed to sense things in grammar and never needed to use the rules she memorized. But spelling appalled her. Words! words! words! dozens, hundreds, thousands, millions of words she had never heard before! How could she master them? There was no use trying. Speaking was one thing, writing was another; for couldn't the same word have several meanings, depending on what letters were used?

But despite these struggles, the twelve months spent at Concordia were a treasure. She had learned as much as she was able to absorb and had formed lasting friendships with some of the teachers and students.

CHAPTER XXVIII

To Forget Trouble

In Northwood and the surrounding country an epidemic broke out. Kjersti offered her services, ignoring the danger that there might be to herself; she could work only so long, however, before she had to go home to rest. Wherever there was sickness, Kjersti was in demand; going into poor homes, she made the sick comfortable first, then gradually cleaned the house and baked. She didn't mind inconveniences, nor poverty; no home was more lowly than the one in which she had grown up. She always wondered if she did enough work for the money she received, and she was happy when she could give extra service. When she had to spend any time at home she often used her spare moments to sew garments for little children.

It was midwinter. The room Kjersti had fixed up as a parlor had become a bedroom with two beds. Ragnhild had occupied one for a long, long time; Mor had the other. Kjersti was sitting by Mor's bed. As she looked at the long deep scars on Mor's left arm, she wished she could hear more about the time the doctor had made a long trip to save Mor's arm, and her life, when she was a young girl in Norway. But Mor had said she wanted to forget the terrible incident when she had been caught by a belt and pulled into a machine. Aloud Kjersti said, "Mor, when you were young, were you afraid the morning you found that the girl who shared your bed had died in the night?"

"The touch of her cold hand startled me, but I wasn't afraid."

Kjersti thought that when Mor only answered questions instead of talking, she had better change the subject; so she said, "Tell about when I was a baby."

At first Mor didn't seem to hear, but she finally replied: "Many years have passed since you were a baby. I have forgotten much, but I remember you never gave me any trouble. I fed you and kept you clean and you slept most of the time. I still have one of your baby caps in the big chest upstairs. Here is the key if you want to get it."

Kjersti closed the key in her hand; it was so large that both ends stuck out. How it grated in the old lock when she gave it a twist! She raised the heavy lid of the chest and leaned it against the wall; out of a side pocket in one end of the chest she took a tiny bundle of faded garments she had seen Mor use for patterns. Yes, there was a cap made of pink calico and lined with flour sacking. She took the cap, locked the chest securely, and went downstairs. As she returned the key to Mor, she said: "I am going to cut a pattern of my baby cap. There are so many children who need caps, and this is easy to make."

As she sat with Mor, she thought of Aagot; she must tell her sister the disturbing news even if it caused worry. She wrote at once.

DEAR SISTER,

We got another letter from you today. You scold because we don't write. It has stormed every day and has been so cold that Far hasn't been in town after the mail for two weeks. Another reason we haven't written is because Mor has been sick. A small sore started on her nose, and then it spread; her face was so swollen she couldn't see. Dr. Peterson calls it *rosen* [erysipelas]. She had to lie still in bed for three weeks while I kept cloths dampened with medicine on her face. She is almost over it now, but the doctor says she can't go outdoors for a long time.

I have to leave again, but Tosten is going to bring in wood

and water and do the milking. He always says he does not know how to milk, but he knows how when he has to.

You ought to see how fat the yellow cat is. Every morning the cat watches Tosten while he dresses, and when he takes the milk pail the cat jumps on him and crawls inside his overcoat and goes along to the stable. The same thing happens in the evening. While Tosten milks the cows, the cat sits on the straw near by. Every so often Tosten sends a stream of milk into the cat's mouth; the cat shuts his eyes and licks and swallows so fast that you can hear the gurgles way off. We haven't much milk; so I don't dare to tell Mor about it.

To keep the cold out Tosten found some old boards and made solid shutters for the bedroom windows. He put hinges on them so they can be opened and closed. We generally open them a little to let the light in. On sunny days we keep them wide open.

We bought some herb pills from a peddler, for Ragnhild. She doesn't like them, but if they are going to help her she must take them.

Tosten knows the notes now and can sing very well. Ole S—— comes over evenings to get Tosten to teach him to sing. The stable is so cold that the newborn calf can't live there yet; so we have him in the cellar. Ole S—— has a very deep voice. One evening when he and Tosten sang the calf began to moo. That made Tosten feel embarrassed. When he expects Ole S—— over he tells Mor to give the calf an extra amount of milk.

A young girl whose name is Lina Myrold holds religious meetings in schoolhouses and homes.

Do you remember the kind of caps Mor used to make for us when we were children? I am going to make caps like them for poor children where I nurse.

I must close now and go to Northwood.

Your sister,
KJERSTI

Before leaving, Kjersti washed, ironed, baked, and cleaned so that there would be no heavy work for Mor. Tosten could do a lot, and Aagot would be coming soon.

For Aagot, returning home always meant constant work, both indoors and out. It was good to come back to the old log house to Far, Mor, and Ragnhild, and it was good to come back to the sweet earth and all that grew on it. Yet sooner or later poverty, heavy work, and discouragement often so overcame Aagot that she became irritable, despondent, and difficult to live with. She knew that feeling ugly was very wrong, and she fought against it. When she wasn't able to master herself she would say to Mor: "I shall hurry and do up all the work because I must go to the minister's for a few days. I think they need help."

The moment she was on the road, her burden seemed to drop. Three miles was nothing, and when the Tollefsens moved farther away, five miles wasn't anything either. When she came near enough for the children to see her, they came running. Sturdy blue-eyed Olve was in the lead; he had so many questions to ask that he couldn't say anything—the whole boy was one big question mark. Dark-haired Edgar, serious, insistent, scowling, followed close. Patient, sunny Elsie with the golden curls was far behind; she called, "Stand still, stand still!" Aagot waited until she had Elsie on her arm. In the distance was tiny Anna, the girl everybody said looked like an angel; she was lifted up on Aagot's other arm. In the door stood the ever kind-hearted Reverend Bernhard Tollefsen, smiling his usual welcome and calling, "Well, here comes Goodness again!" The kitchen revealed Mrs. Tollefsen, who left her work long enough to wave and smile her welcome.

Yes, there were questions and answers, but Aagot didn't come to visit; she felt the need of these people and came to live with them. With such a big house and so much to do, there was work for many hands. Washing, ironing, cleaning, baking, and cooking where everything was handy was a pleasant change. The spirit of refinement, love, and understanding which radiated in the Tollefsen home sank deep into Aagot's soul. She often repeated to herself, "Father, I thank thee! I thank thee!" Before the children went to bed there was the story hour, and after they went to sleep there was the minister's library. But her most joyful moments were those when she could sit unnoticed with her handwork and listen to Pastor Tollefsen and some friend discuss the deeper meanings of books and of life.

As the years went by, Aagot gave the Tollefsen family many times the value of that ten-dollar bill in service, but she herself received much more. Whenever she went home from the Tollefsens she had a new lease on life. It proved to be one of those friendships that never fail.

Kjersti had written to a big hospital in Minneapolis. As a result she was busy making big white aprons and blue-and-white-striped cotton dresses. Now and then she looked at the letter from the hospital, which stated how many different articles she must bring and how they were to be made. The trunk stood open so she could put things in as they were finished. Her thoughts worked with her hands. Mor had said, "You must learn to wait; we all have to learn that." She was glad she had learned to wait; so many had needed her, and Mor most of all. Aagot always said, "Do your duty first; then do the things you like." Well, Aagot had learned that from Mor, too. It had been hard to wait and still harder to do work she didn't like, but Kjersti was sure now that it was the best way.

Through waiting she had found Tim. Through waiting and doing many kinds of work she had found herself and her life work. Her dream had grown with her until it had become a big thing that had absorbed everything else. She still had a hunger for beautiful clothes and beautiful surroundings, but it was overshadowed by her dream. There was something bigger ahead — a life of service; the hunger to make life better for those in need was greater than that for beautiful things.

Kjersti was suddenly stopped in her work by a shooting pain that reached from her throat to her very fingertips; she leaned back in her chair and closed her eyes till it was over. Three years in a big hospital — she would learn to take care of sick people and see how a hospital was built and how all the work was done; there they would know how to make her well, too. The pain came again. She called, "Mor, I am so dizzy. Will you put my things away and close the lid of my trunk?"

That night Kjersti was taken violently ill with vomiting. The next day Dr. Carr was called. He had often met Kjersti in homes where she was taking care of sick people. When he entered he teased in his good-natured way: "What do you mean by lying down now just as you were ready to leave for Minneapolis? It must be that you are too much of a baby to go so far away from home."

When he had examined her, he became serious and talked in a different tone: "You have had an ingrowing goiter for many years. It has affected your heart, your nerves, and your stomach. What you need most is rest. You must eat only certain foods, and you must take some medicine."

Dr. Carr didn't have the heart to tell Kjersti that she wouldn't be able to go through a three years' course in nursing; he explained that to Aagot so she could make it clear to Mor. They were to tell Kjersti to rest now and to work part time later; then all would be well.

CHAPTER XXIX

The Revival

Kjersti was bewildered, but so was everybody else in the old neighborhood. Serious Lina Myrold had come into their midst, carrying a Bible and a guitar. She had won the friendship of many by visiting in their homes and teaching that love and charity are the greatest things — others matter very little.

It was the first time a woman had called any kind of meeting in Newburgh Township. An hour before the services, the schoolhouse was packed with eager listeners. Kjersti sat with Mor in the rear of the room. It was comforting to be near so many people interested in something outside themselves. Kjersti listened to snatches of conversation carried on in low muffled voices.

"When Lina doesn't wear her plain black dress she has a white shirtwaist and a black skirt; but she always wears the black sailor hat. Paul says we must tell the girls not to pay so much attention to clothes."

"Even likes to see us well-dressed, but he believes with Lina that we should not spend time thinking about clothes nor be proud and vain over them."

Anne joined in, "Clothes take a lot of money, time, and care, which we could spend on things that would mean more."

"Yes," said Maria, "we have been feeding our bodies and starving our souls. I have had time for pretty clothes but no time for the things that last. From now on I am going to be different."

Kjersti didn't hear any more because she became absorbed in herself. Had she sinned in her longing for pretty things to wear? A feeling of disgust crept over her; the desire seemed to have gone; it was good to be rid of it. What would Aagot think about this? She too had the hunger for pretty clothes. Kjersti thought of the time Aagot had been so angry that she had run outdoors and cried because Far had opened the Bible and showed her I Peter, chapter 3, verses 3 and 4, which emphasize the real things that make women beautiful. She didn't think it was necessary for Far to show her this when she had only one dress and no shoes! Far meant it well; Aagot was named for his mother and he wanted her to be a real woman. Aagot was called the "gray girl" the summer she prepared for confirmation because she wore a gray cotton dress all the time. At school they named her the "calico girl."

Lina arrived at the hall; Kjersti's thoughts took a different turn. Many of the new hymns had stories in them and were sung to lively tunes that made her feel happy. She had money to buy two new songbooks. Had Lina brought them this evening? Yes, she had a package.

Lina had no sooner placed the large bundle of songbooks on the table than the crowd filed by and bought them all. Her fingers struck chords on the guitar; her voice took the lead in song after song that rang out in the still night. When she laid down the instrument she had the attention of everyone in the room.

As she read the text her voice was serious, her gaze direct — she looked at them and not at the Bible in her hand. The prayer she offered was simple and direct, like that of a child. The sermon that followed was a series of statements about the happiness of a life based on love and forgiveness. By the time the meeting was over, tense forms had relaxed,

hard faces had softened; a sob here and there broke the stillness.

Far was seen in the crowd near the door, but he disappeared when the closing hymn was sung.

Lina walked among them, shook hands, and talked about
the love of Christ and what it could do if people would admit
it into their hearts. When she came to Mor and Kjersti,
they reached out their hands without speaking — they felt
too unworthy.

The crowd seemed unwilling to leave. Mor and Kjersti
walked slowly into the quiet night, each busy with her
thoughts. Kjersti was debating with herself whether she
dared to ask Far to explain some of the things that were
happening; somehow she felt sure he could.

On reaching home, they found Far in his accustomed chair
by the stove, poking the fire. When he looked up there was
friendliness in his glance. Kjersti blurted out her questions.
Far gazed at her so long that she thought he was not going
to reply at all.

At last he said: "You will have to think this out for yourself. But I will tell you a true story. Joan of Arc was the
daughter of a poor but God-fearing peasant of France. She
herded her father's sheep on hillsides until she was sixteen
years old. While she was doing this, she listened to the whispers of nature, and voices from on high guided her actions.
France at that time was in a sad condition and was about to
lose everything.

"One day the voices told Joan to go to the king and offer
to lead the army. She did not want to do this, but she dared
not disobey. She finally went, was accepted, donned armor,
mounted a horse, and led the army of France to victory.

"The Bible says if you have faith you can move mountains. If you believe that you can do a thing, you will be
able to do it."

In the months that followed, enough happened to puzzle
even the wise. Mor and Kjersti seldom missed a meeting.

There were times when Far went, too. While Kjersti kept on repeating, "You must think this out for yourself," she weighed and measured in her own mind everything she heard and saw. She wondered what Tim would think about the revival. She must write him, and Aagot too.

HATTON, N. DAK.
February, 1898

DEAR SISTER,
  You won't know this neighborhood when you return. Lina Myrold is preaching in all the towns: Mayville, Portland, Hatton, and Northwood. Besides this she holds meetings in schoolhouses and homes all over the country. There are such crowds at the meetings that if you come late you can't get in. We all have songbooks and many have bought guitars. On moonlight nights we get into bobsleds and go miles and miles to meetings. We have the best time singing, going and coming.
  After much singing, Lina reads the Bible and talks; when she is through she asks if anyone else would like to say something or pray. One evening twenty people got up and told about the mistakes they had made and asked forgiveness of those they had wronged; then they asked God's forgiveness.
  The revival has changed most of the young people. Those who used to cause their parents sorrow have begged forgiveness and lead different lives. The first thing people say when they meet is, "Have you found peace?" Then they either rejoice or offer help. Tosten gets up and talks and prays like a minister, but he will have to go to school to become a real minister.
  And such a sale of Bibles! People bring their Bibles to the meetings, some because they are interested, others to see if Lina adds anything to what she is reading. But she is honest; I am sure she wouldn't do that. It is strange, though, how many different meanings can be got out of the same Bible verse. Some say you should stand up when you pray, some say you should kneel, and some say you should go into your own room and lock the door and pray all by yourself so that no one can hear it. Others say that if you don't pray in public you are not a Christian.
  (Two weeks later.) So much has happened that there has been no time for writing. You should have been with me in Northwood! There was almost a fist fight right in church! A man found a place in the Bible where it says that a woman should not speak in public meetings; another man arose and said a woman could speak in public if her head were covered. (Lina always has her hat on.) A third man got up and shouted at Lina, "You ought to be at home attending to your housework!" But Lina hasn't any home. It got so bad that dozens of families left the church and

hold meetings in a big hall; they are going to hire a minister who agrees with them in their understanding of the Bible.

When Far first came to the meetings everybody turned and looked at him. I don't know if it was because he never goes to church or because they remember he was under *kjerketukt* [church discipline] for drinking, when the church was first organized. I don't see how they can blame him for not coming to church after having been put out. Do you remember how ashamed we used to be when we were teased about this?

Mor and I have not prayed in public yet, but we pray at home by ourselves.

Your sister,

Kjersti

The revival gave Kjersti much to think about. She wrote in her diary:

There are so many things I don't understand about the revival, but I know it has done a lot of good. Years ago when the Andersons were in need Aase let them borrow $800; they gave her a note and promised to pay interest, but after they got the money they seemed to forget everything and even turned against her. When the time came they would not renew the note, either. Aase felt terrible; she was sure the money she had saved for her old age was lost. Now the Andersons have been converted. They asked Aase to forgive them; they renewed the note, and the whole family is going to save and pay back what they borrowed from her.

I know many people who don't need to be converted to do right; there are Nick Berg, Osten Pladson, Lewis Thompson, Lars Mark, and E. M. Sondreaal. I guess people are born with different natures.

Kjersti was often lost in thought even while at work. They said at the meetings that if you hated those who did you harm, you were not a Christian. No one she knew had been wronged more or had suffered more than Mor, and still Mor harbored no ill feeling. Her patience was like a stream without end. Kjersti felt sure that Mor must be a Christian; she acted like one even if she did not pray in public nor ask others if they were converted.

Pastor Albert Johanson, who was the Northwood minister,

wrote a book, *Et indblik i striden,* to explain his attitude toward the revival. The Reverend B. Tollefsen had said, "Ministers make mistakes, too. Only God is perfect."

Bit by bit the old story about the Reverend Mr. Kjelstrup went through Kjersti's mind again. He was one of the finest-looking ministers the people of Hallingdal had ever seen; he was good-natured, too, until he was crossed; then he became so angry he didn't know what he was doing. One evening some young boys who knew his weakness rolled a huge stone in front of his door. Mr. Kjelstrup was so strong that he rolled the stone away again all by himself, but while he did so he swore. The boys who had done the mischief were hidden behind some big boulders some distance away. When they heard him they called out, *"En mand some sverger meget skal fyldes med uret og plage skal ikke vige fra hans huus."* ("A man of many oaths is filled with iniquity and the scourge departeth not from his house"; the English verse is from Pontoppidan's *Explanation.*

The Reverend Mr. Kjelstrup always preached best when he had had several drinks. Sometimes he whipped those who came to him with their tales of woe. It finally got so bad that the people came to Far and asked him to copy a petition they had drawn up so that they could get rid of him. Far did this. Pastor Kjelstrup stayed on, but had to hire an assistant to officiate in his place.

What else had Kjersti heard? "Suffering and self-denial are necessary if you are going to amount to something." It all seemed very difficult, but what others had done she felt sure that she too could do. She walked out into the night repeating, "You will have to think this out for yourself." The sky was clear, with no moon; but there in the heavens were the stars — the patient, untroubled stars.

Education and Change

CHAPTER XXX

Moving Shadows

Though Dr. Carr had told Kjersti she couldn't work hard for a long, long time, that didn't keep her from following her bent. She brought home Per Brendon's sick motherless baby and cared for him until she saw that no more could be done; then she called Per, who held the little form while life ebbed away. Kjersti felt that the baby might have lived if he could have been given proper care in a hospital. But these thoughts were soon pushed aside by other interests.

She had been looking for a nice spring day so long that she had almost given up when she heard a meadowlark, harbinger of spring. In a minute she was outdoors looking at the sky and feeling the balmy air. Soon she was on the road, the pony pulling her in the old buggy, which was half full of quilts.

It was dusk when Kjersti returned with the bundle of quilts upright by her side. Mor opened the door; the two helped the bundle down and into the house. When the pins were out and the quilts came off, out stepped Anne Lundmoen Berg, the gentle old lady who had to live with an unkind daughter-in-law. Anne had been young and beautiful and had had quite a bit of money when she married Mor's uncle. Now she was poor, old, and almost blind.

Having Anne in the house for two months meant much

169

extra work, but everyone in the family profited by it. Anne was cheerful and appreciative, and, by doing things for her, the family forgot themselves and their own troubles.

During the summers Syrian and Arabian peddler women, who lived in Grand Forks, came wandering through the countryside carrying heavy packs on their backs. Kjersti always hailed their coming, for they made the most beautiful lace she had ever seen. Even though Far didn't like to have them in the house, Kjersti managed to let them bathe and wash their clothes. When Kjersti went to Grand Forks they took care of her in return.

Dr. Carr and Kjersti had become good friends. Whenever he had a case that needed a nurse, Kjersti was his helper. As she grew stronger again, her aprons and uniforms were in almost constant use. Under Dr. Carr's guidance, she studied nursing; he got books for her, assigned her lessons, and taught her. He kept up her courage by telling her that if she did this for a year or two it would shorten her stay at the hospital and save her both time and money. Most of her earnings she put in the bank; the rest she used to buy materials and make things that Tim and she would need some day.

She hemstitched linen tablecloths and napkins, crocheted lace for pillowcases and top sheets, embroidered tidies and doilies. She smiled as she thought, "In a few years I'll be ready. It isn't hard to wait when there is something beautiful to look forward to. Oh, the shadows are moving, moving; some day they'll be gone!"

Kjersti often wondered about Aagot, who was growing more and more stern; her life seemed to consist of work, duty, and books only. Aagot would have been different if she hadn't given up Anton. What would Aagot do this fall? All summer long she had plied every trade she knew and had saved every penny she earned; but no matter how she figured, she knew there wasn't enough money to take her to Moorhead and back and to pay for even three months' tuition at Concordia

—and she would have to spend nine months in school this year if she was going to get anywhere. She looked at her clothes; two winters at Concordia had worn them threadbare and there was no money for new ones. She grew so despondent and difficult to live with that even Tosten's sunny nature couldn't dispel the gloom which surrounded her.

One day she heard Lars Mark, Beata's father, say that the Mayville Normal School was a good school; his daughter had attended it. Only those who had finished grade school, however, were admitted. The fare to Mayville was only fifty cents, and at the normal school tuition was free and textbooks could be rented for very little.

Aagot had once heard, "When you can't choose, take what you can get and make the best of it." That came back vividly now and helped her to decide at once. Grade school? What did she know about grade school? She had been in school only fifteen months in all her life, but she would walk up to the normal school, open the door, and sit down at one of the desks. The teachers surely couldn't put her out. Aagot was good-natured once more. Mor and Kjersti packed a jar of butter, a can of gooseberries, a small bag of flour, some bread, and potatoes into a trunk; on top of these Aagot put her bedding. Tosten took her to Hatton, where she purchased a ticket for Mayville.

As the train started out, Aagot had but one thought, "I must get into the normal school; I simply must." The thought went around and around in her head until she was dizzy with it.

Soon the conductor called, "Mayville! This is Mayville!" Aagot stepped off, carrying the suitcase that contained all her personal belongings. She must find a room before dark.

There were rooms, all kinds of rooms, ranging from twenty dollars to five dollars a month, but Aagot couldn't pay so much. About dusk she found a tiny upstairs room for two and a half dollars a month. She must get her trunk. Next door she saw a child's wagon and borrowed it. Back to the depot she went; with a piece of rope she tied the trunk onto the wagon and started off. She heard laughter and looked back to see the young station agent making fun of her. A hot flush of resentment passed over her, but it soon died; other things were more important. She would go by way of the alley so as not to be seen. She was used to lifting; so she could get her trunk upstairs alone.

Did she hear Mor calling, "It is time to get up and milk"? Where was she? The air was stuffy, breathing difficult. She opened her eyes; light was streaming in through the one window. Memories of yesterday and last night came with a rush. She jumped out of bed. This was the big day; she was going to the normal school. She was hungry; she remembered that she had not eaten supper.

As she ate of the good bread and butter from her trunk, her thoughts were busy. "I must buy some wood — not stove lengths, that is too expensive — and saw and chop it myself. I'll ask for empty grocery boxes and make a cupboard for books, food, and dishes. A knife, fork, spoon, plate, cup, saucer, and kettle won't take much room." The hot flush of resentment came again as she thought, "I'll carry the boxes home after dark so that no one will see me." She polished her shoes with a bit of paper and made sure there were no spots on her clothes.

The red brick normal school loomed in the distance. Aagot raced past everybody, entered, and was at the head of a flight of stairs when a kindly voice stopped her. "Are you looking for someone?" She glanced up and saw a dignified man whom she could not pass. Courage fled; she stood still; she couldn't even speak. The kindly voice spoke again, "Maybe you want work? We have some scrubbing and cleaning to be done. Come this way."

So this was the end of the big day! Good-by to books and all that. Ahead were only miles and miles and miles of houses to be cleaned and scrubbed, messed and mussed by untidy people, then scrubbed and cleaned again. An endless circle of fruitless work — and far in the distance were the books, piles and stacks of books about beautiful, wonderful things — books she could never, never touch.

They reached the office. A girl addressed the man with the kindly voice as President Carhart. He was the head of the normal school. Mr. Carhart pushed back his skull cap; there was a merry twinkle in his eye as he continued, "We pay a dollar a day for such work if it is well done, and you look as if you can do it well. Can you begin today?"

The air seemed filled with sympathetic understanding. Her courage was returning, but she kept her eyes on her worn dress and red hands as she spoke, "I like to scrub and clean, but I must go to school now. I simply must."

"Oh, you want to come here to school! You are three weeks late. Have you brought your credits?"

Credits! credits! What would she do! Tremors ran through her body, her hands twitched, she couldn't hold back the tears much longer.

Mr. Carhart seemed to understand. When he spoke his voice was very kindly. "Come into this room and we'll do some writing."

For hours she was left alone writing answers to a list of questions. When Mr. Carhart came into the room occasionally, she felt that he was studying her. When she was through, he gave her a slip of paper and told her to go to the library for the necessary books. What did he mean? He hadn't even looked at what she had written. Was Kjersti right? Were the shadows really moving?

Could Aagot live in a room with only one window? The kerosene lamp gave off an unpleasant smell; it was better when she left the door open. She would have to get six grocery boxes. That would mean two trips uptown to different stores — she couldn't ask for six at the same place.

Three boxes made a good-sized cupboard that looked nice with the old cheesecloth curtains that Kjersti had discarded. The box made into a washstand looked really lovely, covered with cheesecloth and topped off with wrapping paper on which stood a bright tin basin. The box used for stovewood was left uncovered. The sixth box was covered with an old calico apron — but no one could tell it had been an apron. Aagot could sit on the covered box while a caller was using the only chair in the room. Because she needed all the sun, air, and light that the little window could admit, she strung only a ruffle of cheesecloth across its top.

Mrs. Hoiland, the widow who owned the house, had noticed Aagot's woodpile; she came to the open door.

"My, how pretty your room looks! I am glad you are here. I think you are going to be quiet. The ax and saw are in the shed; use them any time, just so you put them back where you found them. Good night."

When Aagot said her prayers that night she had nothing to ask God for. She simply repeated over and over and over, "Father, I thank Thee," until sleep came.

CHAPTER XXXI

Have You Ever Seen Steam?

School was over for the day. Aagot was hurrying home. She felt that she had suffered great shame that day because she had answered incorrectly and because of her clothes. She could still feel all the students' eyes on her and hear the echoes of their laughter.

It was largely her own fault. If she hadn't sat in the front row and stared so at the professor he might not have asked, "Have you ever seen steam?" She had remembered the teakettle on Mor's stove and had said, "Yes." One of the students, Ragnvald Nestoss, who later became governor of North Dakota, had shouted, "Cut out a piece and bring it to class tomorrow so the rest of us can see it too." Everybody had laughed and looked at her.

Then too, she had heard whispers, "The calico girl, did you hear the calico girl?" Ashamed and shrinking, she had looked down at her old calico dress.

When she was back in her room, her hands set the books on the table, but her mind was still at school feeling the eyes on her and hearing laughter and "the calico girl." Her fists clenched; she wanted to go back and hit right and left until only books and those who loved them remained.

Then her thoughts went back to the day when she had come to the normal school. President Carhart had faith in

her; she must make good; she would make good; she couldn't
fail. She had copied one of his mottoes on a big piece of cardboard and had hung it on the wall above her table. She
looked at it now — "Nothing is impossible to him who can
will and then do." With a will she went after doing, until the
taunts gradually faded.

In her classes Aagot sat beside high-school graduates and
men and women who had taught school. Some of them had
so much of the milk of human kindness that they never refused to explain when she had an important question — and
she had many such questions because of her strong desire to
know the reason for things.

Every holiday except Sunday, and every Saturday, she reviewed all the assignments and work that had been covered
in classes, besides studying the fundamentals she should have
had in the grades and high school. After she learned to know
the teachers she felt free to go to them with any problems
that she could not solve in any other way. The teachers also
helped her make up the three weeks of work she had missed
by entering late.

Aagot kept a record of President Carhart's talks to the
students. In one of them he had emphasized the value of
wholesome food, but how could she eat that when she
couldn't get her money to stretch far enough? He had said,
"Those who live on bread and butter only will think bread
and butter thoughts." Every evening she had mush, made
from home-ground meal, with milk. Sometimes she dreamed
that she drank a whole quart of milk with her mush, only to
wake up and realize that milk was five cents a quart and that
a quart must last for four days. Her other meals were bread
and butter. Sometimes a gnawing hunger troubled her so
intensely that she had to buy a meal and pay for it by
working.

The first quarter came to a close too soon. When the examinations were over Aagot was a sick girl, broken in spirit.
She was certain that she had failed in two subjects and

barely passed the rest. Christmas vacation followed. Stacks of work awaited her at home and in the old neighborhood. But the first day she sat by the kitchen stove with hands folded and head bent. Mor paid no attention to her. As usual Far went in and out; when the evening neared, he said something about the sunset. Then Aagot roused herself and went to the woods. The elms and oaks stood strong and majestic in their naked beauty; they had withstood the storms of years. There was gold in the sky and gold on the snow. An owl called, "Who, who, who are you!" She began to answer, "Yes, who am I?" The power of the infinite gradually permeated her being; she went in comforted. Hard manual labor, good food, and sleep soon set her right.

When Aagot returned to register for the second quarter, she was placed in classes with those who had passed. She was so sure there was a mistake that she went to the office to see about it. There she was told that she had passed in all the subjects. She was so surprised that she returned a second time, only to get the same reply.

Had she passed? She walked out and then stood still and closed her eyes. Off in the distance a tiny spark seemed to be moving toward her, growing as it approached until it was a brilliant light that enveloped her and became part of her. She was a new being. She had fought, and won.

The winter quarter found Aagot with poorer clothes and less to eat. Since she had gained faith in herself, however, and her vision reached beyond clothes, she felt her hardships less. Then, too, she was winning those who had laughed at her by learning to laugh with them. On her wall was another of President Carhart's mottoes, "Nothing but your own death will excuse you."

Aagot was glad when the wealthy Andrew Stavens asked if his daughter Hannah might share the small one-windowed room. The rent and the fuel bill would be cut in half. Hannah, with her sunny nature and her quiet studious habits, became an inspiration and a comfort.

At the close of the winter term Aagot started on her eighteen-mile walk home. Breathing deeply, she stepped out smartly. The world was wonderful and so was everybody and everything in it, for this time she was sure she had passed. She was glad to have hours in the open to work out a problem not to be found in schoolbooks. She felt the coin in her pocket. Three more months of school, and only fifty cents left!

"I am glad I share my room with Hannah Stavens," she thought. "Rent for each is a dollar and a half a month. I'll pay four-fifty for three months. I'll ask Mrs. Hoiland to keep my clothes and trunk as security; then when school is out I'll work and pay her before I leave town. I'll ask Far if Tosten can take me back to Mayville and bring enough stove-wood for us. Book rent and fees are five dollars. A week's vacation to help at home, but surely the neighbors will need some sewing done during that time. Food? I'll get that some way and —"

A voice sounded, "Do you want a ride? You look as if you need it, carrying that big bundle."

Aagot was used to climbing into the spring seat on top of a wagon with a double box. In no time she was seated beside the farmer. He spoke again. "I see you are carrying books. You aren't attending school, are you? You look too old for that. You look as if you can hustle; we need a girl for spring work; twelve men in the field; my wife busy with our ten children and the turkeys and chickens. We pay well; if you make good you can stay."

Aagot felt the hustle and bustle of the big farm and could almost see the mother with ten children for whom she could do so many things. If she listened much longer she would be hired out. Her reply was, "Please stop the horses." To his amazement she hopped down and started to walk in the opposite direction. His words, "You look too old for that," were ringing in her ears. She had always felt old, old, old, and now she knew she looked old! But there were many old teachers; so that was all right. She must excuse the farmer; he didn't know she was going to be a teacher.

The short vacation was over. Aagot was packing her bundle for the next day. The neighbors had not needed any sewing. She tried to keep up her courage by repeating, "I am going back to school." There was a knock at the door, and good-natured Anne B——— entered and said, "Aagot, I want you to come along to a meeting."

Aagot, who was too discouraged to talk to anyone, framed an excuse, stammering, "I am busy — I am leaving tomorrow."

"This time you have to come with me; I need you."

The word "need" was enough; Aagot went.

The meetinghouse was crowded. After some singing a man arose and made what Aagot thought a very strange speech; then he handed her an envelope containing thirteen dollars. At first she was too bewildered to speak. "This isn't mine; I haven't earned it; I can't accept it," kept hammering in her mind. Then everybody laughed. This relieved the tension, and she held out the envelope and begged: "Please take it back. I have done nothing to deserve this; I just can't take it."

Then Anne spoke up. "But you need this money now. When you are ready to teach we expect you to return it in service by giving our children extra help. You will have a chance to earn it then."

Aagot sank down on the bench. She would take the money, since she could work for it; and she would work, and work, and work. A party followed, with lunch, laughter, good cheer, and song. And to crown it all, kind-hearted Kjersti sent her a surprise: material for a dress.

With a new dress and money in her pocket, Aagot returned to school feeling that life was beautiful — a bit of the heaven she had dreamed about.

June came, and the close of the school year. Aagot didn't know she was thin until Far asked if she had been sick. For weeks she had studied almost night and day; others could afford to fail; she couldn't. She was starved for sleep, but there was Sunday, and Monday was a holiday when she would be alone at home with Mor and Ragnhild. Oh, she would soon catch up with sleep! Was she bent, too? Tosten corrected that by laughing and calling, "Stooped!" and then walking like an old man every time she saw him.

Thin? One quart of milk wouldn't have to last four days now. And there were green things growing in the woods; sour grass! she must have some sour grass! Shoes and stockings came off, and she ran, a wild thing, across the footbridge, along the old trails once more.

CHAPTER XXXII

Where There's a Will

Aagot had met Barbro, whose real name was Annie Gunderson, during her last few weeks at Concordia. Now they were attending summer school for teachers at the Mayville Normal School.

Aagot wasn't quite satisfied with the motto she had written and put up, "Visit only when your hands and feet are busy with useful labor." She felt she ought to add, "and then only when you can't occupy your mind with anything better."

When Barbro read it she laughed and said, "Well, I hope this will keep us from visiting when we ought to study, but we have more to talk about than any other two people I know."

"We shall have to do our visiting on the way to church or when we have an errand uptown," said Aagot seriously. "I have been promised the home school, and the clerk in the neighboring district said you could have a school. Summer session lasts only six weeks; and in order to pass the teachers' examination I shall have to talk and act school only."

"I shall have to do that too," Barbro replied. "If my Minnesota certificate held good here it would be different. As it is, I shall have to pass all the examinations."

It wasn't quite time for chapel, but Aagot and Barbro took their books and went. They needed a bit of fun; and Helga, who managed to sit next to Aagot, could provide that. They were no sooner seated than Helga started: "Don't sit with your nose in a book all the time. Look at the crowd. Let's count all whose mouths droop at the corners. Oh bother! there are too many of them. Most of the men are bald; so we will count only those who have healthy-looking hair."

"But, Helga, it is wrong to make fun of people, especially of those who are guiding and directing others."

"I am not making fun of them. I am only trying to get you to see them as they really are! Preachers and teachers are only human beings and have faults like the rest of us. They are not hired to think for us; if we are going to get any-where we shall have to do that ourselves."

This chat set Aagot thinking, and she eagerly awaited the next day, when she would be near Helga again.

When they were once more together, Helga continued as if she hadn't been interrupted: "See the one who recited so long in methods class yesterday that the professor had to ask her to sit down? Pity the poor children who have to listen to her all day! It's a good thing she can't see what is going on inside their heads; they can have a good time inside and she won't know it."

Aagot thought of some of the long sermons she had heard; she knew the reason she had not enjoyed the sermons was that she had not understood them.

Helga spoke again. "How severe most teachers look! They are dictators who tell children what to do and what not to do till the children have no ideas of their own. Most teachers think they are doing grand service and instead they are com-mitting crimes by keeping children from working out their own problems and deciding for themselves. I am not going to be a teacher, but you are; so you better take notice. It will give you an idea of your own looks a few years from now."

"If you aren't going to be a teacher," said Aagot, "why

do you come to summer school, which is only for those who have taught or are going to teach?"

"I am here to humor my mother, but this is the last time. I am going to find some work where I won't have to be responsible for the manners, morals, and life-after-death of those with whom I work. I don't want to be a pattern for others. I want to earn what I get and then do as I like."

Barbro, who had been listening, now joined in. "I have taught school myself; so I know there is much truth in what Helga says. But if children were allowed to think through their own problems and decide for themselves they would make a great many mistakes and there would be no discipline. And if a teacher wants to get along with superintendents and school boards she must have discipline. I heard a speaker say once that some children never have a chance because they are too carefully guarded by parents and teachers; the speaker thought both young and old learn only by trying out things. He added that some children succeed in spite of parents and teachers, and this, I think, is true."

Then, turning to Aagot, she whispered, "But we'd better not bother too much about what Helga says because her ideas are not going to help us when examination time comes!"

They were again in their room, where the shelves were stacked with books and old examination questions. They would study a while, and then one would be the teacher and the other the pupil until it was time to go to bed.

Instead of "Good morning," Barbro would say, "How are your bones this morning? Please name them all."

Aagot would reply, "My bones are fine." Then she would proceed to list them and wind up by adding, "I always get the ulna and radius confused and the tibia mixed with the fibula."

Then Barbro would think of some device to get the bones in Aagot's mind unmixed. But when they were studying circulation, no device could help straighten out the superior *vena cava* and the inferior *vena cava*.

As they were cooking meals, eating, and washing dishes, the studying went on. One would command, "Trace a drop of blood through the body." When that was done, the other would then demand, "Tell the story of a slice of bread from the time it enters the mouth till it is waste matter."

Aagot enjoyed learning from books the physical culture drills prescribed in elementary schools. If she were to be questioned as to the value of the subject she knew she would have to depend on common sense. At the end of the six weeks the walls of their room were covered with drawings of hearts, ears, eyes, alimentary canals, skeletons, and what not, with all the parts properly named and labeled. Aagot was especially anxious about these subjects because they were not part of her regular school work.

When rural teachers who had been long in service got together, they had much to say about "busy work." By questioning, Aagot found out that busy work was something that the children in the lower grades could do with their hands — work that would keep them from thinking of things that might cause a disturbance in the schoolroom. You would have to have almost an endless number of such devices because you generally couldn't keep children interested in the same pattern very long.

Aagot made a large notebook of light-colored wrapping paper and she made friends with as many teachers as possible. At the end of the short term she had so many patterns and devices that she felt sure she would have no trouble with her lower grades when she began teaching.

On the first page of the notebook she had a full description of how to make paper chains and straw chains, with such hints as "Be sure to have the pieces of paper as small as possible and the straws as short as possible to keep the children busy longer. Children don't care much for chain making, but if you are strict they will do it."

On the second page she wrote: "With chalk write words or draw pictures on their desks. Have the children outline these properly with kernels of wheat—not corn or beans; they get through too quickly."

"A box of toothpicks will provide an endless variety of work for idle hands. All kinds of buildings can be made by sticking the ends of toothpicks into tiny squares of raw potatoes or beans that have been soaked."

"Draw outlines of almost anything on cardboard; have the children prick holes in these outlines very close together, with darning needles. The children then sew the outlines with colored thread."

"Often boys refuse to do busy work but if told that all who do not finish the work assigned will stay after school, they will do it."

The rest of the book was filled with similar suggestions. Aagot became a collector of colored paper, cardboard, toothpicks, needles, thread, string, and anything else that could be used. She also borrowed books and pamphlets from older teachers.

At the close of the short session, Aagot returned to the farm, filled with ideas she ached to try out. She had been promised the home school, but she had to pass the teachers' examination first. From then on her body worked in the house and field, but her mind was on the coming test and all that it meant to her. She studied far into the night.

Barbro and Aagot were in Mor's kitchen putting up a big lunch of bread, butter, and *primost*. They were to be gone three days, and this time they must have enough to eat. A two-gallon jug filled with sweet milk was kept in the spring till they were ready to leave. Aagot gave her orders. "Barbro, put the lunch in a box, our things in a suitcase; then put them and half a sack of oats in the cart while I run to get the horse Mrs. William Olson promised me I could borrow."

But when she got there, Mr. Olson, who had not been present when the horse had been promised, did not dare let Aagot have it; he knew she was not a very good driver. For a minute she was stupefied; then she began to run. She was aware of only these things: it was noon; Sherbrooke was twenty-six miles away, and must be reached that night; and tomorrow was the day set for the teachers' examination!

On the way back she passed big-hearted E. M. Sondreaal's home, where Sten Willand was working. When he saw Aagot coming he called, "Why such a rush and why do you look so glum?" She hurriedly told what had happened and had started to run again when Sten shouted: "I have a white horse I know you can drive. The field is dead ripe and must be cut, but if Sondreaal will let me use one of his horses you can have the white one."

When Aagot knew it depended on Sondreaal she also knew the white horse was hers to use, for Sondreaal was never known to refuse help.

By the time Barbro had packed everything as ordered, she saw Aagot coming up the hill with the harnessed horse. They hitched it to the cart. Mor stood in the doorway and watched the rig disappear down the hill.

While urging the horse to an easy trot Aagot said, "We are late starting; so we can't afford to make a mistake. How shall we avoid Golden Lake, sloughs, and closed section lines between here and Sherbrooke, and get there before dark?"

"The road is as new to me as to you," Barbro replied, "but the sun will guide us in the general direction and I'll take care that our things stay in the cart and watch the road ahead. When we get into serious doubt as to what is the best road we had better drive up to the nearest farmhouse and ask."

Until sundown Barbro and Aagot thought of the road only; when they saw that the horse was beginning to lag, they stopped. They had sat in a cramped position with their feet on top of suitcase, feed sack, and food box, and the cart had no back support. It felt good to get out and stretch. Aagot removed the bridle so that the horse could graze by the roadside. Barbro spread the lunch for their feast, but stopped in her work. "I have never seen a lovelier sunset on green hills," she exclaimed. "Were I a painter I should make a picture to last forever!"

"Even if you were a painter," Aagot replied, "we haven't the time. If we keep looking and thinking and feeling as long as the sunset lasts maybe we will remember it forever, which will be just as good because then we can take it with us wherever we go. Now, we must call at the nearest farmhouse and get the exact location of the farm where Jens Berge lives; it is supposed to be about two miles from Sherbrooke. Jens has often bought wood from Far and not paid for it because he is poor. We will go there and sleep and not use your money. All I have is enough to pay the examination fee."

When they finally arrived at Jens Berge's it was so late that everybody was sound asleep. Repeated knocking brought the oldest girl to the door; after much talking back and forth they found that there were only two beds in the house, one downstairs where Jens and his wife slept and one in the loft where the girl slept with the younger children. The girl insisted, "I'll wake the children; we can sleep downstairs on a blanket; you must have the bed."

Aagot remembered that the haying season was over and she knew the hayloft must be full of new, sweet hay. The problem was solved. "We'll put the horse in the stable and sleep in the haymow." The girl had to give in and let Barbro and Aagot do as they pleased.

It was pitch dark. Barbro and Aagot moved quietly till they had slipped off their dresses and shoes and were cuddled snugly down in the soft hay near the door of the loft. Then Aagot called out in a loud voice, "Barbro, tell me the function of the medulla oblongata."

She never got a reply, for over in a far corner of the loft a voice yelled, "What is all this racket? Who are you? What do you want?"

When Barbro and Aagot had answered the questions, the voice spoke again, "I am the hired man. This is where I sleep. I work hard and need my rest; I wish you would shut up!" They soon heard the hired man's snores, and it wasn't long before theirs were mingled with his.

On the second night the children had been moved downstairs, and Barbro and Aagot had to take the vacant bed.

During the three days of writing, the white horse stood tied to a post back of the courthouse and in the cart was a lunch box and some oats. At noon each day the horse munched oats while Barbro and Aagot took the box into a vacant room and reviewed subject matter as they munched good *primost* sandwiches and drank milk.

Aagot had studied physiology and hygiene in school for only six weeks; the rest of her knowledge on that subject she had gleaned by herself. Physical culture and theory and practice were subjects she had never had in school. In writing answers to the questions on these she had to depend largely on reason and common sense. She always remembered how she put her left hand under the table and opened and closed it to work out the answer to one.

Six o'clock the third day found Barbro and Aagot headed homeward. They reached the log house at two o'clock in the morning. While waiting to hear from the superintendent, Barbro went to her family in Minnesota and Aagot hired out to Andres Huus and his wife, east of Hatton, who needed help badly.

Days passed into weeks and Aagot grew thin with anxiety over the letter that didn't come. But one day, three weeks before school was to open, Andres Huus returned from town bringing a large envelope postmarked Sherbrooke. Aagot hurried upstairs and locked her door. She was sure the letter contained one of two things, a third-grade certificate or a "not passed" slip. She opened the letter to find a second-grade certificate; she even had good marks in the subjects she had studied by herself! Aagot ran downstairs, and, to the great delight of the children, chased them in play, around the house and stable and through the trees, till shouts of laughter echoed and re-echoed.

CHAPTER XXXIII

Kjersti's Discovery

Kjersti was in Dr. Carr's library. As she studied and searched, she put back one medical book only to take down another. Her pulse quickened and her eyes shone as she read on and on. By studying she was making a wonderful discovery, but before she tried it out she must be sure it would work — she couldn't make a mistake.

It was a hazy peaceful September day. Aagot, who had just returned, was so lost in worries and plans for getting ready to teach the home school that she hardly noticed when Kjersti entered. Mor and Kjersti had much to talk about but they waited till the rest were asleep. Mor liked to have Kjersti at home, but this time she didn't understand her coming. "Is anything the matter?" she asked. "Don't you feel well?"

"I know you all think it strange that I came home this time, because no one sent for me and Aagot will be here working mornings, evenings, and week ends; so I am not needed for that. But something is the matter." Kjersti chuckled as she looked at Mor. "No one is going to be sick abed in this house any longer. Ragnhild has been in bed now for three long years and has been cared for like a child. I don't mean I can cure her from the hurt she got when an infant, but I can make her walk once more."

189

On Mor's face there was a dazed questioning look that soon gave way to a puzzled stare. She was living again the weeks that had merged into months and years when she had carried food into the bedroom three times a day. Could it be possible she wouldn't have to do this any more? At night she had slept with Ragnhild to keep her covered and warm. So many baths and so much care for three long years — but Ragnhild had no bedsores! The worst of all was that Ragnhild had not talked in all that time; Mor had guessed at many of her wants. Would she talk and sing once more? When Ragnhild first fell sick she had lain in a stupor for weeks. That had been followed by months when she couldn't bear any noise. After that she had just lain there. The doctor had called it brain fever.

When Kjersti didn't get a reply, she continued: "You need not be afraid to let me try to get Ragnhild up again. Dr. Carr says I can take better care of sick people than most graduate nurses he knows, and I have found out so much in books that I know I can do it. I'll start tomorrow; you will be right here to see what I do."

Tosten was working out, saving money so that he could go away to school after Christmas. Aagot was lost in her school work. Far's presence was ever a comfort when he wasn't in the Shadows — and he never was any more. Mor was so absorbed in watching Kjersti teach Ragnhild to walk that she often left her work.

For days there were short periods of much coaxing and some massaging. Then followed days of getting Ragnhild to sit up in bed; after that, helping her from the bed to a chair. It was a great day when Kjersti had Ragnhild standing up, coaxing her to put one foot in front of the other until she got her into the other room. When Ragnhild could do this fairly well, Kjersti took her to the pump. Later came a trip around the house. In all these walks Ragnhild leaned on Kjersti and was supported by her. The trip to the stable, where she saw the little white calf, was the greatest accomplishment, because when she put out her hand to touch the silky hide, she exclaimed, "*Aa so fin! so liten!*" (Oh, so beautiful! so tiny!) Kjersti could hardly wait until she got in the house again to tell Mor that Ragnhild had talked!

For weeks after that Ragnhild, who had not talked for so long, talked almost incessantly. For three years she had only felt, and seen, and heard; now she had to tell all about that. When she began to sing, the tunes were those that Mor, Kjersti, and Tosten had learned during the revival and had sung at home.

By Christmas life had taken long strides. Ragnhild was able to take care of herself most of the time, Kjersti was again nursing for Dr. Carr, Tosten had earned extra money threshing, acting as separator man and engineer, and Aagot had taught school three months.

On Christmas Eve, 1899, a tragedy occurred that Aagot was never to forget. The Andrew Stavens home burned to the ground, and the gifted Hannah, who had been Aagot's roommate for six months of the previous year, died in the flames. School work had been easy for Hannah; in the short period she had been at the normal school she had earned high grades with little effort.

Christmas vacation was over. Tosten was leaving for Minneapolis to attend school. Aagot helped him get ready. "I am glad Mrs. Tollefsen taught me how to do up shirts and press clothes. See how nice these look! I'll put the books and bedding in the bottom of the trunk, then your clothes. I wonder if you will be able to make up the fall term."

Tosten laughed and replied, "How long do you think the books will remain in the bottom? Maybe I'd better label the trunk 'This side up; handle with care.' You made up three weeks' work at the normal; I'll make up three months' work. By the end of six months I'll come home with credits for a school year. You are foolish to worry so much about everything — especially your work."

"How can I help but worry? I didn't do very good work

for the $105 the school board has given me. When I worked
at Reverend Tollefsen's his brother Engebret tried to talk
me into becoming a nurse; maybe I should have done that."

"You did your best, and that is all anyone can do."

"Of course I did my best, but that doesn't excuse poor
work. I was sure the theories and aids gathered from books
and teachers would cover all kinds of problems and last for
months, and when I had taught four days I found most of
them worthless and the rest used up! The director let me
close school for a day so I could observe an older teacher at
work. It helped some, but after that I ran to Barbro after
school with my difficulties. When the plowing was done and
the big boys came, the fights began and I didn't know what
to do. Then a teacher told me I could solve every problem if
I read a book called *The Evolution of Dod.* I read and tried
to follow it but things got worse. Then I knew something very
different had to be done. Do you remember the Saturday I
borrowed a horse and drove south? Later Ole Gjellereit from
Enger Township came and offered me a six months' term,
which I accepted. The director doesn't like it that I am leaving but I have an experienced teacher to take my place.

"I will go to Enger and start all over again; I have learned
a lot from my mistakes here. I know now that reading and
studying about any kind of work is one thing, and doing that
work is another. If Mor had merely talked to us about saving money it wouldn't have done much good; it was having
to save that taught us the lesson."

In the new school Aagot discovered new problems that
were more difficult than those she left. She taught school
and fought troublemakers in her sleep, often awakening in
a cold sweat. She arose with the dawn. As she walked across
the snow she looked furtively down the road, hoping that
something would happen to keep certain pupils home; then,
when they did come, the war was on for the day. Would she
be able to hold out until the first recess? And if she did,
would she be able to hold out until noon? There were times

she was sure the clock had stopped. The afternoon was a bit better; and when the last recess came, there was only an hour and a half left; she would live through that some way. After the children were gone she sank exhausted into her chair by the desk, only to get up again to prepare school work for the next day, when the same experience was repeated.

No matter how bad the school day was on Friday, it was good—because at four o'clock she felt free to go, leaving her burdens behind her. As she hastened northward she thought: "It is a good plan to get up before sunrise Friday morning; lessons prepared, a clean schoolroom, and plenty of kindling, wood, and coal will make it easier to start again on Monday morning. Some of the children come at eight o'clock, so the schoolroom must be warm. Sometimes little children freeze their hands and faces; they must be taken care of." How deep the snow was! Ten miles, and the sun was sinking. Often her hands grew numb; she had to stop and beat her arms around her shoulders. When the moon came up she walked in a fairy world; millions of diamonds sparkled on the snow and on the frost-covered trees. When she finally reached home they merely exchanged greetings, but she felt that she was needed and that comforted her. Oh, she would never tell Mor about her school troubles! Mor had enough; Aagot must not add to her burden. Seeing familiar objects and planning Saturday's work again made life simple.

The long walk and the cold had tired her; a drowsiness crept over her; she sank into a dreamless sleep. Up early on Saturday morning, she lived the busy life of past years, laboring until midnight, when she considered that the Sabbath began.

Sunday morning she slept late; that day was her own. She would return to her school district by way of the Tollefsens; that made the road longer, but the thought of the children watching for her at the window and of the minister and his wife reaching out their hands to her grew until it became a desire that had to be satisfied. On the way she thought: "No, I won't tell them anything about my school trouble; they could only sympathize and that wouldn't help matters. They might even pity me and that would be a shame." But she received strength and courage from these people, though they never knew it.

Monday at dawn it was often so cold that she saw sundogs, but she wasn't aware of the weather. The schoolhouse was ahead and so were battles, but she was ready to begin once more. She kept Carhart's mottoes before her constantly and decided to stick out the term at any cost.

Her chest was hurting; she had been to see Dr. Carr. She would have to see Dr. Wadel at Portland. Troubles in school multiplied until she felt as if she were standing on the brink of a volcano waiting for it to erupt. The crisis came when she discovered an undercurrent of immorality promoted by one of the big boys. Not knowing how to deal with this problem, she had to send for a member of the school board and later for Superintendent Butler. The superintendent brought his lunch and sat in the schoolhouse all day. When the children were gone he said: "You have improved in your teaching; most of the trouble is in the way you feel. I know a little slip of a teacher who can handle any school situation because she thinks she can. If you feel you can do a thing, you can do it." A long discussion followed; Aagot had many things to ask about.

When Superintendent Butler left he suggested that he call at the homes of the troublemakers, but this Aagot insisted he must not do. She remembered Far had said, "That will be for you to decide." She wanted to know how, but she wanted to do the deciding herself.

All these varied experiences were changing her mental attitude so that when it came to a showdown and she had to fight, she did so and won, although there wasn't much glory in the victory. During the last three months of the term she came into her own and knew that she loved to teach school.

The wholesome life of the family she boarded with had helped her more than she realized at the time. The memory of Ole Gjellereit, his wife and children became a source of moral comfort.

Again spring came. Kjersti was at home with Mor. There was a knock, the door opened, and there stood a stranger, suitcase in hand, saying, "Could I sell you anything, ladies?"

When they heard the voice both Mor and Kjersti exclaimed, "Is it you! How tall you have grown! How fine you look! How well you speak! But school isn't out and you came home?"

Smiling, Tosten pulled a slip of paper from his pocket. "See my grades. I made up what I missed last fall, and before I left I went to the professors and found out what is to be covered the rest of the year. Feel how heavy my suitcase is — full of books. I'll study by myself and take the examination in the fall when I return. My money gave out; there were so many things to hear and see in the big city that I had to take them in, but I have learned all kinds of things that you can't hear about in classes."

School had closed; Aagot was to stay at home during the summer, but first she would have to go to Minneapolis to see a specialist about the pain in her chest. Attired in a percale dress, carrying a suitcase, she walked to Hatton and boarded the night train for her first visit to a city. Far and Mor thought she went to see the wonders Tosten had told about. The night brought so many shifting scenes that it seemed but a short while till it was broad daylight again and the conductor called "Minneapolis!"

Crowds, noise, confusion! Everything and everybody seemed to be moving in all directions at the same time. She stood still, feeling that life had at once become one snarled web. She must get out of this — save herself. Holding on to her suitcase, she elbowed her way through the jumble. What did she care if people glared at her and shouted to her?

When she finally got onto a quiet street she asked to be

directed to the address where the Pauls, the Yankees she had
worked for long ago, lived. She was told: "The house you are
looking for is in a fashionable district a long way from here.
Street Car——— will take you near it." There were all kinds
of names and numbers on the street cars and they were running in every direction too. Aagot wasn't going to risk getting lost; so she walked.

The hard streets she walked on were different from the
soft earth she was used to. Houses everywhere shut out fresh
air, too. Tired and wet with perspiration, she reached the
fashionable district about noon. The Pauls had moved from
the small town to the big city, where they had prospered.
The little girls she had once taken care of were young ladies
now. It gave Aagot a queer feeling to be treated as a guest
where she had once been a servant. She thought everything
in the big house beautiful except the rugs, which looked
faded and had frayed edges. Mrs. Paul explained, "They are
oriental rugs and cost thousands of dollars."

For days Mrs. Paul gave all her time to Aagot, showing
her how to know any city and find its treasures. There were
shopping trips, too. Aagot bought a hat, jacket, and coat,
and goods for a new dress. When she bade the Pauls good-by
they thought she went home, but instead of that she spent
several days visiting factories and poor districts where people
of different nationalities lived. She had heard a lot about
nuns, so she also called to see them.

By asking questions she discovered that there were no
charges at the university clinic. She went through it, to be
told she had overstrained her heart muscles and had a growth
in the left breast. Through the influence of one of the medical
students, she was examined by a specialist who charged
only five dollars. Both had told her not to work hard and
not to think about her ailments. She could do the latter, but
how could she manage the former?

When Aagot returned home, life had become complex.
She worked absent-mindedly; there were so many things to

decide. She was offered the home school again, should she take it? They wanted her to return to Enger Township; should she go? Her certificate was good for another year but she felt that she lacked knowledge and shouldn't teach. She realized that a teacher must know a great deal more than just what she is trying to teach. The specialist said her chest trouble wasn't serious if she would follow his instructions, and she would do that.

In the woods life was simple. She took the family washing to the river and, while she worked, it became clear she must go back to school. She reasoned: "To do your own work is one thing; to get others to work is something entirely different. I must learn this. I was among the best hired girls; I must be among the best teachers, too. It will take three years; but I still have over half of the $315 I earned teaching. It would be easy if I could go farther west and teach summer terms as so many do, but Mor needs help during the summer and it wouldn't be fair to Kjersti, who helps the rest of the year."

CHAPTER XXXIV

Guideposts

Tosten was leaving to teach a short term of school. He had been upstairs all day getting his clothes and books and papers in order. When he discovered Kjersti's diary he dropped everything else and read:

If we want to know what pleases or displeases Far we can listen to what he says to Mor or to some of his friends. I think he suspects that Tosten smokes a cigar sometimes, because this morning when Tosten was eating breakfast Far said to Mor, "Since I was a young man I have spent about twelve dollars a year for tobacco. Imagine all the good books I could have had for that money!"

When we do not have any visitors in the house Far likes to have it quiet because he reads all the time. Once he said, "If speech had been very important God would have created animals so they could talk too, especially when abused." Mor and I have decided to talk only when we are outdoors working.

Asle, one of Far's friends from Norway, has been here a week. He was a rich man who owned large tracts of land, money, and race horses; then he lost everything and came to America. When Asle and Far talk about things that have happened you feel as if you are living it all. We like Asle; so we put all the blame on those who had cheated him. Far must have heard what we said because the next day when we were all present Far said to Asle, "When we first came here I could have filed on three quarters of land as so many did; I had the same chance as the rest; I myself am to blame for not doing it. I am largely to blame for the mortgage on our land, too — if I had kept clearheaded it never would have happened." Far doesn't want us to make the mistakes he made nor to blame others nor pity ourselves.

Far and Thomas Mark have had many discussions about church denominations and the points in favor of each. At last Far said, "It does not make any difference to what religious denomination you belong; what counts is a Christlike life."

When Guttorm comes to visit Far he always stays for dinner and afternoon coffee. One day Guttorm complained a good deal about his wife and said he wished that she would keep the house as clean and cook as good food as we do. Far waited until Guttorm was through talking; then he said, "The only advice I can give you is that you write the word *patience* on the wall with letters so big that you can read it no matter where you are." Since then Guttorm has never mentioned his family problems.

Ed Erstad has trouble with one of his boys; he talked about nothing else for hours the last time he was here. I wondered why Far let him keep on, but at last Far said, "I can't think of anything that would be worse than to have children turn out good-for-nothings." Far wanted to say this so we would hear it.

I remember one winter we had a lazy hired man who complained about having to work. Finally Far asked him, "Have you ever heard of people who stand in the middle of the week and gaze toward both Sundays?"

It is a terrible thing for a girl to go wrong. I was telling about what had happened to Sissel and everybody began asking questions, but we were stopped by Far saying, "Those who stand had better see to it that they don't fall."

When Tosten came downstairs he looked at Kjersti as if he had not seen her before. She felt his gaze, turned and walked up to him. He whispered, "I wonder where you get all your wisdom." This pleased her greatly, for Tosten was dearer to her than either of her sisters.

Tosten went away again and so did Aagot, but Kjersti remained. It was a good thing she did and that she was capable. As usual Far had been over on the hills for his morning walk. When he returned he came close to the stove where Kjersti was preparing breakfast; he began to tremble and shake and would have fallen to the floor if there hadn't been a chair near by. Kjersti got him to bed, warmed stove lids, wrapped them in paper, and put them at his feet; she rubbed him and covered him with blankets. As soon as Kjersti dared to leave she hitched up the pony and went to the Reverend Mr. Tollefsen's place for Aagot. The two were soon hurrying home as fast as the pony could go.

On the way Kjersti told all that had happened and added: "You know Far would never let on when he wasn't feeling well, and it is the same now. I asked him if he was in pain; he tried to smile and shake his head. When I asked him if he still felt cold he said, 'No, I am as warm as a live coal, and you know how hot that is.' I brought him bread in a bowl of warm milk and told him he must try to eat some. When I returned I saw he had hardly touched it but he said, 'Oh, it was good; I have eaten ever so much.'"

During the week that followed Aagot and Kjersti worked in the hayfield. At first one of them would make trips into the house to see about Far. He always said "Thank you" for the least thing done for him. They soon understood he would rather be left alone to help himself as best he could. There were times when his hand moved quickly to his heart and he would stifle a moan. If anyone saw this Far would say, "I tried to prevent a yawn."

When Far finally arose from his bed he was very weak and shaky, but he tried to hide it. He began to sort his papers. One day he piled his books on the table and, without speaking, gave Kjersti the Bible; Aagot, *Pilgrim's Progress*; Tosten, the Book of Sermons; then he shoved the rest over to the end of the table where Mor was sitting. Then he rose and went for a long walk in the woods, returning in time to go to bed.

That fall was a busy one. Kjersti helped Mor indoors. Aagot had used a wheelbarrow, spaded earth, and banked it all around the house, away up under the windows. Now the click, click, click, of a hammer could be heard as she flattened old tin cans and covered the holes in the roof. They had become so large that when it rained, instead of slow drips there were streams that filled pans very quickly. It was fun to be on the roof; she could look over the treetops and across the river to the hills beyond. The days were growing shorter; cold winds would be bringing snow and keep sifting it through the tiniest crack. At least the larger holes were covered!

"Come down," Kjersti called, "it is time for afternoon coffee." Then she added, "Don't you think it would be better to buy some shingles and hire someone to cover the roof properly?"

"Yes," Aagot replied, "that would be better, but you know there's no use spending money here nor making any improvements because it is only a question of a few years till we have to leave. Far gave Gunder Stavens a mortgage deed when he borrowed money from him to pay the bank. The land has increased in value and is worth more than the loan now; so if we pay the taxes and some of the interest, Gunder Stavens won't lose anything on us. When the mortgage is due, the land will belong to him."

Kjersti pondered a while, then spoke slowly: "I am glad no one will lose anything on us. I could never be happy if I knew any of us owed anybody. Tosten often spends money before he thinks; I wonder what will happen to him. It will be hard for Mor to leave this place, and for Far, too."

"Yes, it will be hard for all of us," Aagot replied. "We shall have to find another place for Ragnhild, Mor, and Far to stay. The house, stable, and granary haven't any value now; only the land. We could have made this the prettiest place along the river by planting berry bushes, fruit trees, and shrubs. Yes, and we could have built a summerhouse and covered it with vines. But all that would have taken much time, and work, and money. And what would have been the use when we have to give it all up? Some of the neighbors think we should have done it anyway."

"Well," Kjersti said, "when the mortgage is paid in full and we live so that we never have to accept anything from anybody, we won't mind what the neighbors think; until then we shall have to put up with criticism. The drought treated everybody alike, but those who have no debts to pay can get along with what the cattle bring. You and I will have to pay the taxes this year, too, and some of the interest."

Aagot agreed and then added: "Tosten says gambling is betting or risking money on cards and races, but there is another kind of gambling just as bad. In order to get what they wanted the Andersons bought on credit at the stores and from machine companies, hoping they would be able to make money someway so as to pay for it — and when they couldn't they didn't seem to care. They called it bad luck and said lots of other people had failed, so they weren't the only ones. There are many, many people like the Andersons."

"What is this about money and many people?" said a merry voice. There stood Tosten, who had come home unexpectedly. "If we take care of our own affairs that is all we need to worry about. I don't want to mix into the affairs of others and I don't want them to mix into mine. Mor says she and Far have had their coffee and if we want any we will have to get it ourselves, so you had better come."

With Tosten, gloom vanished. But in her own mind Kjersti carried on the conversation. "Yes, I know it could never be right to risk other people's money. But I suppose each person has the right to do with his own what he likes so long as he isn't hurting anyone by doing it. Farming is risking, too, because you put seeds in the ground hoping you will get a harvest. But you don't know. So many times grasshoppers, rust, hail, and drought take everything. Those who learned to live within their means from the time they were small do not make the mistakes others make. Osten Pladson and E. M. Sondreaal always seem to know what to do."

Kjersti was interrupted by Tosten's asking: "How much money have you in the bank now? What are you going to do with it?"

"After I pay for the big operation the doctor says I must have, I won't be able to work for a long time. That doesn't seem at all bad because I will have money enough for the operation and for my keep till I can work again. And you know about some of the other things we need money for."

"It is a good thing," Aagot chimed in, "that we can help ourselves. Far isn't well any more, Ragnhild will always need care, and Mor isn't as strong as she used to be."

"For a long time," Kjersti said, "nothing has been really bad nor hard — not since Far quit drinking. He did it all by himself, too, while some of the prominent businessmen of Hatton and Northwood had to take the cure."

CHAPTER XXXV

Why? Why? Why?

The three years following the patching of the roof were so busy for Tosten, Kjersti, and Aagot that to them the seasons merged rapidly one into the other.

For Tosten time divided itself into two periods, the long season when he had plenty of chances to try out the many kinds of work he prided himself on being able to do well, and the short season when he attended school in Minneapolis and spent what he had earned at his numerous jobs.

Aagot lived so intensely in the school term that for her there seemed to be but one season. She worked at home during the summer and earned what she could doing extra work in the neighborhood, but her thoughts and interests were all in the new life that was unfolding through books.

Kjersti's periods of time were mixed and difficult. As she began to realize that the dream which had been dearest to her could perhaps never be realized, Kjersti became a serious woman, often despondent. Dr. Carr had gradually made it clear to her that she wasn't strong enough to go through a course for nurses. She was always questioning, "Shall I ever have that big house where I can take care of those who need it?" Then she would think of Tim and look at all the things she had crocheted, embroidered, and sewed for her home and his. But at times the thought would come into her mind —

would it be right for her to marry Tim? She might become a burden to him. When she wasn't needed at home she began going farther and farther away, always seeking a remedy. After one of her long absences Mor was surprised to see Kjersti looking so different.

"What is the matter? Are you sick?" inquired Mor.

"No, I am not sick now. I have had that operation. I had to stay in the hospital a long time, and after that I had to go to a place to rest. I haven't any money in the bank now, but I can earn some more."

"You could have come home and rested," Mor said.

Kjersti looked at Mor and forgot to reply. Mor's shoulders stooped; there was no color in her face; her skin was dry and deeply lined; her hands were thin and worn. It suddenly dawned on Kjersti that Mor was growing old. She must see Mor's eyes and hear her voice again. When Mor didn't get an answer she looked up and continued: "Ragnhild was in bed for three weeks; I was afraid I wouldn't be able to get her up again. Far doesn't seem to have any strength; he sleeps a great deal. He takes little interest in what is going on and doesn't talk much."

Kjersti was so taken up with watching Mor that she didn't pay much attention to what she said. She felt a wave of thankfulness when she saw that Mor's eyes had the same direct kindly gaze and heard the same friendly notes in her voice.

They heard the sound of steps, and Far entered. Kjersti glanced anxiously at him. His movements were slower and his steps lagged; otherwise he looked the same. Ragnhild seemed the same, too. It was only Mor who was growing old. But Kjersti would make Mor young again; she would stay at home and do all the work so Mor could rest, so her shoulders would become straight once more. Kjersti would prepare good food; she would tell stories to make Mor laugh. The deep lines would have to disappear and the color come back to Mor's cheeks. And she would stroke Mor's hands until the worn look vanished. Kjersti was glad now that she had not come home to rest; she must never add to Mor's cares.

As Kjersti set about her work, Mor became cheered and rested. Happy contentment spread over her face and she stooped less. By the time Kjersti left again she had become used to Mor's changed appearance and finally even forgot that she had looked old.

At the normal school Aagot still stayed in the background, but her head was up. She hadn't accomplished anything wonderful in the year she spent out of school, but she hadn't failed, and that was a lot. Her clothes were not good, but they were better than they had been the first year. She was the oldest sophomore, and overgrown, but she had taught school; teachers had prestige and were looked up to by those who had not taught. What interested her most were the advanced studies that required little memory work and much reasoning.

She no longer accepted a statement because it was made by someone who was supposed to know; she had to find proofs herself. An incident occurred in science class that was of the greatest importance to Aagot. A student gave a perfect book answer to a question, but when Professor Willard asked for her own reasons she couldn't give any. Willard then told the following story:

"The new teacher asked, 'How do you know the world is round?'

"The boy replied, 'Because teacher last year said so.'"

Aagot soon discovered that everything that came within the reach of her senses had a "why"— nothing existed without a reason for existing. Her life became an endless string of "whys"— Why? Why? Why?

It was at the close of the zoology course that Professor Willard saw Aagot rolling up a very long sheet of paper and asked, "What have you there?"

"I kept a notebook of the lectures you gave us and the material I found in reference books; then I made a diagram beginning with the amoeba and ending with the most complex forms. I had to make it almost as wide as it is long; there are so many branches."

"Why did you make this diagram?"

"Because I wanted a clear picture of how animals have developed and why."

The diagram caused a lot of discussion and Aagot was often called upon as an authority on the subject.

Geology disclosed a changing universe; the elements became tools that made or destroyed whole worlds. Landscapes took on a new meaning. A winding river spoke of youth, one with a direct course expressed old age; volcanic mountains became regions in the making, and rocks told the truth of ages past. She began to see "books in the running brooks, sermons in stones, and good in everything."

Botany became a world by itself. On Sunday morning during the spring months Aagot would rise at dawn, put on an old dress and a pair of worn shoes, and go to the woods. As she gathered specimens of all the growing things she could not name, she spoke to the violets, trilliums, and wood anemones — they were childhood friends. How wet her skirts were! And her shoes were soaked! Well, she had saved her only school dress, so she wouldn't have to wear her best dress to school. When she got back to town she would reach her room by going through back alleys. While she ate her breakfast she thought of the botany teacher and the extra work she would cause him Monday after school — he would have to help her name and classify what she had found. Work with the microscope revealed beauty in nature she had never dreamed of.

Aagot feared she would be called into President Carhart's office when she purposely stayed away from an examination; and she was. She thought of that first visit, which seemed so long ago, and repeated to herself: "Carhart is the greatest man I know. What a shame he has to reprimand me! But I couldn't help it. I just couldn't help it."

Carhart motioned her to a chair and said, "Will you please state why you did not take the algebra examination?"

Aagot looked straight at Carhart as she replied, "I couldn't take an examination in something about which I know nothing.

"Why don't you know anything about algebra? Hasn't Professor Travis done his duty as teacher?"

"Yes, he has. The fault is mine. No amount of explanation can help. I have to think it out myself. I'll come to summer school and do it over again."

Travis, who had also been called in, looked at Carhart when he spoke. "I have given her a passing grade on her class work. She has never missed class and has done all the assignments. What isn't clear to her now will be at the close of the second semester."

Aagot started to object to the passing grade but didn't get a chance, for Carhart announced: "The matter is closed. We are dismissed."

Then later came geometry. Aagot called at the office and asked to substitute studies she knew would help her as a teacher. Carhart listened patiently and then said, "It isn't like you to give up that which is difficult."

"It isn't because it is difficult that I don't want geometry; it is because I don't see any use in it."

"Obstacles are necessary for growth, and strength of character depends on overcoming obstacles. The poet says, 'Then welcome each rebuff that turns earth's smoothness rough.' I think you will stand the test."

As she realized the number of precious books she might have read, Aagot's resentment against geometry grew. She had to spend every week end reviewing what she had covered previously. It was some time after the final examination that Travis said to her, "You don't seem very anxious about your grade, but you made 98 in the final test."

"If I did, I don't deserve it because I am never sure when a thing is proved."

Travis added, "You ought to have a medal for what you have done in geometry."

"Yes," Aagot said, "if people are given medals for doing things just because they have to, I think I should."

As she learned to reason she became more independent, more opinionated, and more daring. She finally became known as "the girl who dares to contradict the teachers."

To Aagot it wasn't *what* was in a certain place but *why* it was there that was of interest. It wasn't *what* people did but *why* they did it.

Astronomy was not included in the course Aagot was taking, but the more she thought of it the more she felt the need of it. Pictures etched into her memory long ago came to life. She heard herself once more making up stories about the stars to satisfy Kjersti. Far had helped them locate the Big Dipper, the North Star, and the Pleiades. She saw herself again lying flat on her back on top of the haystack looking up at the sky. On the heavens appeared a being formed out of clouds, the shape of a man so large that he covered most of the heavens. She had thought: "It must be God; He has come to destroy the earth. Will everything vanish so that there will be emptiness only?" The thought had made her jump off the haystack and run into the house.

She felt that she had to know the meaning of what she saw in the heavens. If she used her time carefully she could take an extra subject — and she did.

On starlight nights Professor Travis, who taught astronomy, helped the class to locate heavenly bodies, explaining difficult questions as they were asked. For Aagot astronomy was a revelation. So many Bible passages took on new meaning. The glory and power of God overshadowed all. She herself became less than a mere speck of dust.

In connection with the study of English history there was a long list of books to be read, including *Kenilworth*, *When Knighthood Was in Flower*, *To Have and to Hold*, and *Put Yourself in His Place*. Aagot tried to hold on to the belief of past years that it was wrong to read novels, but at the same time she eagerly reached out toward the forbidden fruit. She had a delightful excuse, "They are part of the course and have to be read." She felt it her duty, however, to tell the professors that certain books should not be on the reading list, and that certain items and passages in other books ought to be omitted.

Professor Grosvenor, head of the English department, always listened patiently to Aagot's criticisms, and when he couldn't laugh her out of her faultfinding, he would say: "That is no criticism of you and no criticism of the book. It is simply proof that you are not far enough developed. You will change when you get your eyes open."

"Not far enough developed!" she repeated. "I hope I'll never change so I'll like that which is wrong."

Grosvenor would reply, "Does your thinking it is wrong make it wrong?"

Aagot could not reply to this. But when she read *The Merchant of Venice* and found some oaths in it, she came right back. All Grosvenor said was: "We generally find what we look for. Life is nothing but a looking glass — we see ourselves in our contacts."

While Aagot was arguing with the teachers, she used every spare moment to read everything she could lay her hands on. It was a good thing that it had been ground into her bones that duty must come first. So with lessons now. She frequently did not finish them until midnight. But after that she often read till the gray of dawn. Then she arose and shoved the book down to the bottom of her trunk. As she shoved, she thought: "I am ashamed to be so weak that when I see a book I can't leave it alone. I have only one hour at noon; so I can't take time to unearth the book, but if it were easy to get to I would find it and read and read and read until I forgot everything else."

CHAPTER XXXVI

With Glory

During the opening week of school, some of the seniors were chatting in a vacant classroom when Aagot entered. A chorus of voices called out, "What makes you look so happy?"

"I'll give you three guesses," she replied.

"Are you going to get married?"

"No!"

"Are you going to have some beautiful clothes?"

"No!"

"Have you inherited a lot of money?"

"No! I have been to a funeral; that's why I am so happy."

"Happy because you have been to a funeral?" They stared at her and at one another.

"Yes, I have buried my algebra and geometry textbooks! I mean I have sold them. I am free; I shall never have to look at them again. I am a senior now, and what is more, I can choose my own studies: science, psychology, philosophy, and literature. The dearest thing in life is mine; freedom to choose and read the books I love. I won't have to hide books any more to keep from reading them."

Instead of having to spend week ends in reviewing what she considered useless, Aagot now spent that time in reading. Literature took her by storm.

The characters in the novels of Scott, Dickens, George Eliot, Thackeray, and the rest became real people with whom she lived and loved and suffered. The same was true of the poets: Shakespeare, Milton, Browning, Tennyson, and others. An author and one or two of his books would be assigned for study. To Aagot this was merely an introduction. She would continue reading books by that author until she had to leave him for another. When some of the younger students, who read only their class assignments, asked her why she did this Aagot replied: "An ordinary dinner is made up of three courses: soup, main dish, and dessert. Are you satisfied when you have eaten the soup?"

"No!" the chorus answered. "We enjoy the main dish and dessert more."

"So with our school work. Soup is what we get in class. Main dish and dessert are what we get by ourselves. If you aren't careful, your minds will starve to death!"

"Oh well," they said among themselves, "Aagot is queer. She never goes to picnics or parties of any kind; she misses a lot of fun. But she knows a great deal about books, and some of the teachers hold her up as an example."

Aagot couldn't leave George Eliot's books until she had read them all. No matter what others said, she decided that George Eliot was the greatest psychological novelist. And she felt real grief when she realized there were no more books like hers.

Through the novel Aagot had glimpses of the big movements in history. The French Revolution lived again in *A Tale of Two Cities*; the old school system of England was disclosed in *Nicholas Nickleby*; in *Oliver Twist* she felt and saw slum life; Tennyson's *Idylls of the King* took her to palaces; Shakespeare included the problems of all humanity. On and on she read — hearing, seeing, feeling the life of past ages.

While reading she kept a notebook in which she listed all kinds of information. She would have to go on a trip some day. That would be years and years from now, but she would have to go and see for herself if things were really as they were described.

Aagot was gradually changing her opinions about many things. She whispered to herself, "It isn't the novel, it is the kind of novel you choose that makes the reading of it wrong."

No matter how difficult science was, she never tired of it because in it she found reasons for things in which she was vitally interested. Because of the many erroneous ideas she herself had formed, she had to go through a period of painful reconstruction; but that was soon replaced by the joy she found in the real reasons for things. She would often say: "Truth is beautiful. God is truth. Then truth must be the greatest thing in the world." Again she heard faint echoes of the owl's calling, "Who, who, who are you?" And she would reply, "Oh, I am not much, but I know that the greatest thing in this world is truth."

She soon discovered that threads of mythology ran through both history and literature. She dug into all kinds of ancient myths and fairy tales, only to feel no response to them in herself. She was beginning to realize how starved her childhood and youth had been.

President Joseph Carhart taught psychology and philosophy. He was a man great of body, great of heart, and great of mind — a born teacher and philosopher. It was in his classes that Aagot spun and wove the web of life that stood the test of years.

When those who needed props and crutches and made excuses for broken promises came to Carhart for aid, he often would say: "Put different-sized potatoes into a bucket and shake them. The big ones will come to the top, the small go to the bottom. Which do you want to be?" At other times he would say, "A promise cannot be broken; it is a debt which must be paid." And, "Those who accept aid weaken themselves."

Only those who had fought and won against the greatest

odds were held up as examples; Abraham Lincoln was a favorite. Carhart put the greatest emphasis on will. Of all his sayings, Aagot treasured most highly the following, "Nothing in this world can keep you from finally gaining that which you desire most." And, "We are fathered by heredity, mothered by environment, but we make ourselves." And, "Be the captain of your own soul and the master of your own destiny."

Another treasured gem was Browning's line, "All service ranks the same with God." Labor of any kind — so long as it was honest — became exalted. Aagot was still making furniture of grocery boxes, chopping her own wood, and doing her own draying, but with a very different feeling. She did these jobs in the light of the sun and was not conscious of passers-by. Because she was gaining that larger faith in God, in herself, and in life, Aagot was filled with a happiness so great that she saw only good in her surroundings.

Without realizing it, she made her way to the front rank among the seniors. Her opinions were asked, her advice sought. But the joy of being in demand played havoc with her judgment and caused her to give where giving was unwise.

Four months before graduation, Aagot's money was all used up and her clothes were again threadbare. Instead of worrying about it she began to plan. When she heard that Hilda Lynner, a classmate, needed someone to work for her, Aagot took the job and thus earned room and board. Miss Lynner was a sunny companion and her house was a home. Congenial surroundings and nourishing food brought an overflow of vitality, which on occasion turned into sheer fun. Aagot's smiles turned into deep chuckles that sent vibrations of thankfulness through her soul for all the good things that had come her way. She felt that she was receiving more from Miss Lynner than she was giving in services but decided that she would watch for an opportunity to make it up. Her thoughts went back to her junior year, when two schoolmates, Olga Koppang and Anna Sando, used to bring her eggs, milk, cream, bread, and sauce. These she had refused to take as gifts, but when they had assured her that the food would spoil when they were gone over the week end, she had accepted. They knew Aagot lived on little, but they did not know she sometimes went hungry. If they had, they might have insisted on feeding her and that would have been too humiliating. She was interrupted in her retrospect by someone's telling her that a package had arrived for her.

Upon seeing the package, Aagot exclaimed: "A bundle of clothes from Sylvia Warren! She left school and married a well-to-do man. It is lucky for me that she tires of her dresses; I wish she were as big as I, so I wouldn't have to make them over. But you watch! I'll be all dressed up for the senior parties and picnics." Then she thought of the fun she had had with Margaret Carhart, who was worried about her party dresses. Aagot had advised, "I can tell you something my mother does that never fails; when anything is too short she cuts it off at the top and pieces that onto the bottom, but if it is too long she cuts it off at the bottom and pieces that onto the top." Margaret had stared at her and said, "I am going to tell my father that he ought to have graduated you long ago!" Aagot was uneasy about this, but nothing happened; Carhart had an unusually keen sense of humor.

Food, clothes, shelter, and everything related to them were once more forgotten as the one word, "thesis," demanded her attention. A list of subjects had been posted on the board. To the surprise of students and professors, Aagot chose "The Novelist as a Teacher" for the subject of her thesis.

Aagot was again interrupted in her work by a message from home: "Far has had a stroke. Come home at once." She packed books, papers, and some necessities into a suitcase and reached Hatton after dark. It felt good to walk alone along the familiar road to the old farm and sniff the air, laden with spring odors of plowed fields and budding trees.

She was anxious about Far, but "The Novelist as a Teacher" had to be planned. Before she reached the house that night she had worked out the introduction to her thesis.

Far was very ill and needed constant care. Mor and Aagot took turns staying up with him at night. The thought of her thesis never left Aagot. What would she do? What could she do? One night as she was sitting by Far's bedside, she remembered a final examination in literature. The students had expected the customary ten questions, but Professor Grosvenor had stalked into the room and had written on the blackboard, "Discuss the relation of literature to life." She had been stunned at first; then she had written for two hours without stopping. She had written about what books meant to her and that was easy. She decided to do the same with her thesis.

A message had been sent for Kjersti. When she came, Aagot had been at home a week. During that time she had done the necessary housework and had made a complete outline for her thesis.

Back in school, Aagot found writing easy because she wrote of those things which had touched her most vitally in the four years she had been at the normal school. Aagot was a homespun girl expressing herself in homespun language; she pushed reference books and the ideas of others aside and concentrated on her own thoughts.

By working for her room and board, and dressing in discarded clothes, Aagot had managed very well with little money. But graduation was drawing near and she had to have a white dress and things to go with it. The diploma would be five dollars, and the pictures would cost something. After much thought she wrote Sven Huus, an old friend of Far's, and asked him if he dared lend her thirty dollars, stating she had a school engaged for fall. A letter came with the money enclosed. One sentence Aagot always remembered, "I both can and dare lend you thirty dollars."

How swiftly time passed! Kjersti wrote that Far was much

better. Aagot's graduation dress was finished; her thesis was handed in. She and her chum had made the rest of the seniors laugh by saying, "We are sure to be chosen to read our theses; we'll make a reading duet out of them."

A week before the big day, a group of seniors came to Miss Lynner's house and asked for Aagot. When they saw her they shouted, "You are one of the three chosen to read your thesis!" She thought it was a joke and laughed with them over it.

But the next morning, when she received a direct notice from the office, she knew it was no joke. She dressed hurriedly and went to Carhart's office. He asked her to take a chair and said, "I am glad you came; you are one of the three chosen to read at graduation."

"That is what I came to see you about. Will you excuse me and let one of the other girls read? Many of them are anxious to appear in public, and I would much rather not." Carhart looked at her and smiled but made no reply. She went on, "The other girls know so much more than I do, and they speak much better English."

Carhart finally spoke, "It isn't like you to shirk."

"Oh, I don't mean to shirk. I am giving the chance to another who can do it better than I."

"You have been chosen to read and you will read, that's all. Here is your manuscript. We will go outdoors and you read it to me."

When she was about half through, she mispronounced a word. Carhart said, "If you mispronounce that word commencement evening, I'll faint."

Aagot replied, "I'll faint long before I get that far — I have never appeared in public." Carhart only laughed.

She then read a second time, standing several rods from him. He told her that she spoke clearly and loudly enough. He added, "When the time comes, you may hold your essay so you can glance at it in case you are uncertain, but you must not read from it."

Aagot read the essay to Miss Lynner's cow, to the hay-stack, and to the chickens; she went to the woods, where she pretended the trees were her audience and she the preacher.

When the great evening came she was ready and in her white dress. She sat on the platform with the rest, staring into a sea of faces. Everything was unreal and blurred; she herself was floating in space. Suddenly she discovered her cousin Ole Haugen and his wife — they waved. And there was Kjersti. Life became real once more.

Kjersti, ever patient and kind, glad for the good that came to others, had come to see Aagot's success. Kjersti smiled and waved; then she became engrossed in her own thoughts: "If I could only have brought Mor to see all this! But Mor always feels unworthy and would have been shy among so many well-dressed people. Far would have marched right up in front and faced the crowd and talked to them if necessary. Poor Far! He does not know Aagot is graduating — he is so sick he is out of his head."

The exercises began. The girl next to Aagot tried to call her attention to the program. Aagot whispered, "I don't want to know when my turn comes." But when Carhart brought her a glass of water, she knew. As she drained the glass she heard his low voice say, "I have faith in you."

Aagot felt as if she were on a teeter board, but she couldn't fail Carhart. She stepped forward and read to him and to Kjersti. Whenever Aagot glanced at the audience they seemed to move like billows on a sea and she would come back to Carhart and to Kjersti — they held her.

It was over. There were flowers and congratulations. She heard Professor Grosvenor, the teacher of literature, with whom she had discussed and argued the most, say, "Oh, she covered herself with glory." And Carhart added, "It is will power rather than ability that accomplishes great things."

CHAPTER XXXVII

Victory

Graduation exercises were over. As Kjersti hurried homeward her thoughts were in a jumble. "Maybe I shouldn't have left Far and Mor, but I just had to see Aagot graduate. Crowds and crowds of people — beautiful music — Aagot on the platform in a lovely white dress — I wonder how she feels! Far was so much better; then he had a relapse. I got one of the neighbors to stay till I get back. Aagot steps forward; she is reading, 'Books may be divided into two classes: books of information and books of inspiration' — I could hardly keep from telling Aagot about Far, but I am glad I didn't; it would have spoiled the evening for her. In a few days she will be coming home; it will be time enough to tell her then. The horse is tired, but I wish he would go faster. If Far only lives so I can see him once more!"

When Aagot arrived and discovered what had happened at home and how Kjersti, for her sake, had kept everything a secret, she began comparing herself with her sister and felt that Kjersti was far her superior.

Far lived, and gradually gained so that he could be left alone at night. Aagot was to remain at home, as she then thought, the rest of her life. Kjersti was once more free to do as she liked. Tosten was away, earning money and going to school.

The day Kjersti left, Far was able to be up and walk around. When he saw Kjersti's trunk put into the wagon he looked at her, turned away, and walked off. He knew he would never see her again; he couldn't say good-by.

Mor often wished that Kjersti hadn't gone away. There were eleven cows to milk. Aagot had to do that alone most of the time because when Far was awake he had to be watched. After the last severe stroke his mind was blurred and his step uncertain, but he tried to resume his old walks on the hills and in the woods. There was grave danger of his falling into the river or getting tangled up in undergrowth and bushes. Mor would try to divert his attention and when she didn't succeed she called Aagot, who was swift of foot. They wanted him to feel free to go and come and do the things he liked; so Aagot kept at a distance until she saw he needed help. Then she would go up to him and say, "Mor is steeping coffee. She sent me to call you," and he was willing to be led home. More difficult were the times when he wanted to follow the old habit of going to town for the mail or to some of his good friends, who lived so far away. The biggest problem came when the field was to be harvested — he didn't want it touched.

Aagot, absorbed in daily problems, barely read complimentary letters and an offer of a book job that came from a representative of P. F. Collier and Son, who had been at the commencement exercises. He had bought her essay; thousands of copies were printed and used in connection with selling books for that firm.

One day Mor had been to the far woods for berries. When she returned her voice betrayed anxiety. "We are in for it now; the cattle have broken the fence." Aagot knew what it meant when cattle broke a fence and found good fodder on the other side. From that day until the cattle were put in the stable for the winter they were a constant worry. Aagot could dig post holes and fasten the wires with staples and hammer, but she couldn't stretch them tight enough. The cattle would look at her work and walk right through. She finally had to go to E. M. Sondreaal to get help, but by that time the cattle were so efficient at getting through that they found new places and made their escape. Mor had to begin herding. She enjoyed this except when the cattle got away from her and she had to walk too far; she often came home and sent Aagot on the long trips.

Kjersti frequently wrote home to inquire about Far. Aagot finally replied.

DEAR KJERSTI,

I promised to write if Far took a turn for the worse, but he is about the same.

Andres and Lukris Huus, Far's lifelong friends, have called; Far was so glad to see them that he talked incessantly. It was pitiful to see Far when it dawned on him that he could not make himself understood. Ole Swenson came yesterday; that was even sadder — you know he and Far have been bosom friends and now Far couldn't talk to him.

Far is so appreciative for the smallest favors and tries so hard to help himself that I sometimes have to leave the room to hide my tears.

I fell asleep in church today. When we were children you remember we were told that feeling sleepy in church was the work of the devil; now we know it happens when we are worn out.

At present we can get along; but it is going to be hard when I have to begin teaching in October.

Greetings from Mor and me.

AAGOT

With all this, Aagot was not unhappy. As she worked she lived in the wonders she had discovered at school. She would be walking down the streets of Stratford on Avon to the house where Shakespeare was born, then over to the church where he lies at rest. Another time she would be in Scotland in the tavern where Souter Johnny and Tam sat and then would go with them down the road past the old kirk and across the Brig o' Doon. She would rest under the trees where Burns and his Highland Mary used to wander. There was no end to the places she visited and the things she saw in her imagination. She would wind up every trip by saying: "Oh,

I am going across the ocean some day! It will have to be a long time from now, but I am going!"

October came and school opened. Aagot had to rise at five in order to milk the cows and feed the calves. When she returned from school she had to get the cows and repeat the same chores. Mor had all she could do in the house.

On the nineteenth of October when Aagot came in from work, she saw that a change had come over Far. His suffering was intense, his breathing heavy, but he uttered not a complaint nor a moan. At midnight, with Mor and Aagot holding him, Far passed to the unknown from which no traveler returns. Aagot closed his eyes; then she and Mor retired to the kitchen.

They needed to occupy themselves with something; so they built a fire and put on the coffeepot. They talked about all the good things Far had done and said — and these were many, because Far had not been mean. Aagot finally said: "Our home could have been different in many ways, but in spite of all it has been good. When I listened to Carhart, I thought of so much. The things he said that were of highest importance I had already learned from you and Far — Carhart only made them stand out clearly. Far suffered because of the mortgage too. After he realized he had been tricked he was never the same — he talked less and seldom laughed. Whenever M——— called, Far would arise and politely tell him to be seated; then he would leave, to return when he was sure M——— had gone home. The burden he never mentioned."

"Yes," Mor said, "much could have been different. Far could have been helped more. Students Peter Nykreim and Iver Tharaldson, who helped to organize Hol congregation back in 1874, were only young visiting evangelists who had too much work to be able to call on anyone." Aagot thought of how Nykreim had been criticized for having married people when he was not an ordained minister. Nicolai Berg and Tonetta Heskin, Andrew Stavens and Kari Haugen had

been married by him — and there must have been others.
But could it be wrong to perform the work of a minister
when the services of one could not be obtained? Aloud she
said, "Tell me more about Hol congregation."

Mor's face brightened as she replied: "The congregation
was organized on August 17, 1874. In the spring of 1875,
after a year's visit in Norway, Reverend B. Hagboe, the
mission minister of the district, returned to his work and was
the first ordained pastor to serve Hol, at a salary of fifty dollars per year and offerings. On September 28 of that year we
joined the congregation. It was named Hol because most of
the early members were from Hol, Hallingdal, in Norway."

Other questions followed and Mor eagerly gave replies.
"Hagboe was a kindly man and a real minister. Because he
served many congregations that covered a large territory he
came infrequently, and when he did he could not make
friendly calls. He had to attend to official duties: marry
couples, baptize children, give the sacrament, settle disputes,
and perform *jordpaakastels* [a religious ceremony of casting
earth upon the coffin or grave] for those who had been buried
in his absence. He was criticized for not being a fluent
speaker."

Aagot led Mor on to talk about the Reverend M. J.
Waage, who was called in 1878 because he was a good
speaker. He had a smaller territory to cover and could have
given personal aid but instead he stressed the Ten Com-
mandments to the extreme. Whenever it was brought to his
notice that members of his congregations did not conform he
immediately put them under *kjerketukt*. They knew of several such cases. When rumors grew that Waage did not live
strictly within the Mosaic law himself, Hol called the Reverend B. Tollefsen, who came in 1887. He and his beautiful
bride Malina were young, shy, and serious, unwilling to
meddle in other people's affairs. *Kjerketukt* was abolished.
Mor and Aagot agreed that the Tollefsens were living examples of the Prince of Peace.

After a long pause, Mor's face changed as she said: "We must think about the present now. You will have to make the five-mile trip to the parsonage and ask Reverend Tollefsen to preach Far's funeral sermon." She paused and then added, "We have so many debts to pay we shall have to keep the cattle until spring; we wouldn't get much for them now. There is hay enough. We can have an auction in March and sell all the cattle and horses and old machinery."

It was still dark when they realized that it was four o'clock in the morning and that they needed help. Aagot lit the lantern and started across the river and through the woods to E. M. Sondreaal's house. At dawn he and Aagot returned to comfort Mor and to make plans for the funeral. It was the busy threshing season, but Sondreaal took his hired man and team from the machine and went to Northwood to send a telegram to Kjersti and to bring back the coffin.

When they returned Aagot had Far ready for burial. All they needed to do was to lift him into the coffin and carry that to the granary, where he had often slept during warm weather.

On the day of the funeral Kjersti brought cut flowers from the city and Aagot made a wreath of the wild flowers and colored leaves that Far had always loved. There was a crowd, and friends from far away came. But all Kjersti and Aagot remembered afterwards were bits of conversation. One had commented on Far's youthful and handsome appearance in spite of his seventy-seven years; another wondered how soon the family would have to move.

Early Saturday morning Aagot hitched the pony to the old cart and went to Lewis Thompson for her voucher; then on to Hatton where she cashed it. With money jingling in her purse she drove into Sven Huus's yard. She was no sooner inside the door than she called: "Good morning! I finished my first month of school yesterday. Here is your thirty dollars and two in interest for five months. Thank you ever so much."

Sven looked up and replied: "You were so glad when you got the money that I knew you would be prompt in returning it, but I did not expect it as soon as this. But as for the two dollars, I shall have no interest."

"You must take the interest; others charge ten per cent and you must take this."

"The interest is already paid. When I used to buy firewood from your father he often gave me some extra. Once he let me chop willows for summer wood, for nothing, saying it was a good thing to be rid of willows — the grass in the pasture could grow better."

Aagot finally had to be convinced. She stayed with these good people until the next morning. As she drove on home, she thought she had never seen a Sunday so wonderful. She felt sure now that the deed returns to the doer and that a kind act or thought is never lost. She began to sing old school songs she had learned from Gospel Hymns. It was Sunday; she could take her time.

In the months that followed Aagot found that she needed all the resources her mind had access to. Remorse began to overtake her. When she thought of Far she thought of all the things she could have done to help him, things that in her blindness she had neither seen nor done.

Mor was broken in spirit; it was only work and the care of Ragnhild that held her. A man was hired to help with the stock, but he could not be trusted to feed the cattle and he didn't know how to milk. Mor often ailed; then Aagot had to rise before dawn, and, in cold ranging from 30 to 40 below zero, go to the stable to feed and milk the cows, and still be ready to build a fire in the schoolhouse by 7:30 in the morning.

There were times when Aagot didn't know whether or not she could hold out until spring, when the cattle would be sold. One morning she was met at the stable door by a new-born calf. Would she be able to milk the mother and feed the new baby and do the other chores and still get to school on time? She knew she would, because she had to. After that there were more calves.

When conditions seemed impossible Aagot thought of the position Mr. White of Portland had offered her: a clean warm schoolroom, few grades, nice clothes, a good place to board, fellow teachers, friends. Then she would hurriedly turn to her books. While at the normal school she had found no time to commit poems to memory; she could do that now on her way to school, to church, to town, and back. Thus she learned gems from English, American, and Norwegian literature.

Aagot, being a teacher, often had to take part in young people's programs; then she was glad she had some poems on the tip of her tongue. When she was asked to give a talk on "Envy" she had to revert to the teachings of Carhart. She wove the following into many a talk: "Don't envy another woman her diamond necklace. She had to spend money for it and has the care of it, and when she wears the necklace she can't see it. All you need to do is to enjoy it; so it is really yours. Whatever you enjoy in this world is yours."

In March, the day before the auction, Aagot stayed up all night making doughnuts and sandwiches. When the cattle, horses, and old machinery were sold there was a neat sum of money with which to pay the debts. After the auction Aagot hunted up all the old bills and wrote people to whom she thought Far might owe money. She paid out one dollar here, two there, five and ten elsewhere. There were no notes, but there were proofs of the debts. She even sent five dollars to a man in Iowa who had once done some work for Far and had not been paid.

Money had been made on the cattle. By planning and working as they had done, the mortgage, too, had been kept down so that by selling half of the 160 acres to pay it off, they would have 80 acres left. Aagot knew that by teaching several years she could save the farm, but she shrank from the additional sacrifice and decided that the 80 acres had to go.

That same spring, when Aagot had finished at the home school, Lewis Thompson, one of the prominent men in the township, offered her extra pay to teach a three-month term in a school that other teachers couldn't manage.

An early thaw had set in that made sloughs out of hollows; zero weather followed, covering the landscape with ice; a blanket of snow finished it off. This wasn't bad, as the daily six-mile round trip could be shortened by walking across fields and sloughs. But one day when the final spring thaw had arrived Aagot, still hoping the ice would hold, fell into a deep hole up to her armpits. Wet through and covered with mud, she reached a farm home near by. That evening a two-day rain set in. The flood came with a rush; the river overflowed its banks; those who lived on bottom land had to evacuate their cattle. Mor was glad to offer the empty stable for Vesle Mikkel's herd during the flood period. When roads became passable again, Aagot was glad to hitch the pony to the old cart for her school trips.

In the new school Aagot had to settle a legal point. She was glad now that Carhart had assigned *The North Dakota School Laws* as lessons for a week when he was to be away. When he had returned and it was found that she was the only one who had read it, the rest of the seniors had all laughed. Carhart had asked, "Why did you read it?"

"I read it so I would know where to find information."

Tosten returned from Minneapolis. Kjersti, who had been back only a few days for Far's funeral, was again called home. All was set for the sale of the 80 acres, but difficulties soon arose that they were not able to handle. Then Aagot again went to Sondreaal, who helped to put the transaction through. After the 80 acres were sold, Gunder Stavens was paid his money, in full. He returned the mortgage deed, and a new deed was made out for the remaining 80 acres.

When Aagot saw that the new deed contained not only Mor's name but Aagot's, Ragnhild's, Kjersti's, and Tosten's as well, she turned to Sondreaal with a surprised look. He answered it by saying: "I did it for the protection of all of you. Now, no one can, by cunning or threats, get your mother to sign away that which you all have sacrificed to save."

The following evening Mor and her grown children were seated around the kitchen stove in the old log house. Tosten was the first to speak. "Are the debts really paid? Aren't there any small bills left anywhere?"

"Every cent is paid," Aagot replied. "We owe no one."

"Victory!" exclaimed Kjersti. "Now we don't have to care what the neighbors say. I knew we could make it if we just kept on. And we did."

"Yes," Aagot added, "I am glad we lived within our means. I am glad we dressed in calico. I am glad Mor taught us to put honor first; she has done the most."

A great light came into Mor's face as she answered. "You offered to help me carry the burden; I did not ask you. You kept your word. Without you I could not have done it. And remember Gunder Stavens has always been fair with us." There was a hush; no one spoke; Mor seemed transformed. At last Tosten reached for the Bible and read the Thanksgiving Psalm. Mor led when they sang, "Lover Herren" (Praise the Lord).

CHAPTER XXXVIII

This Time I'll Never Return

"You can't say anything now! No one can! We have paid our debts! Every cent is paid! We are clear!" As she said the last word, Aagot awoke with a start. In her sleep she had relived not only the day before but years past. Wide awake, she listened to the low tones of the organ and to Mor again singing "Lover Herren"; Kjersti was joining in. Aagot's thoughts went back to her first year of teaching, when she had bought that old organ for Mor. She had asked Far for the horses and then had gone fifteen miles to get it. Mor had sat up late that night, fingering the keys and humming softly, trying to get the tones of the organ to harmonize with tunes of the hymns she knew and loved. The music stopped and she heard voices. "Mor, I wish I could play using both hands as you do. Did your uncle, the organist, play as you do?"

"My uncle was a teacher; he knew the notes. He played the organ in his home church in Norway for twenty years. My other uncle, Halvor Berg, taught school, too, and understood music."

For a while there was no sound; then Kjersti's voice came again. "I guess it must be true that we inherit all kinds of characteristics from our forefathers. That must be the reason Uncle Nils knew so much about music that he was chosen *klokker* [precentor]. He also made a violin."

"Yes," Mor said, "my brother Andreas was *klokker,* too; so was my brother Ole."

As Aagot rose and dressed she couldn't understand why she didn't feel happy like Mor and Kjersti. She had imagined the great happiness that would come after the mortgage was paid, but the joy seemed to have been in working and planning to pay it. Was this what Stevenson meant when he wrote, "The joy is in traveling not in arriving"?

Tosten, too, had turned serious. He had a problem he didn't know how to solve, and no one could help him with it. As far back as he could remember he had wanted to become a preacher. But during his senior year in college he felt a strong desire to study law at the University of Minnesota. To the surprise of everybody, however, he now announced that he was going to stay at home and farm the 80 acres. He bought a team and a plow, and began the summer fallowing.

Mor worked in the woods all day long and sang as she worked. Aagot couldn't understand this either. She thought of the two years when the Reverend Mr. Halvorson had lived in the neighborhood, how Mrs. Halvorson and Mor had visited back and forth, and how Mor had borrowed many books and read. Aagot felt she must stop all this outdoor work that Mor was doing.

"Mor, you don't have to grub away all that underbrush. There is plenty of grass for the one cow we have. Why don't you stay in the house and read instead?"

Mor looked troubled. She hoped they wouldn't take work away from her. "I have to be outdoors; when I am sitting still I think too much. Those years when I feared we would lose everything it was often hard to work. I enjoy it now because I know I can live here as long as I want to; and, besides, work has become a habit."

The change in those around her perplexed Kjersti. She wondered why it was that as soon as one problem was solved, another more difficult arose to take its place. Would a person never be through with trouble? Discord entered where harmony might have been enjoyed. Tosten and Aagot weren't friends as they used to be, and Kjersti knew why. She again heard them talking.

"I have broken off with the girl to whom I was engaged."

"How could you do that! Breaking an engagement is a great wrong," Aagot replied.

"She is a nice girl and I was interested in her. But after I returned to school and we began to correspond I soon realized I had made a mistake. Since I don't care for her, wouldn't it be a greater wrong to marry her and make her unhappy the rest of her life?"

"You should have made sure about caring before you became engaged," Aagot argued.

Tosten had tried to laugh Aagot out of her critical mood, but hadn't succeeded. Aagot felt bad because she thought the girl would never get over it. Kjersti began to wonder if anything in this world could be permanent, but she kept that to herself. And after all, wasn't Tosten right? It would be awful to live with someone you didn't love. But Tosten would have to be more careful, Kjersti thought. That wasn't so easy; everybody liked him and he could have his choice of girls.

Because of the disagreement, Aagot didn't even congratulate Tosten on being the first college graduate in Newburgh Township, nor did she say that she was glad he had worked his own way through school. Aagot was destined to become the second college graduate from Newburgh, but that was years later.

Kjersti felt neglected; Aagot gave her love and companionship to friends who had the habit of depending on others, and she neglected the sister whose companionship she should have cherished. Aagot, in later years, paid heavily for this error in keen remorse.

After teaching a year, Aagot had been granted a teacher's certificate valid for life; but she wasn't satisfied. From the day Tosten decided to stay at home and farm, Aagot began to plan once more. When she heard that Kjersti wanted to

stay with Mor for a while she was ready to leave. Aagot had
little money, but she knew how to make it go a long way.
She went to the World's Fair at St. Louis, where she saw so
much that she decided that unless she could stay three
months and make a study of what she saw, three days were
enough. From there she went to the University of Minnesota
and entered as a freshman.

Entering several weeks late and working for board and
room wasn't easy at a large university. And there was trigo-
nometry — how was she to get around that? She went to
Professor Maria Sanford, her class adviser, and was told
that by registering as a special student she could choose her
subjects. That difficulty was solved. Physical culture was
compulsory — Aagot couldn't take time for that. Being a
special student, she was excused from that also.

To Aagot the university seemed like a city. So many
people, so many buildings, and such trouble to find what you
wanted! Even the classes were in different buildings, far
apart. In this maze Aagot felt very insignificant. There were
many outside interests that complicated matters. One of her
English teachers took her to the Walker Art Center to study
paintings and later to a large establishment to learn about
fine china and oriental rugs. She wanted to hear the best lec-
turers that came to Minneapolis. She met the understanding
Sarah Foss, who always gave more in friendship than she received; how the two talked as they tramped the city in search
of treasures! Sarah could inspire; Aagot could always do
double duty after being with Sarah. Sarah knew how to dress
and she sat at table with a group of alert students; Aagot
was asked as guest. When she listened to the table discussions shared by all, she realized what she had missed by living too much by herself.

Before the end of the year Aagot also realized how crude
her normal-school essay had been; it had won a prize not for
literary merit but for some original ideas.

So much reference work and so many strange assignments!

"Write a paper on Milton as a poet, or write a sonnet." Aagot didn't have time to write a paper; so she wrote a sonnet on "The Mission of the Ocean." She hadn't seen the ocean, but she imagined it must be something like the endless stretches of wheat fields in North Dakota. The sonnet was read in class and later sold to a school magazine.

A month before school closed, Aagot fought one of the hardest battles of her life. She read an advertisement, "Free fare to the Philippines, good salary, easy work as teacher; you can go home by way of Europe." She would sign the two years' contract; she knew she could hold the job. When she went back to her room she soared on shining clouds. She would have to write home and tell of her good luck.

A letter from Tosten awaited her. She tore it open. What was that? "A year on the farm has made it clear to me that my life work is in the ministry. I shall see you on my way to Wisconsin, where I shall teach a summer term. In the fall I'll be in Minneapolis studying once more. Kjersti has left. Mor and Ragnhild are not well, but they can be alone till you come home."

The shining clouds were gone; there was utter darkness. Aagot knew it was Kjersti's turn to be free, and she was glad Tosten had come back to his ideal. She wanted to go home, but she wanted two years to really live first. For hours she fought and reasoned, "I have the right to live my own life now since the debts are paid." Then again, "No, there can be no lasting happiness built on the unhappiness of others, and Mor and Ragnhild will be unhappy if I leave." Breathing seemed difficult; she opened the windows. She would go to bed and sleep, and the next morning she would sign the contract before all these thoughts about right and wrong could begin dinning in her brain again. She looked into the night; below, Maria Sanford was passing.

Aagot now turned her mind to the teacher she almost worshiped, Professor Maria Sanford, the white-haired lady, who always wore the same clothes and denied herself so many necessities in order to pay a debt of honor. Aagot knew the story about the three young men who had come to this great teacher for help, making fair promises if she would but sign a note for them. She had signed, but when things did not turn out very well for them the boys had left her with the debt; she was paying it in full. Aagot saw Maria Sanford shoveling snow in her own yard, saw her in a bare room stripped of comforts, listened to her Shakespeare lectures so full of sound philosophy, heard her severe talks to whimpering students. Aagot decided she would go to Maria Sanford's house, where she had often gone as a friendly helper but not as a guest.

When Aagot entered Maria Sanford looked up in surprise. "What brings you here this time of night?"

"I have a question that must be answered, and you are the only one who can do it. What is of greatest value in life?"

Maria Sanford removed her steel-rimmed spectacles, as she always did when she had something important to say. Slowly and distinctly came the answer, "I think it is the power to stand alone and the power to seek the best."

As Aagot said "Thank you," she clasped the hard, worn hand of the speaker. It wasn't difficult for her to decide now; she saw only one road, and that road led home to Mor and Ragnhild. A great peace came into her soul and she felt happy.

Once more Aagot took up life at home among the pioneers where she had had her origin. A six-month term in the home school, a spring term in a place three miles away, and often a six-week summer term of parochial school became her regular routine. There were church services, prayer meetings, and young people's societies. Vesle Mikkel, Tosten's friend, bought many new books, which she borrowed and read.

The Reverend Mr. Urdahl, a scholar and philosopher, moved into the neighborhood. Aagot had the rare privilege of becoming one of his close friends. She had great pleasure, too, in anticipating her yearly visits to Beata Mark in Winnipeg and in reliving them after she returned. Beata was a musician and had married a doctor. The two had a circle of cultured friends. Then, once a year there was a friendly visit from Beata and her children at the farm.

There were times when longings and desires threatened to break loose again. Then she would work and pray so hard that they disappeared once more. With all this, Aagot had a good life.

To Mor, things were dated from before the debts were paid or after the debts were paid. One evening, in the second autumn after the debts were paid, Aagot received the following message, "Come to the Northwood Hospital at once; I am to have another operation. Kjersti."

Aagot set out on foot and within two hours she was with her sister. As Kjersti talked, her voice betrayed great uneasiness.

"Will you go with me into the operating room tomorrow — and stay right by me until it is over? I may not live through it this time."

"Yes, I will."

"When I have returned to my room, will you sit by my bed till I am myself again?"

"I will."

"I have some money in the bank and Tosten owes me some. If I should go will you pay my bills?"

"Yes, you know I will."

"Then all is well. Be kind to Mor."

For two days Aagot lived and suffered with her sister. Finally the patient fell into natural sleep. When Kjersti awoke she said, "Go and comfort Mor now, but don't tell her how sick I have been."

Kjersti finally came home, but a long time passed before she was able to leave again for Minneapolis.

It was the second spring after the debts were paid. Ragnhild was growing more delicate and Mor seemed to have lost interest in outdoor work. She spent most of her time reading a *History of the World* borrowed from the Reverend Mr. Tollefsen. Her complaints about the old house were increasing.

"The roof leaks worse than ever, the windows and doors rattle, the cold wind whistles through cracks and crevices; we simply can't keep warm."

That summer Mor was happy to see a small, well-built frame house erected. They were comfortably settled in the new home and Aagot had begun to teach again when Kjersti unexpectedly returned. After an exchange of greetings she said, "Mor, I have to rest before we can talk." Many days passed before they could have that visit.

"Mor, the operations have not cured me. I was so sick this fall that I was sure I would never see you again."

"You should have let us know that you were ill."

"No; then you would have worried, and you couldn't have helped me. I feel better already. I think I will soon be so well I can leave again. And, Mor, I—I have so much to do; I am to be married next June."

Then they talked about Tim and Kjersti's new home until Mor could almost see the big house with so many rooms, decorated with the pretty things Kjersti had worked on for years.

Kjersti's good-by this time was cheery. "I'll be back in June, and Tim will be with me. My! won't the neighbors be surprised when they are asked to my wedding!"

Weeks passed. It was Saturday noon. Mor came in all covered with snow. As she brushed and stamped she said: "We have not had so much snow and so cold a January in many years. I gave the black cow extra fodder; I may not be able to get to the stable tomorrow. It is snowing heavily and if a wind comes up we shall have an old-time blizzard."

"We have plenty of food and fuel to last for weeks," Aagot replied, "and you know I can get to the stable."

"Look!" cried Ragnhild, "there are big black shadows outside the window; they are moving."

Both Mor and Aagot rushed to the window. There they saw a team of horses floundering in the snowdrift. They opened the door to admit a man carrying a big something. What was it? Who were they? A low cry, and the man let the body of a woman slide to the floor. He talked. "We tipped twice on the road from Northwood. The snowdrifts are awful."

The shawls and wrappings were untied; the woman was Kjersti. She moaned: "I am very sick; but I won't be any trouble. I had to come home to see you all."

For days and days the storm raged, but no one noticed it. Kjersti was fighting for her life. There were times when the pain eased; then she talked incessantly.

"See the frost pictures on the window. I wanted to draw them on the *tinae.* I have embroidered some on cloth — yes, spider webs and pretty designs in leaves. The snowbirds are on the window sill; I can count them now but I don't want to. Strange how eager we are to learn things and later we don't care! Far said the bird would become part of the ground once more. Now I know everything will become part of the ground once more."

Mor would tell her to try to sleep; she must sleep to get well. But Kjersti would continue: "I wish we were back in the old log house; this house has no memories. I like memories, even those that hurt. There were shadows on the wall; life has many shadows, but we can make shadows move. I wanted to go to Hol, Hallingdal, where Far was born and had his home."

The doctor finally worked his way through the snowdrifts. When he had examined her he said, "Kjersti has gotten over so many serious sick spells before that she will live through this one too."

A change came over Kjersti but Aagot paid little heed to it; she clung to what the doctor had said. It bothered Kjersti when she had to be helped.

"I said I wouldn't be any trouble and now you have to

wait on me. I am so sorry. But it won't be for long; no, it won't be for long. I should like to see the old neighbors, and Tosten."

Aagot reasoned that the roads were almost impassable, and, as for Tosten, the trip from Minneapolis would cost him a great deal. But she too grew uneasy at last and sent to Portland for another doctor. When he arrived he said very little. Kjersti kept on talking.

"Mor, I understand now why the mother bird pushes the baby birds out of the nest; she wants to teach them to depend on themselves. I am glad I left home as I did, but I wasn't able to do as much as I wanted to. There will be no hospital, and no home with Tim. Far often said, 'If you think right and do right all will be right.' I have tried to live up to that. Mor, I am so tired. It will be good to rest, just rest."

One day Kjersti slept for many hours. When she awoke she called Mor and said, "I have left home so many times and I have always come back. When I leave this time I shall never return." She saw Mor crying. "Don't feel bad. You said Birgit has it good; I will have it good. I will never be sick again. Lay me beside Far."

That evening Ole Midboe came to offer help. He sent his daughter Sophia. That night Mor, Aagot, and Sophia took turns watching by Kjersti's bedside. She finally slept. It was four o'clock in the morning when she awoke and called: "Aagot, I am leaving now. No, don't do anything. It is death. There are so few things that are worth striving for; I am glad I can go. Don't feel bad. You will join me on the other side. Mor! Where is Mor! I must say good-by to Mor!"

Mor clasped Kjersti's outstretched hand. "Thank you, Mor, for everything since I was tiny. You have been so kind, so kind. Greet Tosten for me." And Kjersti was gone.

In its shroud of new-fallen snow the big outdoors breathed peace. A lone snowbird fluttered near the window, hesitated, then slowly winged his way into space. Overhead the stars beckoned. The stars — bright, sparkling symbols of eternity.

CPSIA information can be obtained
at www.ICGtesting.com
Printed in the USA
LVHW042303250623
750763LV00005B/81

9 780873 512954